Guide to
Internet Job
Searching

Guide to Internet Job Searching

2004–2005 Edition

Margaret Riley Dikel and Frances E. Roehm

PUBLIC LIBRARY
ASSOCIATION
A division of the American Library Association

VGM Career Books

Chicago   New York   San Francisco   Lisbon   London   Madrid   Mexico City
Milan   New Delhi   San Juan   Seoul   Singapore   Sydney   Toronto

I 95
14
8-24-04

1 2 3 4 5 6 7 8 9 0   QPD/QPD   3 2 1 0 9 8 7 6 5 4

ISBN 0-07-141374-X
ISSN 1527-7410

McGraw-Hill books are available at special quantity discounts to use as premiums and sales promotions, or for use in corporate training programs. For more information, please write to the Director of Special Sales, Professional Publishing, McGraw-Hill, Two Penn Plaza, New York, NY 10121-2298. Or contact your local bookstore.

This book is printed on acid-free paper.

Contents

Foreword

What is the sound of one hand clapping?

Job seekers and employers alike are guilty of aligning their interests so poorly that they seldom meet. The result is that corporations are taking longer than ever to fill their open positions and the candidates they seek are taking even longer than the companies to find the right position.

It doesn't have to be this way.

Armed with the newest edition of *Guide to Internet Job Searching*, you can quickly identify, target, research, and successfully apply for the jobs you want and qualify for. The authors, pioneering experts about how job hunting has been transformed by the Internet, offer well-organized practical advice on how to overcome any job-hunting challenge.

Especially important are the resources in this edition that will help you thoroughly examine and study the companies, firms, and agencies that have the openings you seek. Don't skimp when it comes to research, for the following reasons:

1. On average, companies fill one-third of their open positions with their own employees. That may seem like fewer openings for *you*, but think of it another way. Once you get in, there is opportunity to grow. How important is that to you? Would you willingly pass up a firm that couldn't demonstrate development opportunities? And would you be willing to work extra hard to develop a relationship with a firm that "walked the talk"? Learning all you can on company websites can help you match what they offer with what you really want. If there is a link from the company website's home page for "employees," follow it. What you learn will help you decide whether this company knows how to treat its employees. Look for profiles of employees with backgrounds like yours. When you develop a contact in the firm, you might also ask to get a glimpse of some of the jobs that will be posted shortly to the company's website but are still available only to the staff. Firms with the most successful employee bidding programs will have the most entry-level positions and the best retention. They are harder to get into but worth the effort to prepare yourself to be there.

2. Of a firm's new hires from the outside, one-quarter are the direct result of a current employee referring the successful candidate. Most firms have significantly strengthened their employee referral programs since the Internet

was introduced. Good employee communication via e-mail, the intranet, and the Internet is the key. Some firms are finding 50 percent of all their hires through referrals by their employees. The "half-empty" attitude looks at a statistic like this and sees an obstacle. They feel it is always about who you know, not what you know. The folks who believe the glass is half full realize they probably know or can meet almost anyone. (Of course it helps to have a copy of this book.)

To illustrate the importance of networking, my partner and I know of one Northeast firm that hired a thousand employees in 2002. Two hundred were hired as a result of the resume they submitted on the company's website. Another two hundred were hired as a result of an employee in the company who submitted their resume (or the candidate mentioned the referring employee when applying online). Sounds like these two approaches are equal, right? *Wrong.* The two hundred hires that resulted from website submittals were selected from a total of fifty thousand applications while only six hundred employee referrals produced the same number of hires (two hundred).

Where would you spend your time if all firms had similar statistics? Would the best use of your time be to apply online to every company—over and over (because most recruiters will automatically eliminate resumes more than thirty days old)? Do you want a one in five hundred chance, or a one in three chance? I know where I'm spending my time. I wouldn't apply without researching how to network to an employee in the firm I targeted. Instead of applying to a hundred jobs a week, I would apply to a dozen—and I'd spend the bulk of my time researching, meeting, and networking to employees who could refer me.

Use this book to find leads that will open positions you qualify for. Use it to better research the companies who are advertising these openings, and then use it to network to employees in your target companies who can refer you. What is the sound of one hand clapping? It is the quiet sound of the handshake between a company's recruiter and the candidate the company will hire.

Gerry Crispin, SPHR (Senior Professional, Human Resources)
Coauthor, *CareerXroads* (careerxroads.com)
International Consultant for Online Recruiting and Staffing

Preface

If you hold a copy of this edition of the book next to a copy of our 2002 edition, you will notice that this new one is smaller. This is following the recent trends in the online recruiting industry. Sites come and go, and the mergers of the past few years have left holes where a few major resources used to be. But for all of the apparent downsizing of online employment sites, there is a constant evolution of new sites targeting new audiences, locations, and career fields that were not previously covered.

We approached this edition of the book in a different way. We reviewed each and every listing from the past, deleting several sites that are no longer available and delisting others that no longer meet our standards. The number of sites online allows us to be much more selective about what we will and will not list. We felt it was important to remove some older listings and limit more developed fields so we could include other listings and employment areas not previously reviewed.

This edition also comes at an important time. As we are completing our work, we are experiencing one of the highest levels of unemployment the United States has seen in decades. This makes the preparation of a new edition even more important—so we can be sure you have the best information and instructions on how to leverage the power of the Internet in your search for new opportunities.

But for all this new power, reach, and leverage, if you are spending all your job-search time online, then you are missing the most effective tool available to you. It is the other parents you sit with at your child's baseball or soccer game. It's the other people at your local association meetings. It's even your parents, siblings, and other relatives. Yes, it is the people you know—the people who make up your personal network.

Remember, the Internet is also a network, a means of communication and connectivity. It can help you build your personal network by finding you new places to connect with others. It facilitates new meetings by eliminating the sweaty-palm factor. It alerts you to new opportunities and new organizations. It has the research resources you can use to learn more about the others with whom you are talking. It gives you tips on working meetings and dinners, and it offers sound advice about preparing for interviews and honing your negotiating techniques. What it cannot do is tell an employer that you are indeed the best-qualified person to fill an open position. This is where your personal network comes in, that supportive and truly helpful group of friends, colleagues, and even acquaintances who will introduce you to the right people, make sure you know what to say and how to say it, and even give you the grand tour on your first day of work.

This book is here to offer guidance and resources to help you find potential leads, research potential employers, and connect with others using the great network we call the Internet. We feel that this book gives you the tools you need to navigate the Internet with ease, taking advantage of all it has to offer and making your search a true success. Here's to new opportunities!

Acknowledgments

It's been several years since we lost our close friend and coauthor Steve Oserman, and yet we continue to be inspired by his warmth and good works on behalf of job seekers and career changers. Steve came up with the initial idea for this project and early on provided much of the perspiration behind its success. His vitality and energetic personality were wonderfully inspiriting, and we only hope we can continue to uphold his vision for the book and to follow his example of service to the community.

We'd like to thank Gerry Crispin, coauthor of *CareerXRoads* (careerxroads.com), for graciously agreeing to provide us with a foreword. Gerry was a participant in the very first edition of the book. We are indebted to Susan Ireland, professional resume writer and author of *The Complete Idiot's Guide to the Perfect Resume*, third edition, for allowing us to use so much of her information on electronic resume formats in our book. And we owe a great deal to Susan Joyce, president of NETability and webmaster of Job-Hunt.org, who allowed us to quote information from her website and assisted with the editing of Chapter 1.

From Frances:

This *Guide* represents the efforts and support of many individuals. While there is not enough space to list them all, there are some who have provided so much in the way of inspiration, encouragement, or technical support that I must extend a public thank-you.

> Carolyn A. Anthony and the board members, staff, and volunteers of Skokie Public Library
>
> Sarah A. Long and the staff of the North Suburban Library System
>
> Colleagues and mentors such as Dick Bolles, Joan Durrance, Terry Weech, Carol Kleiman, Maxine Topper, Katherine Sopranos, Jane Hagedorn, Lola Lucas, and others who remind me that it's all about the people
>
> Lenny, who makes our house a home, and Christopher, family, and friends who make my world a better place

From Margaret:

Until you work on something like this you never know how many people it takes to really create it.

Friends and colleagues such as Dick Bolles, Joyce Lain Kennedy, Laura Lorber, Perri Cappel, Fran Quittel, Mary-Ellen Mort, Susan Joyce, Susan Ireland, and

Tom Jackson are priceless. They not only keep an eye on what I'm doing, but they also introduce me to many more good people just like them.

Family is even more important, and my family is one of the true blessings I have.

Many thanks go to my husband, David Dikel, for his patience and love.

And to Misty, who reminds me when I've been on the computer too long.

1

Pounding the
Virtual Pavement:
Using the Internet
in Your Job Search

Using the Internet in your job search is not necessarily easy. The online job search crosses a variety of services and information resources. No single website, online service, or electronic resource will contain everything you need for a fully effective online job search.

Please Note: Unless otherwise indicated by the inclusion of *http://* you must add *www.* to the beginning of each URL listed here.

What Is a Complete Job Search?

Many people think they are working hard on their search for a new job when they religiously scan the Sunday classifieds each week. Unfortunately, what they are really doing is expending 100 percent of their effort on only 25 percent of the possibilities.

A complete job search involves four activities:

1. Networking

2. Researching and contacting employers about possible opportunities

3. Reviewing job leads

4. Preparing a resume and distributing it

Incorporating the Internet into your search means each activity has two facets—offline and online:

Job-Search Activity	Offline	Online
Network	Attend association meetings, have friends and colleagues introduce you to others	Participate in appropriate mailing lists and chat forums, arrange to meet at local meetings or national conferences
Research and contact target employers	Use telephone books and business directories, and then make telephone calls or send letters	Use telephone books, business directories, association links, industry sites, employer websites, and search engines, and then contact via e-mail or telephone
Review job leads	Use newspapers, recruiters, association journals, job postings on bulletin boards	Use online job banks, recruiter websites, news-papers, association journals, employer websites
Distribute your resume	Mail copies to employers and networking contacts	E-mail copies to employers and networking contacts, post in online databases

It's important to remember that as you search for opportunities you must not put all your effort into just one activity or facet. A successful job search includes all of the activities and facets in the appropriate measures. You should spend more time where you will get more value, and focus less on those activities that produce fewer results You are the only one who can measure your comfort level with any activity or environment, but avoiding some of the more difficult ones in favor of others that seem easier will only hurt you in the long run. Look at it this way:

- Networking offline by attending local association meetings means coming in contact with the people best positioned to help you with your search.

- Reviewing job listings online allows you to review lots of job listings in a very short time.

- Telephoning potential employers puts a person behind a name or electronic resume and lets you talk about possibilities and how you can help.

The Internet Advantage

Here are some ways the Internet can enhance your job search:

- You can access current information when it's convenient for you, even if that means doing it at night after the kids go to bed.

- The Internet doesn't take holidays, the whole network doesn't go down all at once, and if one site is down there are always others you can use.

- There are no geographic limits online, so you can take your job search far beyond your regular boundaries. Many employers prefer to hire from their local area, but that doesn't mean you can't set up interviews before moving.

- You can dig deeper into your local area and perhaps find the smaller employer within walking distance from your house who needs someone just like you.

- Using the Internet in your search demonstrates computer skills to employers.

- No one can see you sweat. The Internet lets you meet new people and initiate new relationships with others in your profession or region without the usual "first date" stress.

- You can explore career alternatives and options that you might not have considered. Not quite happy with your current job? Explore! What sounds like fun? Are there any ways to apply your current skills in a new direction? You will find self-assessment tools, career guides, and even lists of local career counselors and career centers to help you if you feel you need it.

But Before You Go Online . . .

You need to know what keywords to use as you search, which means knowing what you want to find. This is important because most of the online job banks and other directories allow you to search their listings using keywords, so to use them effectively you have to know what you want to search. To make up this list of keywords, ask yourself these three questions and jot down the answers:

1. What do you want to do? What can you do? (Skills and Occupations) For instance: *I can type seventy words per minute; I like working with my hands; I'm licensed to drive a forklift.* Along with your list of specific skills, put down general occupations that interest you. Don't focus on job titles such as chief medical officer or vice president of international sales. Think "doctor" or "sales" instead.

2. Whom do you want to work for? What industries interest you, what type of employer? (Industries and Employer Preferences) For instance: *I want to work for an Inc 500 company; I'd like to find a family-friendly employer.* Add specific companies you've always wanted to work for.

3. Where do you want to live and work? (Location) Is there a particular city, state, region, or country you are targeting? For instance: *Southern California; Maryland; someplace with good golf courses and very little snow.* If you are thinking about a particular city, find out what other cities and municipalities surround it, what county it's in, and if the region has a geographic nickname (such as "Silicon Valley" or "Silicon Alley"). Add all this information to your list. Local maps or an atlas can help you here, as can the online telephone books and map services. Your local librarians can point you toward even more useful materials.

JOB-SEARCH TIP

The best way to compile your list of keywords is to prepare your resume. This exercise forces you to define your skills and qualifications, outline your work experience, and determine how you want to market yourself, all of which will help to define the keywords you will use in your search. You also need your resume ready once you begin your job search. Resources to help you write your resume are included in Chapter 2.

If you are having trouble coming up with answers to the previous questions, try the following:

- **Scan some online job banks.** Search some of the job-lead banks listed in Chapter 3 for jobs that interest you. Read the job descriptions, note the skills and qualifications the employers are seeking, and then use these words in your search.

- **Ask a friend.** Friends can frequently see things in you that you can't see yourself. They might also have some good ideas and interesting options for you to consider.

- **Read some good books.** Check your local library for *What Color Is Your Parachute?* by Richard Bolles (Ten Speed Press) or *Cool Careers for Dummies* by Marty Nemko and Paul and Sarah Edwards (For Dummies). These contain information and exercises designed to help you identify your skills and interests, and they suggest some interesting occupations to consider. Your local career center, public library, or employment service center can recommend even more good books and resources.

- **Ask a librarian.** Librarians are usually very good at this kind of exercise, plus they can point you to other helpful books and resources.

- **Talk to a counselor.** If you are truly having trouble figuring out what you want to do, contacting a career counselor should be your next move. A counselor can help you learn more about yourself and your interests and guide you through the process of deciding where to go. We have resources to help you find career counselors in Chapter 14.

The "Dirty Dozen" Online Job-Search Mistakes

Before we start talking about where to go and what to look for, let's talk about some of the common mistakes people make when they use the Internet as a job-search tool. Susan Joyce, webmaster of Job-Hunt.org (http://job-hunt.org), has put together a list of common errors she sees as she works with both job hunters and hiring managers. Review this list so you can avoid making the same mistakes.

1. Posting your resume without worrying about privacy. Protect your identity (and your existing job, if you are currently employed) by limiting access to your contact information.

2. Using your employer's computer (and other assets such as Internet connection, telephone, etc.) to job hunt at work. It may cost you your job by inappropriately using company assets, by violating the company Internet acceptable-use policy, and/or simply by revealing to your employer that you are job hunting.

3. Expecting someone else to do the work (the job sites, a recruiter, your outplacement counselor, etc.). A job hunt is a do-it-yourself project! No one is as invested in your future as you are, and no one else knows what you want as well as you.

4. Not leveraging the Internet's extensive research resources to assist your job search. Use the Internet to identify potential employers, evaluate them, and contact them. Customize your resume and cover letter based on your research, and then dazzle them in the interview with your insight into their products and services, their market, their competitors, etc.

5. Forgetting an e-mail message may be providing an employer with that all-important first impression. Using a crazy, cute, or weird e-mail address (e.g., WonderWoman@yahoo.com or BigStud@hotmail.com) undermines your credibility and almost guarantees a message will be deleted or ignored.

6. Depending on e-mail as your only method of contact. The sad truth these days is that most employers have spam filter software that screens e-mail before it reaches recipients. Your messages may look like spam and be deleted, unread, without notice to you (the suspected spammer).

7. Not virus-proofing your computer so that your resume and cover letter arrive at the employer's inbox containing credibility-destroying surprises. An e-mail message containing a virus is usually quarantined and deleted. It's not viewed! And it leaves a very bad impression.

8. Using the "fire-ready-aim" method of distributing your resume. Posting your resume at hundreds of job sites or "blasting" it to hundreds or thousands of recruiters and employers is a self-defeating strategy. Most recipients will probably regard it as spam.

9. Applying for jobs without meeting the minimum qualifications. Taking advantage of the simple application process to apply for every job that looks interesting, even if you don't have the minimum qualifications, means you will be training recruiters and employers to ignore you.

10. Using only the big-name job websites. In tight budgetary times, employers save money using less expensive niche sites that may have exactly the applicants they want—for example, an association's website or an industry- or location-specific job site.

11. Forgetting that a personal resume Web page or portfolio is a business document. Yes, you can make a razzle-dazzle resume Web page, but, unless you are demonstrating skills required for the job you want, the animated pooping bull or the fluttering butterflies may make a potential employer think you're not very serious about your job search.

12. Limiting your job-search efforts to the Internet only. People are hired by people; the Internet is useful only as a way to reach the people with the job opportunities. Use the Internet as a *part* of your job-search toolkit.

Job-Hunt.org is filled with insightful and truly helpful articles designed to guide you to a better job search. We urge you to visit this site and take advantage of the free guidance provided, including several simple things you can do to stand out from the crowd in your search as well as ways to protect your privacy and identity online.

Now that you know where you can go wrong, let's talk about where you can go right—into an employer's view and onto his or her payroll—starting with finding the information you need.

Make Your Search Less Work: Easy Ways to Find Anything Online

There are two simple ideas that will help you find anything on the Internet:

1. Move from general to specific. The more general sites such as Yahoo.com will help you to find the more specific sites. When you review job listings you want to check the big job sites such as Monster.com and the smaller targeted sites such as ChicagoJobs.org.

2. Browse to learn, and search to find. Browsing allows you to look over a site at your own pace, learn the language it uses and what it includes, and get comfortable with it. Searching gets you to the heart of the matter quickly and efficiently.

TIME TO BROWSE

When you are unsure of where to start or what to look for, browsing is the way to go. It's also helpful in cases in which you've already started looking online but aren't finding what you want. Browsing works well when you have a basic idea of what you want, but you could use some suggestions or pointers to move you in the right direction.

Browsing is a general search and scan process. You use very broad terms from your keyword list to search Internet libraries or directories for information and resources on your choice of occupations or industries, and then you scan the resulting list to see what came up. It's like searching the catalog in your local library: you find a book that looks promising and go to the correct shelf to pull it, but while there, you look around to see what else might catch your eye. You don't just look at the list of links to other sites and resources; you're also interested in the categories of information produced so you can scan the shelves and see what you might find. In most cases, you should start finding information and resources almost immediately, along with suggestions for more paths to explore. You can find job sites, potential employers, links to industry or occupational information, and pointers to resource guides.

Browsing also lets you test your keywords so you can see which terms from your list point you in the right direction or even give you more keywords to use. You also learn which words don't work well and which are taking you in the wrong direction and should be removed from your list. In any case, none of it is wasted activity.

START THE SEARCH

Searching comes into play when you have your objectives identified, you've developed your keyword list and settled on the very best terms defining your needs and objectives, and you have your resume prepared. You know you are ready to search when you have a list of very specific terms defining your skills, the types of jobs you are looking for, and the companies or organizations for which you want to work—a list that was built while you were browsing. You are not looking for long lists of possibilities, but rather the most specific and best-matched ones.

Searching has the advantage of speed and accuracy. You cover more ground online because you move faster and with more determination. You get in and out of the major job-lead banks in ten minutes or less, you're able to review loads of information about an employer in preparation for an interview in twenty minutes or less, and you aren't wasting time scanning hundreds of job leads. Your searches produce a limited number of highly qualified leads and highly qualified employer lists with very little mismatched job-lead spam.

Through browsing and searching, you have already begun to move from general data to specific information. Now you can start expanding this approach to the online resources needed for your search.

Stepping Through the Internet Research Process

Now let's apply the ideas of moving from general to specific and browsing before searching to your search for information online.

STEP 1: CHECK THOSE VIRTUAL LIBRARIES AND INTERNET DIRECTORIES (VERY GENERAL)

Virtual libraries and Internet directories are large collections of information arranged in broad topics by human editors. Because they cover many subjects, they act as general guides to the Internet. They are useful for identifying the best terms for searching and to begin finding helpful resources. Start out by browsing their main categories, and then use their search features, scanning the resulting lists for ideas.

Try this: Browse *education* or *finance* in the following libraries and directories to find information on these topics. Make a note of employers you find and topics you discover.

Librarian's Index to the Internet	lii.org
The Scout Report	http://scout.wisc.edu
University of Delaware Subject Guides	http://www2.lib.udel.edu/subj
Yahoo!	yahoo.com

Many of the search engines listed under Step 3, coming up, also maintain directories of information you can browse.

STEP 2: REVIEW ONLINE RESOURCE GUIDES (BECOMING MORE SPECIFIC)

Online resource guides are sites or online documents dedicated to a specific topic or industry. Like print directories or encyclopedias that focus on only one topic, they are much more specific in identifying industry and employer information and are usually more inclusive of resources. The virtual libraries and Internet directories listed in Step 1 will point you toward online resource guides (look for the indexes or directories under any topic). The best resource guides are those created by organizations or people who are specialists in a particular subject or topic.

To judge the value of a resource guide, look for information on who has compiled it, reviewing the creator's expertise in this area noting why the guide was created. Resource guides can take many forms, as you can see from this short list.

Hoover's	hoovers.com (business information)
NewsLink	http://newslink.org (newspapers worldwide)
The Riley Guide	rileyguide.com (employment information)

STEP 3: SEARCH THOSE SEARCH ENGINES (VERY SPECIFIC)

While a Web directory usually points you to a whole website, a search engine is a searchable database of keywords retrieved from individual Web pages, and these databases are huge. For this very reason, it's best not to use the search engines until you can be very specific about what you want to find. Use search engines to locate hidden information on any topic (occupation or industry) or employer. Remember that each search engine is different in terms of how it works and what it indexes, and none of them, even the biggest, have indexed the whole Web. Use two or three in your search and compare the results. Try them all, but choose the ones you like the best. Don't feel obliged to use the ones that your friends, the local librarians, or even this book might recommend. It's a personal choice. Once you've selected the ones you like the best, become an expert searcher by learning all the advanced commands so you can really *search*!

Try this: Search the names of employers you found earlier as well as specific topics or occupational fields.

AlltheWeb	alltheweb.com
AskJeeves	ask.com
Google	google.com

Now that you know how and when to browse and search and where to look for what you want, you can start your online job search. We'll go through each job-search activity—networking, researching, reviewing job leads, and preparing a resume—and talk about how you can incorporate the online facet of each into your search. Just remember to also work on each activity offline for the best results in your job search.

INTERNET TIP: BROKEN URLS

If you have trouble connecting to a particular Web page, try cutting the address, or URL (for "uniform resource locator"); go back one slash mark from the right end. The file or directory you are seeking may have moved, and by backing up one level at a time, you may be able to find the new location.

rileyguide.com/careercenter/dob.html becomes *rileyguide.com/careercenter/* becomes *rileyguide.com*.

Step One for Your Search: Network

In the foreword for this book, Gerry Crispin reported that one-quarter of the openings that an employer fills by hiring from outside the organization come from employee referrals. Gerry and his partner got this information from surveys of employers. (You can read these on their website at careerxroads.com.) Regular surveys of candidates in transition programs at the outplacement firm of Drake Beam Morin (dbm.com) also confirm from the job seeker's point of view what all the experts repeat ad infinitum: Networking is the best way to find a new job. The problem is networking is also the most stressful of the four activities in the job-search process, which is probably why it is the least pursued. In this case, the Internet can make a difficult situation a bit easier by allowing you to network online.

Advantages of Online Networking

You can break the ice before meeting someone in person. No one can see you sweat.

You can listen, engage, or be engaged as you wish. You won't feel like a wallflower, because no one can see you standing off by yourself.

Many recruiters follow the discussions to help locate interesting and qualified candidates for positions they are trying to fill.

Many employers and recruiters use subject-specific groups to post jobs targeting a defined group of potential applicants.

And the Disadvantages

While making first contact is easier, establishing a true personal relationship online takes more time because you do not have the luxury of the personal touch or a handshake.

First impressions count more than ever, so be very careful with your public postings since any posting may be the first time someone learns about you. You must be even more professional and polite than you would be in person, and you should be very careful with your language.

There are strict etiquette and behavior rules for each group, and they can differ widely from group to group. Any behavior that appears rude or obnoxious will get you blacklisted faster than you can imagine.

The content of each group differs. Some groups allow job announcements; some don't. Some post only professional scholarly announcements. Know what is permitted before you post by reading any available FAQs (frequently asked questions).

The contents of public forums and lists are often indexed by the search engines, viewable by anyone who searches, at any time in the future. So don't reveal anything or write anything that you would be uncomfortable having a potential employer see.

THE FINE ART OF NETIQUETTE

As we said earlier, the stress of making new connections is greatly alleviated through the Internet, but this isn't a fast track to the hidden job market. It is important that you begin these relationships in the right way and maintain them properly. Because you can't use your voice or body language to express yourself, you are limited to making sure that the words used and how they are presented properly represent your intentions. And this warning is not just for those new to the Internet. Many Internet experts need a reminder that the real people behind the electrons make real decisions based on your electronic communication. To all of you we humbly offer this bit of advice: **Do not go boldly where you have never gone before!**

Online networking gives you a unique opportunity to connect with people in hiring places. Take the time to learn some simple rules of Netiquette, otherwise known as the Fine Art of Correct Behavior on the Internet. These simple rules can mean the difference between stepping out in style and stumbling off the online block.

Stop and learn the respective rules of conduct and desirable topics of discussion for any particular mailing list or community forum, and then follow them!

Look for a list of FAQs so you don't ask the same questions that everyone else has and frustrate the other users of the list.

Listen patiently to the groups and forums you have joined and learn the tone, language, and culture of the group before you start posting.

Never post your resume or ask if anyone can help you find a job unless you are participating in a forum dedicated to this activity.

Think of each online discussion forum as an association meeting or an office party where you are the new person in the crowd. You must introduce yourself to everyone, and you want to make a good first impression. Step carefully, speak well, and learn as much as you can about this group of people before you make yourself known to them. Remember the three principles of good networking.

1. Public participation is necessary to get networking contacts. If you don't make yourself visible, no one will know you are there, including recruiters and potential employers.

2. Your participation must count. Enhance the discussions with your knowledge, but limit your responses to topics you know. Offer truly helpful advice or information when you can, but do not overwhelm others by responding to each and every question asked. Earn your place and the respect of the others.

3. Networking is a two-way relationship that must be beneficial to both parties. You must give in order to receive. If you aren't helping others on the list, then it is unlikely they will be willing to help you.

We have listed several books and resources on networking at the end of this chapter, but we suggest the following articles as required reading before you start strutting your stuff online:

• Agre, Phil. "Networking on the Network" (http://dlis.gseis.ucla.edu/people /pagre/network.html). Although intended for graduate and Ph.D. students, the principles outlined here apply widely to anyone considering using the Internet as a networking tool.

• Rinaldi, Arlene H. "The Net: User Guidelines and Netiquette" (fau.edu /netiquette/). This is a complete introduction to appropriate online behavior. It has been adopted by many organizations for their own use.

IDENTIFYING THE GOOD CONTACTS AND MAKING THAT FIRST CALL

Now that you are in an online discussion group, how can you identify the people who might be your best contacts? First, look for postings by those who seem knowledgeable about the topic being discussed. You can do this only by knowing the topic yourself, but beyond that, look for people who seem not only authoritative, but also have the respect of others. You want to pay attention to the person about whom others say, "Yes, listen to this person." Then check the person's organizational affiliation. You might be able to decipher this from his or her e-mail address, but it might also be in a signature at the end of the message. These signatures usually give a person's name, his or her employer and job title, and more complete contact information. While such signature information is not a guarantee that this person is good, it's at least a statement that the writer is not afraid to identify him- or herself and the affiliate organization.

Once you have selected some forum participants you want to contact, prepare your approach carefully. Because you know them from the Internet, your first contact should be through the Internet, specifically by e-mail. Be sure your message is professional and especially polite, and double-check for grammar and spelling errors before sending it. In addition:

- Be sure to contact the person or persons directly, not through the list or open forum.

- Be concise, identify yourself, and state why you are contacting the person. List some of your interests and where you noticed some correlation with his or her postings. Never use this contact to ask for a job or if he or she knows of any jobs.

- Request a follow-up to your message, via phone or e-mail, but give your contact the choice of how to continue.

- If you are contacting more than one person, do not copy the same message to each of them. Send each person a separate e-mail message. It not only looks better but also avoids the possibility of fueling any hidden rivalries that might work against you.

WHERE TO NETWORK ONLINE

There are numerous places to network online, including mailing lists, chat rooms, Usenet newsgroups, and Web forums. The principles regarding Netiquette and making contact with participants that we outlined earlier apply in all of these areas. The marvelous thing about all these online forums is that they are a great way to begin those casual relationships that later turn into great opportunities. Various forums are used to announce meetings, projects, proposals, and products. Participants also discuss recent developments in their occupation or industry and ask questions of one another. Anyone involved in a job search or career exploration can benefit from following these online public discussions, learning about current trends and developments and the interests and concerns of those involved.

It's important to remember that while there are hundreds if not thousands of discussion forums out there, the best ones for your job search will be those dedicated to professional topics representing your particular employment field, the industry that interests you, or research topics in your field of study. While the rec.pets.dogs newsgroup is a great place to get to know other dog lovers, it will truly benefit only dog walkers or pet sitters in terms of networking for employment. Once you identify the forums that carry discussions for your field or industry, it's also possible that you'll find job announcements crossing these forums, making these yet another targeted service for your job search.

WEB FORUMS

Web forums, sometimes also called online communities or message boards, are discussion groups that operate through the Web. Many sites offer them, and the easy Web interface makes them popular with users. All you need to participate is usually a valid e-mail address (for registration purposes) and a Web browser. Check out the Web forums at these sites to see how they operate and what they offer.

Fast Company's Company of Friends	fastcompany.com/cof
MSN Groups	http://groups.msn.com
Vault.com Message Boards	vault.com

USENET NEWSGROUPS

Usenet newsgroups are discussion groups that operate on the Usenet, another network that makes up the Internet. Like mailing groups and Web forums, the newsgroups on the Usenet cover a variety of subjects from highly professional to highly personal to just plain odd. To access the actual Usenet, you must use software called a *newsreader* and the computer you are using must also have access to the Usenet. (Users of Microsoft's Internet Explorer should look for their newsreader under Tools/Mail and News.) Fortunately, Google offers you a way to view and post Usenet newsgroup messages through a convenient Web gateway.

Google Groups (Usenet archive)	http://groups.google.com

MAILING LISTS

Mailing lists are discussion groups that operate through e-mail; anyone with an e-mail address can use them. A central computer (sometimes called the listserv, listproc, or majordomo) runs the list. (The name varies according to which list manager software is being used.) To participate in a mailing list, you must first subscribe to the list by sending a message to the list's host computer asking to be added to that particular list. The computer will then send you back a message to let you know your status. Once it says you are successfully added, you will automatically begin receiving the messages from that mailing list in your e-mail account. This ease of use and delivery makes them very popular.

Like other online discussion forums, mailing lists cover a broad variety of topics and fields. They carry occasional job postings, usually in advance of print announcements, and they are a good resource for networking contacts, industry trends, and other developments. Mailing lists are popular among the traditionally academic professions, making them particularly useful for persons looking for work in colleges and universities. In fact, Sarah Nesbeitt of LibraryJobPostings.org reported in *American Libraries* (Vol. 34, No. 6, June/July

2003, p. 116+) that a survey she did shows that mailing lists are the number one source for job listings for librarians in all work settings.

INTERNET TIP: FREE E-MAIL

If you don't have an e-mail account available where you access the Internet, or if your account is through your employer, register with one of these free Web-accessible e-mail services.

Eudora Webmail   eudoramail.com
Mail.com   mail.com
Yahoo! Mail   http://mail.yahoo.com

These directories can help you find relevant mailing lists for your networking. They can be searched using keywords that describe the subject or occupational area in which you are interested or browsed by major topic.

Catalist   lsoft.com/lists/listref.html

Topica   topica.com

Yahoo! Groups   http://groups.yahoo.com

Some mailing lists are also archived online, making it easier for you to get the feel of a list before you subscribe to it. The archives are fairly limited in the number of groups they cover, but they can still be helpful. These sites offer archives of mailing lists.

eScribe   escribe.com

Yahoo! Groups   http://groups.yahoo.com

There's one more thing you must remember about mailing lists, and that is how to control them. When you are first added to a list, you should receive a brief message with explanatory commands, including the ones you need in order to suspend mail while you are on vacation or to unsubscribe from the list should it not be right for you. Save this message somewhere, along with the e-mail address of the person who manages the list! Other list members do not appreciate it when you have to write to the list to ask for this information. To learn more about the basics of mailing lists, along with the rest of the Internet, we suggest the following books.

• Kent, Peter. *The Complete Idiot's Guide to the Internet*. Alpha Books.

• Levine, John R., et al. *The Internet for Dummies*. For Dummies.

Both of these are updated frequently, so look for the most recent editions.

Step Two for Your Search: Research and Target Employers

The Internet is a huge collection of databases just waiting for you. Tap the resources provided by the thousands of companies, colleges and universities, governments, and news and information services to do extended research into your target occupations, industries, and employers.

Have you ever gone into a hardware store and asked the manager if there were any job openings for day-care providers? No, because you know it is unlikely a hardware store would have any need for someone with those skills. This is why you research employers, to find those that have a need that you can fill. You want to know what they do, how they function, and how you might fit into the organization.

In the same vein, if you are invited for an interview, you cannot walk into an employer's office and say, "So, what is this job I am interviewing for, and how do I fit into your organization?" Employers today expect you to know who they are, what they do, what the job entails, and how you might fit into the company structure and culture before you arrive. Researching the employer in advance will get you past the small talk and into the real purpose of your interview: convincing the employer that he or she needs you and that you will be a valuable addition to the team.

Think of a job interview as a sales pitch. You have a product to sell (yourself). You need to know who is buying (the employer) and what he or she needs (what skills are required in what jobs). Once you've determined the situation, you send in your marketing brochure (the resume and cover letter), noting the company's needs and specifying how your product fills those needs. If you've done it right, you'll be invited to make a live presentation (job interview), and possibly make the sale (be offered a position). All it takes is some advance research. You know the constant refrain by heart: 80 percent of all jobs are never advertised, not even on the Internet. Well, researching the employers and contacting them is one way to get connected to that "hidden market." (The other way is through networking.)

To start your search, you first need to find lists of companies to review. Then you must research them to weed out those that don't interest you, leaving only two or three. These few must be very aggressively researched until you find the points that match your desires, and, one hopes, the right people inside each for you to contact.

Business directories and yellow pages directories are good ways to find lists of companies. Many of these online sources will include links to the company's website. The business directories will also give you some information about the company so you can begin to weed out those that do not interest you and highlight those that do.

CorporateInformation	corporateinformation.com
Smartpages	smartpages.com
Superpages	superpages.com
Thomas Register	thomasregister.com

Once you have a list of possible employers you can begin the three-part process of researching the company itself. As you go through this process, you will prune your list even further, leaving yourself with a few core companies to target.

1. Start your employer research at the employer's website. The company website is a book about the employer by the employer. Read it and print out the pages that interest you or have information you want to double-check.

   Look at anything that says "News" or "What's New" for the latest information on what is happening and possible clues on new areas or projects where you might be able to contribute necessary skills.

   Read all mission statements or descriptions of services to learn how this organization describes itself. Use this to customize your cover letter to the company's interests.

   Look for annual reports or strategic plans, and read them carefully. These will tell you where the company is going and how it plans to get there.

   Check out the human resources area for more information on current or ongoing job openings and the benefits offered by this company.

   Look over the whole site. What does the design of these pages say to you about this organization? Is the design conservative or freewheeling? Are the pages well organized or difficult to follow? Companies want their websites to reflect the business's corporate image, so the site can say a lot about the institution with very few words.

2. Check business directories and other employer information sources for outside profiles of the employers. This includes brief profiles with financial information such as those found in Hoover's or insider profiles like those from The Vault and WetFeet.com. The reference librarians in your local library can point you toward even more print and electronic resources to help you with your research.

CorporateInformation.com	corporateinformation.com
Edgar (10K reports)	sec.gov/edgar.shtml
Hoover's	hoovers.com
Vault.com	vault.com
WetFeet.com	wetfeet.com

3. Fire up the search engines. Look for more information on an employer anywhere you can find it. Search the employer's name, the company's products, the names of any people in the organization, and so forth in your favorite search engine. Why? As one job seeker put it, "The employer's website told me what they wanted me to know, but I found what I wanted to know by doing more searching online." Anything you find can be useful in your initial search, your sales pitch, or even your decision on whether it's even worth contacting this employer about opportunities.

Step Three for Your Search: Review Job Listings

While searching for employers and opportunities, look for job listings at several levels, again always thinking about moving from general to specific.

Start with the large recruiting sites to get the broadest overviews and largest database searches you can.

Review the online journals, newspapers, and job banks for your target location, industry, and occupation or discipline. Look for recruiters who specialize in a particular industry or occupational group, or who concentrate on one geographic area.

Scan through the various professional or trade association websites to find job listings marketed to your particular job areas, occupational fields, industries, and geographic location. There are also websites for many of the diversity and affinity groups with which you might identify yourself, many of which carry job announcements.

Visit employer websites, even if you have seen their jobs listed in other locations. Many use the major job-lead banks to advertise generic jobs they are always looking to fill, but they may post the specific openings, along with even more job categories, on their own sites. You may also find a way to contact their human resources departments to learn about any opportunities they haven't posted.

Online resource guides for job and career information contain links to hundreds of Internet employment resources. Using these, you can quickly identify places to begin your job search. The Employment or Jobs/Careers sections of the virtual libraries might also be useful, but you'll likely find these targeted guides better organized and more in-depth. This short list will get you started; a more complete list with descriptions can be found at the end of Chapter 3.

Job-Hunt	job-hunt.org
JobHuntersBible	jobhuntersbible.com

| JobStar | http://jobstar.org |
| The Riley Guide | rileyguide.com |

JOB LISTINGS 102: THE GREAT JOB-LEAD BANKS

Job-lead banks feature hundreds or even thousands of job announcements in numerous fields and occupations. The online classifieds of most major newspapers fall under this category (smaller regional and local papers are generally considered targeted sources, the next category). Almost all of these sites and sources have a keyword searching capability, allowing you to scan all the job listings in a few minutes instead of a few hours. A sample listing follows; a more complete list of the great job-lead banks along with descriptions can be found in Chapter 3.

America's Job Bank	ajb.org
CareerBuilder	careerbuilder.com
Monster	monster.com
NationJob	nationjob.com

JOB LISTINGS 103: TARGETED SOURCES

Many sites are set up to serve a particular industry, occupation, geographic location, or group of people. Professional and trade associations, all trade and industry publications, and even the mailing lists and community forums discussed in the earlier section on networking fall into this category. This book contains hundreds of these sites, so select the chapters that address your needs and scan the index for topics you hadn't thought of. This is just a small example of the variety of targeted resources available online:

American Academy of Forensic Sciences	aafs.org
ChicagoJobs	chicagojobs.org
JobAccess (jobs for the disabled)	jobaccess.org
Power Marketing Association	powermarketers.com

JOB LISTINGS 104: EMPLOYER WEBSITES

As we outlined earlier, you need to create lists of employers for specific industries, filter the list to only those that match your job criteria, and make contact. Business directories and telephone directories can be useful in this part of your job search, as can your local public library or job service office.

Step Four for Your Search: Post Your Resume Online

Yes, you can post your resume in hundreds of databases online with the hope that you will be "discovered" by a great employer and offered your dream job. The problem is it is highly unlikely that this will ever happen to you, especially in the current job market. That's not to say that posting your resume is not worth your effort. Many people have posted their resumes online and gotten calls that have turned into successful new jobs. Articles about such people have appeared in various national publications; many successful posters have even sent the authors accounts of personal experiences or events they have witnessed, but these cases are a very small percentage of all those who are posting.

While we feel that posting your resume online is the least effective way for you to find a new opportunity, it is a way for you to become known to potential employers, so we want you to do it. We just don't want you to waste a lot of time on this activity when you could be doing more productive things such as networking, researching employers, and even reviewing job-lead banks.

If you decide to post your resume online, you must do it correctly. Your resume must be in the right form and format. You must also think about the ramifications of your decision to pursue this activity, and there are a lot of them. Because this discussion covers many topics and requires your full attention, we have devoted all of Chapter 2 to how, why, where, and when to post your resume online.

How to Select the Good Stuff

Now that you've found them, how do you decide which resources best fit your needs? You will have to make the final decision yourself based on your own needs and preferences, but following are questions to ponder as you review everything you find.

What Are You Finding There?

- Is it advertising, or is there useful information for your search? A site that is merely advertising its services isn't giving you any help right now.

- Is it information from experts in this field or comments submitted by others? While some lay users may contribute useful tips, articles from experts will have more authoritative and reliable information.

- Are there lists of employers, including businesses, colleges, schools, or nonprofit associations? These can be very helpful for targeting key firms or linking you to organizations of which you were unaware.

- Are there job listings, job-search tips, and other helpful items? While you are struggling through this process, you may prefer a site with articles about writing resumes and cover letters.

What About the Job Listings?

- Are there real jobs listed here, or just "sample lists of jobs we are currently trying to fill"? Samples are OK, but when you're ready to "buy," pay for only the real thing, even when it comes to free job listings.

- Are the job listings dated so you know when they were added? It is frustrating to you and to the employer to waste time on a job that was filled six months ago.

- Can you look at the job listings without registering your personal information and/or resume? Even if they block the employer's contact information, you should be able to review the listings before you register just to be sure that the jobs are current and relevant to you. We advise users to avoid sites that demand your personal information and/or resume before allowing you to see even a sample of the job database.

How Old Is the Other Information Posted There?

- Are articles and resource lists dated so you know the last time someone reviewed and revised them? Like job listings, these can become dated.

- Are the site's owners updating and adding new materials on a regular basis (daily, weekly, monthly)? If they are not posting anything new, it's unlikely they are working on maintaining current job listings on the site.

- Are the articles retained for an extended amount of time, or are they deleted when new material is added? While it's not necessarily a mark of higher quality, an archive of the older articles is a nice touch.

Who Operates This Service?

- Is there information available about the people who run this site? A simple profile is not hard to write, especially for a group with nothing to hide from visitors.

- What are their backgrounds (recruiters, industry specialists, librarians, etc.)? There are many online job-search services now being run by people who have no background in what they are doing. They are just looking for some fast money and are hoping you'll give it to them.

- Is there a name, address, or phone number for contacting them with questions? At the very minimum, there should be an e-mail address for questions. Again, legitimate services will provide this information. They want to hear from you, and they will also respond if you send an e-mail.

If There's a Fee for This Service, Is It Worth the Cost?

- Can you find other sites and services that offer an equal service at no cost? Don't just pay for this service; be a careful shopper and compare it with others.

- What will your money get you? If you are paying to have your resume forwarded to employers, ask how many employers, in what industries, and demand a list of those who will be receiving it. Have these employers registered with this service as interested parties, or is it a spam list cobbled together from other sources?

- What is the refund policy if you're not satisfied? Again, look for who is running this site, where they are located, and how to contact them.

What Promises Are They Making, and Are These Promises Reasonable?

- Do they offer guarantees? If so, the Federal Trade Commission will want to speak with them. Nothing in a job-search process is guaranteed. There's no exclusive access to the "hidden job market," and there's no guarantee that shooting hundreds of copies of your resume to employers through e-mail will result in your getting an interview, let alone a job.

If You Send These People an E-mail Message Asking for More Information, Do They Actually Respond?

- If they never contact you, consider this a warning that saved you some money.

- If they do contact you, then judge them using your own criteria based on the information they provide. Be sure to ask them all the questions that are important to you, and don't let anyone bully you into buying.

Do You Know People Who Have Used This Service?

- For what purpose did they use the service (posted a resume, reviewed job leads, worked through the career-exploration exam)? How well did it work for them? Did they get calls from recruiters, find good job leads, or get some interesting insight from the exam?

- Did they like what they found? Were the recruiters who called professional? Did they feel comfortable with this service?

- Do they feel it was helpful and worth the time spent here?

As we said at the beginning of this section, the final decision for using any site or service online (or off) is yours and yours alone. Be a careful consumer and buy wisely. If you get lousy service somewhere or pay for services that are not provided in the manner that was promised (or do not produce the promised results), don't take it lying down. Complain to the Better Business Bureau (bbb.org), the Federal Trade Commission (ftc.gov), your state's attorney general, and, if it is an online service, the Internet Fraud Complaint Center (ifccfbi.gov).

After you notify all of them, we hope you will send the authors an e-mail (webmaster@rileyguide.com) because we want to know about it too!

INTERNET TIP: ONLINE PAYMENTS

When paying for any service through the Web, use a credit card. Never send a check or money order, and we don't recommend using a debit card either. Credit cards offer you more protections and recourse should you not receive the services or products advertised. When making a purchase online, look for a locked padlock icon in the status bar at the bottom of the browser before entering your credit card information into a Web page. If the padlock icon is open or unlocked, the data transmission is not secure, and you should not trust it with your credit card information. If you don't want to transmit your credit card information over the Internet, call the company from whom you want to purchase the goods and/or services and give them the information over the phone. If they will not accept your payment information in this way, take your business elsewhere.

Managing Your Time Online

Many people tell us that they always start searching online in the same place, and, well, heck, they spend so much time in those pages that they never get anywhere else.

Every time you connect, start someplace new. Pick out a select list of general resources, use them to find more specific resources, and keep moving. Things change, but not so rapidly that you will miss something important if you check there only twice a week. Plan your online job-search strategy so you don't get stuck in one place and waste time and money.

Here's an outline of what we think is your best plan for spending your time online wisely. It's based on our simple idea of moving from general to specific, but it's up to you to remember to move!

1. **Visit the large information databases first.** These include virtual libraries and large recruiting sites such as CareerBuilder.com and all the other sites we have listed in Chapter 3. Look for links to information in your chosen field or industry. Repeat this search every few days—for example, Monday and Thursday.

2. **Move on to the smaller, more exclusive resources and services, including online resource guides and sites dedicated to your field or industry.** You want to find links to employers or collected information in your field that can give you leads or networking contacts. Repeat this search every few days—say, Tuesday and Friday.

3. **Use the search engines to locate new and hidden resources specific to your occupation and field.** If you are interested in a certain company, search on the

company name, any variations or nicknames by which it is known, and names of its major products. Repeat this search every few days—maybe Wednesday and Saturday.

4. Finally, shut off the computer and spend some time with your family, your friends, and yourself. Take a day to relax, re-center, and remind yourself that there is a world out there and people to talk to. You can update your resume or prepare some cover letters, but don't go online. Take the kids to the park, play with your dog, scratch the cat, sun the iguana, or substitute time with whatever pets you have. Searching for work is a stressful process, and you need to take time for yourself to maintain your physical and emotional health. This positive action will reflect in your search and in interviews.

Probably the Most Important Statement in This Entire Book

The Internet cannot be the only resource you use for your job search!

You must continue to utilize all contacts, information resources, and services available to you to achieve the most effective and efficient search for employment. Attend local meetings, use the resources of your local library to locate employers you may have missed online, and pick up the telephone and call people. Despite all the potential of the Internet, it still doesn't connect everyone everywhere nor does it contain all the knowledge of the universe.

Limit your time online to 25 percent of the total time you can dedicate to your job search. IT and networking professionals may increase this to 50 percent of your time, but make sure your skills are very current so that you can be at your most competitive.

Suggested Reading for Your (Internet) Job Search

Listed here are a few of the many books and online resources available to help you learn how to take your job search online. Your local public library or career service center may have many of the books in its collection along with other titles. Ask librarians for their recommendations. If you'd like your own copy of a particular book to tear apart, mark up, or personalize in other ways, then check your local bookstore or any of the online bookstores. Many of these titles are updated every year or two, so always look for the most recent editions.

- Bolles, Richard. *Job-Hunting on the Internet*, third edition. The Parachute Library/Ten Speed Press, 2001.

- ———. *What Color Is Your Parachute?* Ten Speed Press (updated annually).

- Corcodilos, Nick A. *Ask the Headhunter: Reinventing the Interview to Win the Job.* Plume, 1997.

- Crispin, Gerry, and Mark Mehler. *CareerXRoads.* MMC Group (updated annually).

- Gurney, Darrell W. *Headhunters Revealed! Career Secrets for Choosing and Using Professional Recruiters!* Hunter Arts Publishing, 2000.

- Weddle, Peter D. *Weddle's Job-Seekers' Guide to Employment Web Sites.* Amacom (updated annually).

Job-Search Guidance Online

JobHuntersBible.com

jobhuntersbible.com

This website incorporates Richard Bolles's megalist of job resources online with many of his self-assessment exercises and job-searching advice from *Parachute,* but he still refers to it as a companion to his book.

Joyce Lain Kennedy's Careers Now

tmsfeatures.com/sitemap.htm

Joyce Lain Kennedy has been answering questions on career and employment issues for more than thirty years. She has written many books on careers and job search that have influenced the way thousands of us think about this process, and her syndicated column appears in more than one hundred newspapers. Tribune Media Services maintains a ninety-day archive of her columns, free to all viewers. The fastest way to access it is through the site map. Under Business, look for Workplace and select Careers Now.

Career Resource Library from the New York State Department of Labor

labor.state.ny.us/working_ny/finding_a_job/career_resource.html

The New York Department of Labor has several good guides and tools to help you through your job search on its website.

CareerJournal.com from the *Wall Street Journal*

careerjournal.com

CareerJournal.com offers hundreds of articles and information resources covering all aspects of the job search, and all experience levels from entry-level to chief executive. You'll notice that we mention this site many times throughout the book as a great source.

Interviewing and Networking Advice

Refer to our discussion on networking earlier in this chapter for more resources.

- Baker, Wayne E. *Networking Smart: How to Build Relationships for Personal and Organizational Success.* iUniverse.com, 2000.

- Fisher, Donna, et. al. *Power Networking: 59 Secrets for Personal & Professional Success*, second edition. Bard Press, 2000.

- Kramer, Marc. *Power Networking: Using the Contacts You Don't Even Know You Have to Succeed in the Job You Want.* VGM Career Books, 1998.

Online Advice for Interviewing and Networking

Interview Tips from Monster.com

http://content.monster.com/jobinfo/interview

Among other offerings from this popular job site, you'll find a script to follow for making phone calls, a virtual interview to help you prepare for the real thing, a sample of tough questions to practice answering in advance, and a list of questions to ask a headhunter.

Handling Questionable Questions in a Job Interview

rileyguide.com/dob.html

How do you respond when an interviewer asks you an improper question relating to issues such as your date of birth? This article asked several recruiters and career-management professionals for their advice.

Networking Tips

rwn.org/tips.htm

Authored up by the Rochester (New York) Women's Network, this article is a great guide to networking and includes pointers on working a room—or even working a table during a dinner event.

2

Your Resume
on the Internet

When talking about the job-search process, the action of distributing a resume is rated the least effective of the four activities that make up a complete search. However, job seekers rate it as the second most productive thing they can do online. While we de-emphasize this activity, we do so because in terms of finding you a new job it is not as effective as networking, researching and targeting employers, or even reviewing job leads. Believe it or not, we actually want you to create a great resume for yourself and post it online. We just don't want you to think that this will lead you to job-search happiness.

Writing your resume, actually creating the one that employers and others will review, is one of the most important tasks in a job search, one place where you must take the time to do it right, really thinking about what you want to do before you can start pounding the pavement. Even with our statements on how ineffective it is to post your resume in the many databases online, if you are going to do it—and we think you should—you must do it right.

Your resume is your product brochure, the piece of paper that summarizes all the benefits of you and why the employer should "buy" you. A great resume can help you win the position you want. A bad one will knock you out of consideration, no matter how qualified you are. You must have a great resume, but we are not the ones to help you with that. At the end of this chapter you'll find a list of great books and online workshops offered by experts in this field. They are the ones to help you write a resume. Your local librarians, career counselors and coaches, and bookstore managers can recommend even more books and resources, so don't be afraid to ask should you not find something you like here.

What we're good at is helping you take that resume and get it online, so that is what this chapter will cover. We'll also address the problems associated with posting a resume, how to format it so posting it in websites and e-mailing it to employers is fast and easy, and how to select where to post it. We encourage you to read this before you create your resume and then come back to it when you have your resume ready to go online. Consider the issues and advice we present here, and think about them as you are working on your resume. And remember, you do not need to limit yourself to just one resume. You can have several that are presented in different ways. If you have access to a computer with word-processing software, you are limited only by the available space on your disk or diskette.

Please Note: Unless indicated otherwise by the inclusion of *http://* you must add *www.* to the beginning of all URLs listed here.

The Myth About the Internet Resume

Many people think that the advancement of resume databases, resume-management systems, and keyword searching requires you to produce one resume for paper but an entirely different resume for online. *This is not true!*

When done correctly, your well-written, well-prepared resume will contain all of the necessary keywords to attract attention whether it is being read by a hiring manager or scanned and searched in any database, online or off. You still need only one resume, but now you want to have it in several formats, ready to produce in the proper form as needed, including these:

1. A designed or hard-copy version: a good-looking printed resume with bulleted lists, bold and italicized text, and other highlights, ready to send to contacts through the mail

2. A scannable version: a neat word-processed and printed resume without bullets, bold, italics, or other design highlights, written in a standard font and printed on white paper to send to employers who use scanning systems

3. A plain-text version: a no-frills plain-text file you keep on a diskette for copying and pasting into online forms and posting in online resume databases (See "Preparing a Perfect Plain-Text Resume" later in this chapter.)

4. An e-mail version: another no-frills plain-text file you keep on disk, but one formatted to meet the length-of-line restrictions found in most e-mail systems, making it easy to copy and paste into an e-mail message and forward to an employer or recruiter in seconds (See "Preparing a Perfect Plain-Text Resume" later in this chapter.)

You may also want to consider an HTML version of your resume. This can be posted on a personal website or with any site offering this kind of service. Many job seekers are creating webbed resumes in the hopes of being discovered. It's a great reference for employers who might want to see more than just that flat resume. This format works particularly well for those in a visual arts field, but if it is done correctly and for the right reasons it could serve anyone who wants to present more than what is usually found on a resume.

"Doing it correctly" means creating a simple HTML version of your designed resume, not a hip-hop page of spinning-whirling gizmos, dancing gerbils, and accompanying audio files that take more than two minutes to download over a 56K modem. "Doing it for the right reasons" means turning your resume into an employment portfolio, complete with links to former employers or projects that are already online. If you do this, you must be sure you are not violating any copyright or confidentiality clauses by putting project information online.

The main problem with HTML resumes is the too-much-information factor. Many job seekers make the resume a part of their personal website where there is often a lot of information an employer does not need to know—for example, your marital status, your ethnic background, or your personal interests. Allowing an employer to learn so much about you can lead to all kinds of problems, including discrimination against you for your physical appearance, political beliefs, religious practices, or even just the image you present. When you place your professional image online by posting your resume, it is important that you keep your presence entirely professional by never linking it to personal information of any kind. So if you decide to add an HTML resume to your campaign, post it in a location separate from your personal website, and do not create a link between the two.

Rules for Responding Online

The fastest way to respond to Internet job listings is by e-mailing your cover letter and resume to the person or organization indicated. Yes, your resume and cover letter are still your best bet for winning an interview, but if you mess up the application process, those great documents won't get you where you want to be. The rules are short and simple, so take a couple of minutes to review them before you hit the send key.

- Format your resume correctly for e-mail. If you try to copy and paste the text of your designed resume into the body of an e-mail message and then just send it without preparation, by the time it reaches the intended recipient the formatting will be such a mess it may be unreadable.

- Send your resume in the body of the e-mail message. Do not send it as an attachment unless specifically instructed by the recipient. You have only about twenty seconds to catch the eye of a recruiter or employer and to get him or her to read your resume. If you send your resume as an attachment, the recruiter has to find it and open it before he or she can read it. Your twenty seconds are over before they begin. Put the resume right in the message so the reader will see it immediately upon opening the mail. This also helps you bypass e-mail systems that refuse attachments in this day of rampant computer viruses.

- Always include a cover letter, whether or not you are responding to an advertised opening. Make that cover letter specific to the person or organization you are contacting, and make it interesting. If you are responding to an advertisement, note where you found the advertisement and any relevant job codes. You can create and store a "standard" cover letter in text, but remember to customize it for each job listing for which you are applying, checking the format before you send it.

- Use the advertised job title or job code in the subject line of your e-mail message. This makes it easy for the recipient to sort everything coming in and route your resume and letter to the appropriate person. If you are cold calling, trying to get your resume into someone's hands without responding to an advertised job posting, put a few words stating your objective in the subject line.

- Read the application instructions included in the job announcement and follow them exactly. Sometimes employers want applications sent to a specific e-mail address according to the job location. They might require you to apply through their website using a specific code. It's even possible they will request you attach your resume in Word. Whatever they say, do it. You don't want your application to be delayed because you sent it to the wrong address or person, and you don't want to be perceived as someone who cannot follow directions.

Always remember this as you prepare to e-mail your resume to an employer: *It takes only a couple of seconds for someone to delete an e-mail message.* Don't let that happen to you. Read and think before you respond!

E-Resumes Are Not Just for E-mail

Besides the need to have a well-done plain-text resume for e-mailing, there are hundreds more reasons to take the time to create an e-resume, namely all those places online where you can post your resume. Yes, almost all sites have a copy-and-paste option for getting your resume online. Some even offer to let you build your resume right on the site, but resume expert Susan Ireland doesn't recommend using these forms for the following reasons:

1. It's very easy to have typos if you type directly into the site's form. Working first in your word-processing program (with its spell-check function) can greatly improve your chances of having a perfect resume.

2. The form may force you to use a resume format that you don't like. Most online resume builders insist on a chronological resume, a format that focuses on work history. This will put career changers at a disadvantage because the system doesn't allow you to build a functional resume, a format that focuses on skills.

3. You cannot easily save your resume for other uses because the resume bank is on a website. That means you'd have to repeat your resume-building efforts on each site where you want to post your resume.

The best way to post your resume online is to copy and paste it from a prepared copy you have already formatted to look great online. For the best results, that means transforming the hard-copy version of your resume before you copy and paste it into the website's resume form.

Protect Your Privacy when Cutting and Pasting! Susan Joyce from Job-Hunt.org notes that people frequently sabotage their own privacy by copying the top of their resume (with all of their contact information) into the body-of-the-resume blocks on Web forms. While the job site blocks access to the contact information input into specific labeled fields, you the job seeker have accidentally revealed the information in the text block fields of the resume form. Be careful with the copy-and-paste process!

Preparing a Perfect Plain-Text Resume

Preparing a resume for electronic mail is an easy process, and anyone creating a resume should take the extra few minutes needed to generate a plain-text version. Most word processors and resume-writing programs will let you save a file to plain text. The next step, altering the format, is simple. The following instructions prepared by Susan Ireland will help you take that hard-copy resume and turn it into a perfect plain-text document for posting online. Ireland even talks you through an easy way to format it for e-mailing. Why is this a separate process, and why do we suggest you have two different plain-text copies of your resume? Because e-mail has more formatting restrictions than most online resume databases, but we know what those restrictions are. To find even more complete instructions on creating resumes, cover letters, and even various formats for your e-resume, visit Ireland's website (susanireland.com).

Please note that these instructions assume that your resume is in MS Word for Windows 2000 or earlier. If your resume is in another word-processing application or on a different computer platform such as Macintosh, you may need to consult your word-processing manual for specific instructions. Users of Word XP will find conversion instructions for this application at susanireland.com.

Step 1: Check keywords. Be sure your resume has all the keywords that define your job qualifications.

Step 2: Save your resume as a Text Only document. A Text Only document works best for an electronic resume because you can adjust the margins and formatting to suit the database or e-mail system in which you are working. To convert your MS Word resume to Text Only, do the following:

1. Open the MS Word document that contains your resume.

2. Click File in your toolbar and select Save As.

3. Type in a new name for this document in File Name, such as "ResTextOnly."

4. Under this is the Save As Type pull-down menu. From this list, select "Text Only (*.txt)."

5. Click Save to perform the conversion.

6. Now close the document but stay in MS Word.

7. Reopen the document you just closed by going to File in the toolbar, click Open, select the file named "ResTextOnly.txt," and click Open. *Warning:* if you exit MS Word and then open the resume document by clicking on its icon in the directory, it will be opened in Notepad, which will work for posting your resume on a website but is not what you want if you intend to use this version to prepare an e-mailable resume!

After converting your resume to Text Only, what appears in your document window is your resume stripped of any fancy formatting. You are now ready to make a few final adjustments before posting it online.

Step 3: Delete any page numbers. If your resume is more than one page, delete any indications of page breaks such as "Page 1 of 2," "Continued," or your name or header on the second page. You are making your resume appear as one continuous electronic document.

Step 4: Use all CAPS for words that need special emphasis. Since Text Only stripped your resume of all bolds, underlines, and italics used for highlighting words, use all capitalized letters to draw attention to important words, phrases, and headings. For the best overall effect, use all CAPS sparingly and judiciously.

Step 5: Replace each bullet point with a standard keyboard symbol. Special symbols such as bullet points, arrows, triangles, and check marks do not transfer well electronically. For example, bullet points sometimes transfer as "&16707," ")," or a little graphic of a thumbs-up. Therefore, you must change each to a standard keyboard symbol. Suggested replacements are:

Dashes (-)

Plus signs (+)

Single or double asterisks (*)(**)

Use the space bar to place a single space immediately after each symbol (and before the words). Do not use the tab key for spacing as you may have done in your original resume. Also, allow the lines to wrap naturally at the end of a line. Don't put a forced return (don't push the return or enter key) if it's not the end of the statement, and don't indent the second line of a statement with either the tab key or space bar.

Step 6: Use straight quotes in place of curly quotes. Like bullet points and other special symbols, curly or "smart" quotes do not transfer accurately and in fact may appear as little rectangles on the recipient's screen. So you should replace curly quotes with straight quotes. To do this, select the text that includes the quotes you want to change. Click Format in your toolbar and select AutoFormat. Click the Options button, and make sure "Replace Straight Quotes with Smart Quotes" is not selected under both the AutoFormat and AutoFormat

As You Type tabs. Then click OK to exit the AutoFormat box, and your curly quotes will be changed to straight quotes.

Step 7: Rearrange text if necessary. Do a line-by-line review of your document to make sure there are no odd-looking line wraps, extra spaces, or words scrunched together in the body. Make adjustments accordingly. This may require inserting commas between items that were once in columns and are now in paragraph format because tabs and tables disappeared when the document was converted to Text Only. Now that you have the plain-text resume for posting, it takes just a few more steps to create a perfect plain-text resume for e-mailing. Again, if you take the time to do this now, you will save yourself a lot of time later.

Step 8. Limit line lengths. Because each type of e-mail software has its own limit for the number of characters and spaces per line, your e-mail may have longer line lengths than the receiver of your e-mail allows. This can cause the employer to see line wraps in unusual places, making your resume document look odd and even illogical. To avoid this problem, limit each line to no more than sixty-five characters (including spaces). Here's an easy way to make line length changes in your document:

1. Open MS Word, click Open, select the file named "ResTextOnly.txt," and click Open. Warning: If you open the resume document by clicking on its icon in the directory, it will be opened in Notepad—not what you want right now.

2. Select the entire document and change the font to Courier, 12 point.

3. Go to Format in your toolbar; select Page Setup; set the left margin at 1 inch and the right margin at 1.75 inch.

4. Select the entire document and change the font to Times New Roman, Arial, or some other standard font you like.

With the side margins set under these conditions, each line of your document will be no more than sixty-five characters and spaces.

Step 9: Save as Text Only with Line Breaks. To save the line-length changes you made in Step 8, you need to convert your Text Only document one more time by doing the following:

1. With your Text Only resume document open, click File in your toolbar and select Save As.

2. Type in a new name for this document in File Name, such as "ResTextBreak."

3. Directly under this is the Save As pull-down menu. From this list, select "Text Only with Line Breaks (*.txt)."

4. Click Save to perform the conversion.

5. Now close the document and exit MS Word.

6. Reopen the resume document (ResTextBreak.txt) by clicking on its icon in the directory. That will open it as a Notepad document.

Step 10: Copy the entire text in your ResTextBreak.txt document that you've opened in Notepad, and paste it in the body of the e-mail message. Now that you have redone your resume in the e-mail format, e-mail it to yourself and to a friend to see how it looks after going through the Internet. This will help you identify any additional formatting problems you need to correct before you start sending it out to possible employers.

RESUME TIP

Never use your current office address, e-mail address, or phone number on your resume. Employers consider the personal use of company time and resources to be stealing, and they also believe that if you'll do it to your current employer, you'll do it to the next one, too. Always use personal contact points, such as a post office box, cell phone, and a personal e-mail account. This will also help you avoid possible monitoring by your current employer.

Where, Oh, Where Should That Resume Go?

With the hundreds, if not thousands, of possible posting sites now available online, you have ample opportunity to saturate the Internet with your resume. After all, don't you want to get your resume in front of every recruiter or employer you can, regardless of who they are? No, you don't.

Recruiters are tired of finding the same resumes for the same people in every database they search. They are even starting to ignore these resume spammers, refusing to give them any consideration for possible job openings. There is also the danger that the further your resume spreads, the less control you can exert over it. To make sure you don't encounter these problems, limit your resume exposure by limiting your postings.

- Post it on only one or two of the large online databases, preferably ones attached to popular job sites. This will give you maximum exposure to many employers and recruiters.

- Post it on one or two targeted resume databases specific to your industry, occupational group, or geographic location. This will give you a targeted exposure to employers and recruiters looking for a smaller yet more highly qualified candidate pool.

If you don't get any responses to your resume within forty-five days, remove it from its current locations and place it elsewhere.

PROTECT YOURSELF ONLINE

Limiting the number of locations is a good way to protect your resume, but it is also important to select those few sites with care. Susan Joyce, the editor of Job-Hunt.org, encourages careful evaluation of the job sites you use, because if you aren't careful, you risk a total loss of privacy. Not only could your resume become visible to anyone who comes across it, but also your personal information might be sold to people who have products and services to sell you. Joyce's article "Choosing a Job Site" (http://job-hunt.org/choosing.shtml) outlines fourteen criteria designed to help you evaluate a site before you trust it with your resume, including the following:

1. Does the site have a comprehensive privacy policy? Look for a privacy policy, and *read it* before your register at a job site! The privacy policy should disclose to you the information that the site collects and what they do with it (e.g., sell or rent your e-mail address, etc.). Pay particular attention to what happens to your resume!

2. Do you have to register a profile or resume before you can search through the jobs? Be suspicious of a site that won't let you perform a job search before you register your profile or resume. You need to evaluate the site to determine if it has the jobs you want *before* you register.

3. Are most of the jobs posted by employers or by agencies acting on behalf of employers? In general, jobs posted directly by an employer are preferable because you will be dealing directly with the people who can hire you.

4. Can you set up one or more "e-mail agents" that will send matching jobs to you when you are not at the site? E-mail agent functions typically compare your requirements with new employer job postings and send you the results via e-mail if they find a match. You don't need to revisit the site yourself and run your search. Your agents will do the searching for you and send you the results.

5. Who has access to the database of resumes? The privacy policy should tell you who has access to the resumes. In addition, you can check out the "employer" side of the job site to see how easy it is to gain access to the resumes. If resume access is free, or there is only a nominal fee for access to the resumes, find another job site.

6. Can you limit access to your personal contact information? The best sites provide you with options to protect your contact information (name, e-mail address, street address, phone numbers, etc.). Options range from blocking access only to the contact information to keeping your resume completely out of the resume database searched by employers. Choose the option that works best for you. If you are currently employed, limiting access can help you protect your current job.

7. Can you store more than one version of your resume so that you can customize it for different types of opportunities? Many sites offer you the ability to store several different resumes and apply for a job using the version of your resume you have developed for that specific kind of opportunity.

8. Will you be able to edit your resume once you have posted it? You shouldn't run into this very often anymore, but check to see if there is an update option for you to access your resume. You can always find ways to improve your resume, and they should allow you to do it.

9. Will you be able to delete your resume after you have found a job? You don't want that old resume still available for view. If your new employer finds it, he or she may be concerned that you are getting ready to leave. Good job sites provide you with the capability to delete your resume and account or to put your resume in an "inactive" mode until you are ready for your next job search.

The bottom line when posting your resume is that *you* rule. Many sites want your resume in their database. You can afford to be choosy about where you will place it and which sites you will use in your search.

BEFORE YOU POST, SOMETHING TO THINK ABOUT

For some people, posting a resume online is a great way to find new opportunities. For others, there is a very real fear that their contact information will fall into the wrong hands, or that the wrong organizations—such as their current employer—will see their resume online and problems will arise. We are also all familiar with news reports about stolen identities. You are the only one who can say how comfortable you are with this decision and how you want to approach the idea of posting your resume. Before you begin, review our "Dirty Dozen" Online Job-Search Mistakes in Chapter 1 one more time, and then consider the following questions very carefully:

1. Do you want your resume public? Once you have posted it, no matter where you place it, you should consider your resume to be public and to some extent out of your control. Anyone can look in the public databases and see what is there. Even the private resume databanks as well as those offering confidential handling of your resume may not let you dictate who can and cannot look at your resume.

2. Are you prepared for the consequences should an electronic resume come back to haunt you? It is a real possibility. Some job seekers fall victim to aggressive recruiters who grab their resumes from the Internet and unwittingly feed them back to the job seekers' current employers, with very bad results for the employee. Others are finding their resumes posted in places they never put them, the victims of unprofessional resume services who copy the documents from other open venues. Some employees have even been confronted by current employers brandishing copies of resumes online, not realizing that the documents were more than a year old and part of the campaign to get the current job. You should always go back and delete any resumes you posted during your search as soon as your search is over, but you might not be able to get to every electronic copy out there so you may need some strategies to help fight this. To help alleviate some of this problem put the date of posting at the very end of your resume as a record of when it was posted or make slight changes to the wording of each copy you post, creating a code identifying where a copy originated. These small alterations will give you some ammunition should your resume float into the wrong hands at the wrong time.

We don't want to scare you away from posting your resume online, but you should be aware of problems that can occur. Susan Joyce of Job-Hunt.org has written two articles you should review before going forward with this task: "Your Cyber-Safe Resume," which offers tips on creating a confidential resume, and "Protecting Your Privacy," which is about ways to protect your identity when job searching online. Both articles and many more on this topic are available on her website (http://job-hunt.org).

Resume Blasters: The Wave of the Future or a New Form of Spam?

Resume-distribution services, sometimes called resume broadcasters, are proliferating online. While you may think this is a great way to get your resume seen, we disagree. In reference to your privacy, Susan Joyce feels that "such wide distribution may offer little, if any, control on where a copy of your resume could end up. Your name, address, and phone number, in addition to your education and work experience, could become completely public for a very long time."

There are other problems too. For one thing, not all those who are on the lists of these services actually requested they be placed on the list. Both authors have received resumes that were broadcast by these services; neither of us has requested such a service. Then there may be problems with the resumes that are sent out, problems that the job seekers may not be aware of because they were not allowed to review their resumes before they were broadcast. One hiring manager sent us the following e-mail commenting on her experience with a resume-broadcasting service.

"A recruiting site for IT and technical professionals started bombarding me with forwarded resumes two days ago (I must have received twenty or so). They told us it was a free service, which I believe to be true.

"Because I had no positions open, and because we respond to every resume we receive, this put a burden on us that we don't really have time to handle, so I asked them to stop sending the resumes. In addition, a large number of the forwarded resumes did not contain contact information for the applicants, which made it impossible for us to let them know we had received the resume, or to contact them in case we might be interested in them. Two of the resumes did not even contain the candidates' names.

"I received an e-mail later saying they had complied with the request to remove my e-mail address from their system. Well and good.

"It went on to say, however, that these were 'current resumes of candidates presently in the job market and who have paid to have their resumes reviewed by recruiters, right now.'

"That outraged me. If an organization is going to collect money from candidates to forward their resumes, then it has (I believe) an obligation to make the process of reaching a promising candidate possible. Resumes without names or contact information are useless to a recruiter, as you can well imagine. I think these candidates should know that they are paying (a) for recruiters without jobs, or (b) to have their resumes forwarded in a way that cannot be responded to. They should use their money for something else."

In this instance, resumes were being sent out without any regard as to whether or not the employer requested it. While the chances of a successful match through this activity are already low, broadcasting resumes to employers who have expressed no interest in receiving them is almost guaranteed to eliminate even the slimmest possibility those resumes will be given any consideration. Then there were problems with the contact information on some resumes. This makes it difficult, if not impossible, for the employer to contact these candidates. If you are going to cold-call an employer, you must give the employer a way to call you back. But the worst part of all this is job seekers actually paid for this service, using their hard-earned and probably limited funds to pay for a service that will provide almost no return on their investment. It is a losing proposition for both the job seeker and the employer. The only winner was the blasting service because it got the money.

Help with Resumes and Cover Letters

Each of the following books and Internet services has good information and guidance for preparing your resume. Almost all will walk you through the process of translating your designed resume into the necessary scannable and e-mail formats, and a couple will even take you into Web resumes. We've also included titles covering resumes for teenagers, international variations, and resumes for positions with the U.S. government. New editions of any of these may have been released between the time we created the list and when you are reading it, so check your local library or bookstore for the most recent edition.

- Frank, William S. *200 Letters for Job Hunters*. Ten Speed Press, 1993.

- Ireland, Susan. *The Complete Idiot's Guide to the Perfect Cover Letter*. Alpha Books, 1997.

- ———. *The Complete Idiot's Guide to the Perfect Resume*, third edition. Alpha Books, 2003.

- Kennedy, Joyce Lain. *Cover Letters for Dummies*. For Dummies, 2000.

- ———. *Resumes for Dummies*. For Dummies, 2000.

- Smith, Rebecca. *Electronic Resumes and Online Networking*. Career Press, 2000.

- Thompson, Mary Anne. *The Global Resume and CV Guide*. John Wiley & Sons, 2000.

- Troutman, Kathryn Kraemer. *Creating Your High School Resume*. Jist Works, 2003.

- ———. *Electronic Federal Resume Guidebook*. The Resume Place Press, 2001.

- ———. *Ten Steps to a Federal Job*. The Resume Place Press, 2002.

Online Guides and Guidance

Online Writing Lab (OWL), Purdue University

http://owl.english.purdue.edu

OWL was set up to help the students at Purdue with writing all types of documents. Under Handouts and Materials, the section called Professional Writing includes help with resumes, cover letters, offer acceptance and refusal letters, personal statements, references, and postinterview letters.

Rebecca Smith's eResumes & Resources

eresumes.com

Rebecca Smith has been promoting the electronic resume since 1995. Her website is not about writing a resume, it is about taking that resume and turning it into the best tool it can be for your online search. She also looks at online networking and how to make it work for you.

The Resume Place

resume-place.com

The Resume Place is the resume-writing service operated by Kathryn Troutman, author of *Ten Steps to a Federal Job* and *Creating Your High School Resume*. On her website you'll find free articles and advice on preparing what you'll need in order to create your resume. If you are considering applying for a job with the federal government, then you must review Troutman's information, as she is an expert in the federal resume (which is very different from the resume you need for the private sector).

Susan Ireland

susanireland.com

Susan Ireland's website has terrific information and samples for the job seeker. You will enjoy her online workshops for resume writing, e-resumes, and cover letters, along with the many samples of resumes, cover letters, and thank-you letters.

3

The Great
Job-Lead Banks

Job-lead banks are the sites and services on the Internet known for their collected job listings. They cover multiple fields, industries, and occupations, providing leads for almost every job you can think of. While many are based in the United States, they do not necessarily limit themselves to job listings for just this country. This chapter is divided into three categories:

1. **Online recruiting services:** recruiters and other organizations posting job announcements on the Internet

2. **Online newspaper collections:** directories of links to newspapers from around the world

3. **Online guides to the job hunt:** directories that point you to good resources for your search, including job-search and career advice

Please Note: Unless indicated otherwise by the inclusion of *http://* you must add *www.* to the beginning of each URL listed here.

JOB-SEARCH TIP

Save some time and effort in online applications. If you use one Internet job service frequently and have had good luck finding appropriate positions advertised there, consider registering your resume with that service. Some job databases automate the application process, letting those with a registered resume at the site forward it in response to a job announcement with a single mouse click. It's also likely the same recruiters and employers who post jobs here also search the resume database, increasing your chances of being found.

Online Recruiting Services

Many of the sites listed here include both U.S. and non-U.S. opportunities. Those job banks primarily serving non-U.S. audiences are included in Chapter 12. Sites that are intended for use by minority or other diverse populations are included in Chapter 13.

America's Job Bank

ajb.org

This site is a joint effort of the two thousand offices of the state employment service and the U.S. Department of Labor. You can search the database by occupation or keyword, and transitioning military personnel can search by military specialty codes, easily matching your skills to jobs in the public sector. AJB also links to the databases of the individual state, district, and territorial employment services. We recommend searching both the local job bank and the main AJB database to review all available jobs in any given location. AJB is one of the largest job sources online and is not limited to the continental United States. Visually impaired job seekers can access AJB by phone through America's

Jobline at 800-414-5748. More information on this service is included in Chapter 13.

BestJobsUSA.com

bestjobsusa.com

This site includes job listings plus articles from *Employment Review Magazine*. Job seekers will benefit from the many additional resources, services, and information links found here.

CareerBuilder

careerbuilder.com

CareerBuilder has evolved into one of the larger and more dynamic sites for job and career information. Registering with them allows you to store your resume online without posting it in their database, and you can create up to five personal search profiles that will track new jobs added to the database and e-mail you when a good match turns up.

CareerExchange

careerexchange.com

This service covers the United States, Canada, and international jobs and allows you to search for jobs by category or keyword and narrow your choices to postings from particular dates. You can easily apply for jobs by pasting your plain-text resume into the form provided.

CareerJournal.com from the *Wall Street Journal*

careerjournal.com

This free site features articles, information, and jobs. While some of the articles are from the *Wall Street Journal*, many are written specifically for CareerJournal.com. They have a great job bank to go with their terrific job and career content. This site has something for job seekers at all levels of experience.

Careersite

careersite.com

This site has a lot to offer. You can start with a very simple quick search by selecting a category from the list on the front page. They are partnering with several local newspapers, which gives this site good in-depth job coverage.

College Grad Job Hunter

collegegrad.com

Don't let that title fool you! This website, based on the book of the same title, is a cornucopia of resources and information to guide you through a complete job search. It has job databases for internships, entry-level job seekers, and experienced job seekers, along with a searchable database of more than eight thousand employers. And to top it all off it offers great advice on careers, the job search, resume preparation, and more.

Cool Jobs

cooljobs.com

Cool Jobs includes listings and links to resources for many diverse industries and job fields. Some listings are viewable only by those who pay for Premium Accounts, but job seekers in some fields represented here may find the small monthly fee a good investment.

DirectEmployers

directemployers.com

DirectEmployers is an employment search engine that allows you to search for jobs posted on many employer websites through this one source. Operated by a consortium of employers, it directs you to their websites to view jobs and apply directly to the employer.

Employers Online

employersonline.com

You'll find diverse job offerings here, including professional, medical, and clerical.

EmploymentGuide.com

employmentguide.com

Formerly known as CareerWeb, this site includes job listings from the regional *Employment Guide* magazines as well as the many employers that are customers of this service. The site has good career and job-search information for all job seekers.

FlipDog

flipdog.com

FlipDog uses Web-crawler technology to review employer websites and copy the job listings to its own site. Employers can also list themselves here voluntarily, and they have the option of paying to have their job postings featured in a more prominent position. Job seekers are encouraged to register and use the one-step application process, but it is not necessary. FlipDog is owned by Monster.com.

Futurestep from Korn/Ferry

futurestep.com

Futurestep is a search service for midlevel management professionals brought to you by Korn/Ferry International. Registering with Futurestep is a free and confidential process and will cover more than just your standard resume. You will be considered for searches the site is doing, but your information will never be given to hiring companies without your express approval.

The Hiring Network

hiringnetwork.com

The Hiring Network features employment opportunities with leading employers in midsize local markets like Des Moines, Iowa; Charleston, South Carolina; Dayton, Ohio; and Lubbock, Texas.

HotJobs

http://hotjobs.yahoo.com

Search for jobs by keyword, company, or location, or select a career channel and limit your search to just the postings in this area. HotJobs is owned by Yahoo!.

ItsYourJobNow.com

itsyourjobnow.com

ItsYourJobNow.com is a job ad distribution service, assisting employers in posting their announcements to several sites online. The site also takes those postings and lists them in their own database for you to review. You can review their Niche Network for sites targeted to specific locations or industries.

JobBankUSA.com

jobbankusa.com

A good site for many jobs in all kinds of fields, JobBankUSA.com offers information organized and accessible through a variety of means. You can search the job database by keyword search, refining your search by location and position type (full time, contract, etc.). You can also scan the list of featured employers and connect to their websites. Please carefully review their privacy policy before posting your resume here.

LucasCareers.com

lucascareers.com

A division of Lucas Group, a national recruitment firm, LucasCareers.com offers a strong database of job positions for you to search. Register to post and edit your resume. When you find a job you like, place a check mark in the box next to it, click on the Send me more Info button at the bottom of the page, and fill out the registration. Have your resume ready to paste into the box.

Manpower

manpower.com

Manpower is the largest employer in the United States today, and not just through placing secretaries and receptionists in offices. The world of the temp has opened up all the way to the chief executive's office. Assignments are searchable by location, and you can submit resumes by e-mail, fax, or the online form provided.

Monster.com

monster.com

Monster.com is probably the most recognized name in the online job-search industry. They offer an enormous variety of job and career resources for everyone from college students to contractors to chief executives, and most are served with their own communities that include job listings and career advice. They also offer several industry/job-field communities, including health care, human resources, and finance.

MonsterTRAK

monstertrak.com

Formerly known as JobTrak, this Monster community is targeted to the college graduate. Your college or university must be a member of MonsterTRAK for you to gain access to the job postings on this site, so call your career center to see if it is a member and ask for access information. MonsterTRAK has been noted as an excellent resource for executive as well as entry-level opportunities, so it is worth it for alumni to take some time to explore this site.

NationJob Network

nationjob.com

This site features an impressive collection of job openings, company info, and a variety of ways to find what you are looking for. It divides into many sources of occupational and industry-related resources, creating an excellent bank of information for all.

Net-Temps

net-temps.com

This site features a company database of temporary and full-time job listings, which can be searched by geographic location and keyword. You can also search a specific job category by job type (contract or full time) and location. The listings cover the United States and Canada.

Recruiters Online Network

recruitersonline.com

This network is "an association of executive recruiters, search firms, and employment professionals around the world who have created a virtual organization on the Internet." Job seekers can search the database of openings posted by the participating recruiters, post their resume for consideration by all members, and search for recruiters working with a particular industry or occupational field for direct contact. This site also includes tips on job hunting and articles on using recruiters in the job search.

Top Echelon

topechelon.com

Top Echelon is a cooperative network of more than twenty-five hundred recruiters. It has some good listings ranging from entry level to well into the six-figure range. You can also search the recruiter listings and contact some of the recruiters directly.

TrueCareers

truecareers.com

This service from Sallie Mae is "designed to help its borrowers and other college-educated candidates find higher-paying or more satisfying jobs." Users can search the database with keywords, select a job category and location from the menus, or search for jobs by employer. To apply to jobs listed here you must register your resume in the database, but you have the option of keeping it confidential or private.

USJobs.com

usjobs.com

USJobs.com offers a "nationwide job search with a local edge." Select a position type, select an optional location, and select your job category to find positions listed here. You are not required to register to use their Apply Online feature as it links you to the employer's website.

Online Newspaper Collections

Newspapers are a very important component in your search for employment. Reading local newspapers for your target search location will help you learn about the community and local employers, identify individual contacts within those organizations, and even connect you with local job listings. Most newspapers in the United States and many around the world are now represented on the Web, making it easy for you to find and review the news for your target location.

News and Newspapers Online

http://library.uncg.edu/news

This is an extensive directory of links to news and newspaper sources from around the world. You can browse the site by location or search by a variety of criteria. The directory is a free service of Walter Clinton Jackson Library at the University of North Carolina at Greensboro.

NewsDirectory.com

newsdirectory.com

This is a searchable directory of English-language media, including newspapers, magazines, television stations, colleges, visitor bureaus, governmental agencies, and more from around the world. You can also search the directory by publication title or search for U.S. regional news links by telephone area code.

NewsLink

http://newslink.org

NewsLink offers lists of and links to newspapers, magazines, and radio and television station websites throughout the world. This directory is operated by NewsLink Associates, an academic and professional research and consulting firm studying electronic publishing and visual journalism.

NewspaperLinks.com

newspaperlinks.com

Operated by the Newspaper Association of America, this site calls itself "a gateway to your local newspaper." You can easily find the news you'd like by either browsing the contents or searching with keywords.

U.S. Newspapers

usnpl.com

U.S Newspapers is a free directory of newspapers for each state plus the District of Columbia. The listings here include the local newspapers, college newspapers, radio and television stations, and local magazines.

Online Guides to the Job Hunt

These Internet guides for the online job search, sometimes referred to as metaguides, gather information and resources to help you use the Internet to find employment. Some will give you notes about the resources, some will give you articles on the job search, but all will take you to more online information for your search.

AIRS Directories

airsdirectory.com/directories

AIRS offers products and services to recruiters to help them use the Internet more effectively in recruiting. Part of their service includes the compilation of resource directories, large lists of links to job boards, newspaper classifieds, recruiters, employers, organizations, and online communities, and these resource lists are open to all users.

Job-Hunt.org

job-hunt.org

One of the earliest guides to the Internet job search, Job-Hunt.org offers numerous well-selected links to job-search resources for the world. You can search for job sites by location, profession, industry, or job type. Susan Joyce, manager of this site, also provides users with excellent articles on job-search issues.

JobHuntersBible.com

jobhuntersbible.com

This online guide to the job search comes from the Dean of Career Counseling himself, Richard Bolles! The Job Hunter's Bible is a supplement to his bestseller *What Color Is Your Parachute?* and is spiced with his comments and observations on the job search and your decision-making process. Part of this site is his Net Guide to the best job-search and career-information sites online. This is an excellent place for you to start your search.

JobStar

http://jobstar.org

JobStar began as a California Job Search Guide, but it has always been a highly useful resource for everyone. This is one of the best places online to find out how and where to look for employment. Among the wealth of information included here are articles on the hidden job market, negotiating salaries, and numerous other topics that work to enhance the choice resources listed, selected because they are the best.

Quintessential Careers

quintcareers.com

This is a metaguide to everything you need for your job search from the authors of *Dynamic Cover Letters*. This site gives you great information and resources from both off- and online publications. The job and career site lists are quite good, and if you have teenagers looking for ideas, there is information here for them too.

The Riley Guide: Employment Opportunities and Job Resources on the Internet

rileyguide.com

One of the first guides to look at the Internet as a tool for finding new employment, The Riley Guide was established in January 1994 and has been going strong ever since. This site links you to hundreds of sources of information for job leads, career exploration, and potential employers. It even has information to help you explore new careers, new places to live, and new education and training options. Readers of this book can use The Riley Guide to check for updates to listings in this book.

Yahoo! Employment and Work

http://dir.yahoo.com/business_and_economy/employment_and_work

Yahoo! links to more than fifteen hundred sites for job leads and other sources of employment information. Don't limit yourself to just this list, though. Almost every category on Yahoo! has a separate employment category, so browse the shelves frequently.

Jobs in Business, Marketing, and Commercial Services

The resources covered in this chapter point to job information in business fields and commercial services provided to a company, such as janitorial services, event management, and equipment leasing.

Those in the fields that are represented in this chapter should remember that companies of all sizes and in all industries couldn't do business without teams of accountants, sales representatives, and others to help them operate efficiently. Your opportunities can be found everywhere, so don't limit yourself to what you see here.

Please Note: Unless indicated otherwise by the inclusion of *http://* you must add *www.* to the beginning of each URL listed here.

Great Business Starting Points

Careers in Business

careers-in-business.com

Careers in Business includes information on careers, including an overview of each area, the skills and talents needed for the work, very basic salary information, resources for more information, and a link to job listings from jobsinthemoney.com.

Job-Search Links, Columbia Business School

http://www3.gsb.columbia.edu/intranet/careerservices/vcrc/links/links.htm

Created by the Office of M.B.A. Career Services at the Columbia Business School, this is a good guide to online resources for job and industry information for the M.B.A.

Accounting and Finance

AAFA: The American Association of Finance and Accounting

aafa.com

AAFA is an alliance of executive search firms specializing in the recruiting and placement of finance and accounting professionals. Search their Careers area for listings posted by member firms, and submit your resume for consideration.

AICPA Online: American Institute for Certified Public Accountants

aicpa.org

AICPA is "the national, professional organization for all Certified Public Accountants." Along with finding good information on a career as a CPA and certification, users can review job announcements under Career Resources. Some resources here are limited to members, but others are open to all.

American Society of Payroll Managers

aspm.org

This association website includes news and information for payroll, tax, and human resources professionals as well as jobs for those in these fields.

Association for Finance Professionals (AFP)

afponline.org

AFP's membership is made up of individuals representing a broad spectrum of financial disciplines. The Career Services area offers terrific resources for association members, including networking groups. The job database is open to members and registered nonmembers. Registration includes posting your resume, but you have the option of not advertising it in the searchable database.

Bankjobs.com

bankjobs.com

Bankjobs.com includes job and career information for qualified banking and financial services candidates in the United States and Canada. To get your free password for the database, you must post your resume. The site offers a nice list of industry links for all visitors.

CFO.com

cfo.com

CFO Publishing's website features international news, articles, resources, and jobs for chief financial officers (CFOs), treasurers, and other senior financial executives in the United States and Canada.

Financial Job Network

fjn.com

This international site lists job opportunities for actuaries, controllers, auditors, chief financial officers, and many more finance professionals.

FinancialJobs.com

financialjobs.com

These are jobs for accounting and financial professionals throughout the United States. Some areas require you to register in order to apply for the jobs, but others don't.

International Market Recruiters

goimr.com

This group specializes in permanent and consultative placements exclusively in the financial services arena. You can review some of its current searches and submit your resume for consideration in the search.

JobsintheMoney.com

jobsinthemoney.com

This site offers good job and career information for financial professionals covering an extensive international market. Browse or search the job listings to be sure there are some that match your desires before registering your resume. Registration is necessary to apply for listings here.

National Banking and Financial Services Network

nbn-jobs.com

This is a large association of recruiting firms with nationwide job listings. This site includes jobs in finance, banking, and credit as well as many more opportunities within this industry. You must register your resume in order to search the listings, but you can do so anonymously and it is free.

Robert Half International

rhi.com

Robert Half International is the parent company for Accountemps, Robert Half Finance and Accounting, Robert Half Management, and four other divisions offering staffing and consulting services in various business areas. You can explore all of the divisions from this site, and each will allow you to submit a resume online.

Tax-Jobs.Com

tax-jobs.com

This small site features job listings for tax professionals.

Actuaries

Actuary.com

actuary.com

This is a directory of resources and services for actuaries and those entering this field, including a free job database. All postings indicate the level of experience desired, ranging from "entry level with no exams" to "fellow."

Northstar International Insurance Recruiters

northstarjobs.com

Northstar is an actuarial and underwriting recruiting service with an array of listings from student positions (those still looking for their certification) to executives.

Advertising, Communications, and Public Relations

AdAge.com's Career Center

crain.com/classified/adage

AdAge.com, the website companion to *Advertising Age*, lists job openings for media and advertising professionals and for various positions with advertising agencies.

AdWeek

adweek.com

AdWeek, the magazine for ad agency executives, includes classified listings on its website. Users willing to pay for the Premium Classified will see listings that are less than seven days old. Those who wait can see the same listings for free after that period. Any user can post his or her resume for free.

Commarts.com Network

commarts.com

This site includes information for those engaged in the communication arts: graphics, marketing, artwork, and other visual methods for communicating with others. It hosts an impressive collection of resources for the industry and the individual and a job bank featuring lots of openings for graphic designers, Web project managers, and writers.

International Association of Business Communicators

iabc.com

The IABC represents writers, editors, public relations directors, and other advertising and communications specialists. The job bank is open for all to review and may include jobs for public relations specialists, technical writers, editorial staff, and directors of corporate communications. Many chapters also maintain individual job banks.

Public Relations Society of America (PRSA)

prsa.org

PRSA's website includes an open job bank and information on starting your own PR firm. Visitors interested in this profession will also want to review the site's valuable listings under Resources.

Appraisers

American Society of Appraisers (ASA)

appraisers.org

The ASA is "committed to fostering professional excellence in its membership through education, accreditation, publication, and other services." Persons interested in this field can learn more about training and certification opportunities, the many appraisal disciplines and specialties available, and the benefits of membership (including a members-only job bank).

Church Business Administration

National Association of Church Business Administration

nacba.net

This is "an interdenominational, professional, Christian organization which exists to train, certify, and provide resources for those serving in the field of church administration." They offer training toward certification as a Fellow in Church Business Administration (FCBA) along with a number of workshops and conferences to assist others in this work. The website features some terrific resources, including job listings and links to additional sources.

Customer Relations and Call Centers

CallCenterCareers.com

callcentercareers.com

CallCenterCareers.com is an online job site for the call center and customer relationship management (CRM) industries. The site includes job postings, a resume bank, industry news, and specialized career services. Registration is not required to search the database or apply for the jobs.

Equipment Leasing

Monitor Daily

monitordaily.com

Monitor Daily features industry news and information for the equipment leasing and finance industry. A service of Molloy Associates, recruiters for this industry, this site also hosts two different listings of job opportunities, one with listings of current searches being handled by Molloy Associates, and the other with listings posted by various employers in this industry.

Human Resources

BenefitsLink

benefitslink.com

This site includes good information for anyone dealing with benefits, from the human resources manager to the actuary trying to figure it all out. You can read the latest news, check the industry links, and review the employment opportunities.

International Foundation of Employee Benefit Plans

ifebp.org

The International Foundation of Employee Benefit Plans provides good resources for those in this field, including job postings. Jobs can be reviewed by posting date, location, or job title, and nonmembers can post a resume here for a fee.

Jobs4HR

jobs4hr.com

This site features jobs for HR professionals at all levels. Registration is not required to search or apply for jobs, but the free registration will allow you to customize certain features of the site.

Society for Human Resource Management (SHRM)

shrm.org

SHRM's website is filled with information for human resource professionals. The HR Careers area is one of the largest databases of jobs for this field and is open to all users.

WorldatWork

worldatwork.org

This professional association for compensation and benefits specialists includes a job bank open to all visitors.

Insurance

Great Insurance Jobs.com

greatinsurancejobs.com

This site lists jobs in the insurance industry. It also includes a resume database and a link to continuing education services from The National Underwriter's Company. Registration is not required to search and view job listings. Great Insurance Jobs.com has a strict "no recruiter" policy, meaning that only insurance companies can post and search.

InsuranceJobChannel

insurancejobchannel.com

This site is a portal to jobs in the insurance industry. You can browse the listings by company name, industry segment, product line, or region. This is not a new job site but rather it pulls together employment listings from virtually all participants in this industry.

Insurance National Search, Inc.

insurancerecruiters.com

This association of recruiting firms specializes in the insurance industry. The site includes searchable databases of job listings and recruiters. Each job listing is less than sixty days old.

You may also want to review the listings under Actuaries earlier in this chapter.

Meeting and Event Management

Professional Convention Management Association

pcma.org

This professional association website includes industry information, a job bank, continuing education opportunities, and much more.

Packaging

PackagingCareerHotline

packagingcareerhotline.com

Operated by Women in Packaging, Inc., and *Packaging Horizons* magazine, this website offers free access to job listings in this field.

Purchasing and Procurement

Institute for Supply Management (ISM)

ism.ws

The ISM website includes their publications, information on careers in purchasing management, and links to related resources. The job and resume databases are open only to members, but the list of additional career resources is open to all. Many of the affiliate websites listed under About ISM have job banks on their websites.

International Purchasing Service Staffing

ipserv.com

This is a recruiting and temporary services firm providing professional purchasing management on a temporary basis. A short list of job openings is available.

Quality Control

American Society for Quality (ASQ)

asq.org

ASQ is the leading quality-improvement organization in the United States, with more than 130,000 members worldwide. This website is a prime resource for those in this field. You must be a member to have access to the employment listings and resume database services.

Real Estate and Relocation

CoreNet Global

corenetglobal.org

CoreNet Global is an association representing managers of corporate real estate. The Career Services section includes a job database that is open to all visitors as well as a list of executive recruiters in this industry.

Employee Relocation Council (ERC)

erc.org

ERC is "a nonprofit professional membership organization committed to the effective relocation of employees worldwide." This extensive website includes job listings in the relocation industry, a great online research library, and much more.

Real Estate Job Store

realestatejobstore.com

The Real Estate Job Store offers numerous job listings for the real estate industry. The opening page is a bit overly loaded with text, so we recommend you select either the See Most Current Jobs link or the Find Real Estate Jobs by Job Title or Company link. This second link also allows you to search by location.

Sales and Marketing

Ludwig & Associates, Inc.

ludwig-recruit.com

This executive search firm specializes in the placement of sales and marketing professionals for consumer packaged goods companies. Individuals in this industry are invited to review the list of current searches and to make contact at any time.

MarketingJobs.com

marketingjobs.com

This site lists marketing, sales, and advertising employment opportunities in the United States.

MarketingPower, the American Marketing Association

marketingpower.com

The American Marketing Association's job bank, part of its Career Center, is open to all users regardless of member status. If you are not a member, you have the option of filling out an online application, but you also have the option of not posting your resume in their database.

Training and Development

American Society for Training and Development (ASTD)

astd.org

ASTD is the premier professional association for the training and development community. Along with all the other excellent resources, a public job bank is available to all visitors. Non-ASTD members can forward their information to employers without adding their resume to the database.

Instructional System Technology Jobs

http://education.indiana.edu/ist/students/jobs/joblink.html

This site lists opportunities in all areas of training, including academic faculty, media developers, and corporate trainers. It is a service of the Department of Instructional Systems Technology in the School of Education at Indiana University, Bloomington.

Jobs in Law, the Social Sciences, and Nonprofit Organizations

The areas surveyed in this chapter have been grouped together for their interest in and connection to society and the public. The social sciences cover many fields, including education, law, and economics, and many of the employers in these fields are nonprofit organizations.

Please Note: Unless indicated otherwise by the inclusion of *http://* you must add *www.* to the beginning of each URL listed here.

Anthropology

American Anthropological Association

aaanet.org

Anthropology is "the study of humankind, from its beginnings millions of years ago to the present day. . . . Anthropologists may study ancient Mayan hieroglyphics, the music of African Pygmies, and the corporate culture of a U.S. car manufacturer." The website from this association includes information on meetings, publications, and careers, as well as job listings.

Archaeology

Archaeological Fieldwork Server

cincpac.com/afos/testpit.html

Individuals seeking archaeology fieldwork opportunities can browse through postings for volunteers, positions in field schools, full-time and contract jobs, and other archaeological openings that are submitted or found on mailing lists and in newsgroups. This service also links to additional resources that may list more positions.

Archaeological Institute of America (AIA)

archaeological.org

AIA is the oldest and largest archaeological organization in North America, with thousands of members around the world. Their website includes information on jobs and fellowships along with publications for all audiences from children to scholars.

Economics

Inomics Job Openings for Economists (JOE)

inomics.com/cgi/job

This is a very nice source for international jobs in this field as well as links to additional resources. Inomics, the host for this service, also maintains information on conferences along with other good economics resources.

International Economic Development Council (IEDC)

iedconline.org

IEDC serves economic and community development professionals and those in allied fields. The website includes information on professional development, certification, and resources for funding and financial assistance. The Career Services area offers a job database for IEDC members, but nonmembers may sign up for a free newsletter that also lists jobs.

Job Opportunities for Economists (JOE)

eco.utexas.edu/joe

This is the electronic version of *Job Opportunities for Economists (JOE)* from the American Economic Association. JOE is published every month except January and July. The listings are grouped into U.S. academic, international, and nonacademic positions, and each grouping is then arranged alphabetically by the name of the posting institution, eliminating the designation *University of.* Several months of listings are available at all times.

Education and Academe

This section is divided into categories based on the types of positions offered, but since many of the resources overlap categories we suggest that you review the entire list.

COLLEGE AND UNIVERSITY-LEVEL POSITIONS

Academic Position Network (APN)

apnjobs.com

The APN is an online position announcement service for academic institutions all over the world. Job listings include faculty, administration, and staff positions, as well as announcements for research fellowships and graduate assistantships.

Academic360.com

academic360.com

This site provides more than two thousand links to colleges and universities advertising their position announcements online in the United States, Canada, Australia, the United Kingdom, and the Republic of Ireland.

American College Personnel Association Ongoing Placement Listings

http://acpant.acpa.nche.edu/onplace.nsf

These listings include jobs for resident advisers, directors of student programs, and others who support the students at colleges and universities.

Christian Higher Education Career Center

cccu.org/career/career.asp

This site posts faculty and administrative positions at the member and nonmember affiliate institutions of the Council for Christian Colleges and Universities. The most recent notices are listed first. The full list of member and nonmember affiliate colleges participating in this association is available.

Chronicle of Higher Education's Career Network

http://chronicle.com/jobs

This site includes career articles and job listings from the *Chronicle of Higher Education*, the weekly publication of higher education worldwide. Many international institutions as well as companies with research divisions advertise here. The job listings are updated daily and are free for all users. Anyone considering a teaching or administrative position with a college or university should look here.

Council for Advancement and Support of Education (CASE) Job Classifieds

case.org/jobs

Specializing in administrative positions in academe and education, the jobs listed at CASE include positions in alumni relations, communications, development/fund-raising, public relations, major gifts, annual fund, government relations, information systems and advancement services, and advancement management.

HigherEd Jobs

higheredjobs.com

This website lists jobs in more than five hundred member academic institutions for both faculty and staff. You can view the postings by category, location, or keyword.

Jobs.ac.uk

jobs.ac.uk

Jobs.ac.uk is the "official recruitment site for Higher Education in the United Kingdom." All types of jobs in these institutions are listed here, including faculty, administration, and support services. Users can easily target their search to particular types of institutions or to specific geographic locations. Jobs.ac.uk has replaced the NISS Vacancies list.

National Association of College and University Business Officers

nacubo.org

The National Association of College and University Business Officers (NACUBO) represents chief administrative and financial officers at more than twenty-one hundred colleges and universities across the country. News, resources, and a link to its job service can be found on the main page.

National Association of Student Personnel Administrators (NASPA)

naspa.org

NASPA is the leading national association for college and university student-affairs administrators. NASPA's JobsLink includes openings for admissions, enrollment management, student affairs, housing, health, and much more.

The *Times* Higher Education Supplement (THES)

thesis.co.uk

THES is a great way to find jobs in higher education worldwide. It carries listings in all categories of higher education job vacancies worldwide as advertised in the *Times* (London). The free registration is not required but it does allow you to save searches and sign up for job alerts.

Women in Higher Education (WIHE)

wihe.com

The Women in Higher Education (WIHE) website offers news and information on issues affecting women on college campuses. The Career Connection posts several academic openings for faculty and chief administrators, and other areas of the site will connect you to many further sources of information for women.

KINDERGARTEN THROUGH TWELFTH-GRADE OPPORTUNITIES

Academic Employment Network

academploy.com

The Academic Employment Network features job listings by state for kindergarten through college educators. Only those states with actual job openings are listed.

Ed Jobs U Seek

http://education.umn.edu/jobs

Ed Jobs U Seek is a free service for professionals in education and human development who seek positions in schools, institutions, and other education-related organizations. Jobs can be reviewed by category, or you can use a map to search for jobs by location. The site is operated by the College of Education and Human Development at the University of Minnesota.

ISM: Independent School Management

isminc.com

This site hosts a Career Center with opportunities for principals and other administrators in private schools around the United States.

SPECIAL EDUCATION

National Clearinghouse for Professions in Special Education (NCPSE)

special-ed-careers.org

NCPSE is "committed to enhancing the nation's capacity to recruit, prepare, and retain well-qualified diverse educators and related service personnel for children with disabilities." The website offers a number of resources for those involved in or considering a career in special education, including an overview of what special educators do, how to enter this field, links to employment resources, and financial aid information.

RECRUITING NEW TEACHERS

These services encourage people to consider teaching as a profession and to make the transition from other careers to this field.

Teach for America

teachforamerica.org

This nonprofit organization recruits college graduates of all academic majors to teach for two years in an underserved urban or rural public school. Applicants at all age and experience levels are welcome, and certification is not required.

Troops to Teachers

jobs2teach.doded.mil

Troops to Teachers provides referral and placement assistance to military personnel interested in a second career as a teacher. This site includes employment resources and listings, information on how to obtain certification, and a list of mentors.

English as a Second Language/English as a Foreign Language (ESL/EFL)

EFLWEB

eflweb.com

EFLWEB is an online magazine for teachers and students learning English as a foreign language. The site includes a resume bank and job-vacancies board.

ESL Cafe's Job Center

http://eslcafe.com/jobs

This site, presented by Dave Sperling, provides a wonderful list of resources for ESL educators. The Job Center includes jobs wanted, jobs posted, discussion boards for ESL/EFL teachers, a journal of job experiences, a teacher-training forum, and links to even more resources.

Law, Paralegal, and the U.S. Judiciary

Federal Judiciary

uscourts.gov

This website includes information on our federal courts, including employment opportunities in all areas supporting the U.S. courts, their services, and areas of responsibility. You can review the listings by location, desired salary, or position title. Please note that not all of the judiciary's employment opportunities are found here; other announcements may exist on each court's website. For those who are interested, this site also links to the Federal Law Clerk Information System and the Supreme Court Judicial Fellows Program.

FindLaw Career Center

http://careers.findlaw.com

FindLaw is a marvelous resource for legal information as well as for job and career information for all aspects of legal work. Positions listed here include summer clerks, legal secretaries, law librarians, and attorneys in practice or academic positions as well as listings for those needed to support the business of a legal practice.

Hieros Gamos, the Comprehensive Law and Government Portal

hg.org

Hieros Gamos is a wonderful source of legal information. The Employment area includes links to legal employment centers online, sources for job listings, related Internet employment resources (including its own list of legal recruiters), publications on searching for jobs, alternatives to corporate practices, and much more.

The National Federation of Paralegal Associations

paralegals.org

This website offers terrific information on work as a paralegal, including information on how to get started, where to study, legal resources, continuing education, and links to international associations and information. The Career Center offers a job database along with a directory of recruiters and a referral service.

Resources for Verbatim (Court) Reporters can be found at the end of this chapter.

Library and Information Sciences

American Association of Law Libraries

aallnet.org

This website includes information on law librarianship, professional development workshops offered by this and other organizations, jobs, and other good resources.

American Library Association (ALA)

ala.org

ALA is the oldest and largest library association in the world, and much of the website is open to nonmembers as well as members. Under Education and Careers you will find links to accredited programs, employment listings from various ALA publications, and much more. You can also look under Our Association for links to individual divisions, chapters, and roundtables, some of which operate their own career and employment sections.

ARLIS/NA JobNet

arlisna.org/jobs.html

The Art Libraries Society of North America provides vacancy announcements for art librarians, visual resources professionals, and related positions.

Association of Research Libraries (ARL) Career Resources Online Service

http://db.arl.org/careers

The Career Resources Online Service provides job hunters with a resource for finding positions in ARL libraries. Any visitor can review all listings currently posted, review only the entry-level positions, or search the listings by region, state/province, or job category.

BUBL Information Service

http://bubl.ac.uk

The BUBL Information Service is an Internet-based information service for the U.K. higher education community. This site includes extensive international information resources for librarians, including job announcements for the United Kingdom, the United States, and worldwide.

LIBJOBS

ifla.org/II/lists/libjobs.htm

LIBJOBS is an Internet mailing list for employment opportunities for librarians and information professionals. Information on how to subscribe can be found on this Web page along with a link to the list's archive.

Library Job Postings on the Internet

libraryjobpostings.org

This guide compiled by Sarah Nesbeitt, a librarian at Eastern Illinois University, attempts to link together all online sources for library employment listings. She also maintains a list of recent job announcements submitted by employers.

Library Journal

libraryjournal.com

Library Journal is the trade journal of the library- and information-sciences profession. Persons interested in this field can review career articles as well as job listings through this website.

Lisjobs.com

lisjobs.com

Lisjobs.com is a guide to online job resources for librarians and information professionals that also hosts its own job and resume databases. The site is operated by Rachel Singer Gordon, a librarian based in Franklin Park, Illinois, and it includes U.S. and international resources.

Music Library Association (MLA)

musiclibraryassoc.org

MLA is the professional organization for music librarians in the United States. Among its many services is the Placement Service Job List, a monthly listing of open positions for music librarians across the United States.

Linguistics

Jobs in Linguistics

linguistlist.org/jobs

This site is updated almost daily with job openings, and it provides links to other sources for job announcements. International job seekers are encouraged to review information on employment standards in various countries, while linguistics students who have not yet earned a Ph.D. can review a listing of fellowships, internships, research positions, and other opportunities open to them.

Xlation.com, Resources for Translation Professionals

xlation.com

For those who work in this field, this site offers tools, resources, dictionaries, glossaries, and jobs!

Ministry

MinistryConnect

ministryconnect.org

MinistryConnect exists to assist anyone interested in providing, finding, and encouraging meaningful work in the service of others. The effort embraces people of all faiths, helping to connect resources with needs in order to bring about a greater good for society. You can view the jobs by type of ministry or geographic region.

MinistryLink: Employment Opportunities in Church Ministry

csbsju.edu/sot/MinistryLink

This online database of employment opportunities in church ministry is sponsored by Saint John's School of Theology & Seminary in Minnesota. You can search the job database for openings for pastors, music directors, religion teachers, and others working in religious centers. Listings are retained online for sixty days.

Resources for Church Business Administration can be found in Chapter 4.

Nonprofits, Associations, and Foundations

ASAE CareerHeadquarters

asaenet.org/careers

The American Society of Association Executives allows you to search its job database, post a resume, or check on careers in associations. Job seekers will also want to check out the ASAE's great resources under Find Associations, People, Businesses for networking and employer listings.

CharityChannel

charitychannel.com

The CharityChannel includes information, resources, and much more for persons interested in working in nonprofits worldwide. Their Career Search Online lists current openings with various organizations, including postings from executive search firms.

Community Career Center

nonprofitjobs.org

This site lists nonprofit jobs all over the United States, from support staff to chief toxicologist to executive director.

ExecSearches.com

execsearches.com

This site features executive and senior-management positions in nonprofit, public sector, and socially conscious organizations.

Nonprofit Career Network

nonprofitcareer.com

The Nonprofit Career Network is dedicated to the nonprofit sector of today's business and economic world. The website is a good source of information on nonprofit organizations and job and volunteer opportunities in the sector.

The *NonProfit Times*

nptimes.com

The *NonProfit Times* is a business publication for nonprofit management. Its website includes several special resources, including the NPT Power and Influence Top Fifty and a Salary Survey. Job seekers will want to review the NPT Jobs, accessible through the link at the bottom of the page.

Opportunity NOCs.org

opportunitynocs.org

Opportunity NOCs (Nonprofit Organization Classifieds) was launched by The Management Center of San Francisco in 1986 as a print newsletter. The site contains all levels of jobs in the nonprofit sector, as well as links to other nonprofit sites and job sites. Jobs listed on the website do not represent all the jobs found in the five regional print editions. Information on and links to the regional editions can be found under Resources/Print.

Philanthropy and Fund-Raising

Chronicle of Philanthropy **Career Network**

philanthropy.com/jobs

The *Chronicle of Philanthropy* is the leading news source for development professionals. Its online Career Network includes employment opportunities, compensation news and trends, career information for those interested in fund-raising, and much more. The links to online resources at the bottom of the page include many more good resources for nonprofit jobs. Some areas of this site are limited to paying subscribers, but the job listings are open to the public.

Philanthropy News Digest **from the Foundation Center**

http://fdncenter.org/pnd

Philanthropy News Digest's website includes articles and information from its print publication and the Job Corner with employment listings submitted by nonprofit foundations. Job seekers will also want to follow the links back to information resources provided by the Foundation Center for more leads to potential employers.

Philanthropy News Network

http://pnnonline.org

Information on the nonprofit world is featured here, including a nice job database.

Psychology and Counseling

Mental Help Net

http://mentalhelp.net

Employers of all types can post their mental health positions free of charge at this site.

NACE JobWire

naceweb.org/jobwire

JobWire is the job announcement section of *Spotlight*, the biweekly newsletter of the National Association of Colleges and Employers (NACE). The most recent listings with openings for career counselors and human resources professionals are available here.

PsycCareers

psyccareers.com

PsycCareers is a free service of the American Psychological Association and includes job and career information for all persons in this field. Anyone can register for free, but registration is not necessary to search the job listings.

The Society for Industrial and Organizational Psychology

http://siop.org

The Society for Industrial and Organizational Psychology website includes information on this field of psychology, current and back issues of the quarterly newsletter (*TIP*), and the JobNet with openings in academic, industry, or government settings, and internships.

Social Work and Social Services

National Association of Social Workers (NASW)

naswdc.org

The NASW maintains this website full of information for social workers, careers in social work, and jobs. You do not need to be a member to view the jobs, but members do have access to more features in this area of the website.

Social Work and Social Services Jobs Online

http://gwbweb.wustl.edu/jobs

This free website lists jobs in all facets of social work and links to additional resources for people in this field. It is supported by the Career Services Office at the George Warren Brown School of Social Work, Washington University.

Socialservice.com

http://socialservice.com

This is a great place to look for a job in social services. If you decide to register, you can customize job alerts and post your resume, all at no cost.

Verbatim (Court) Reporters

BestFuture.com

bestfuture.com

BestFuture is here to tell you everything you wanted to know about court reporting—how it is evolving and moving from the courtroom into new jobs in business and multimedia fields and even working to assist the hearing disabled through captioning technology. The career options section covers the many career paths such as scoping, medical and legal transcriptionists, and captioning as well as the more traditional courtroom services. This information is provided by the National Court Reporters Association.

NCRA Online, the National Court Reporters Association

ncraonline.org

NCRA is working to advance the profession of "those who capture and integrate the spoken word into a comprehensive and accurate information base for the benefit of the public and private sectors." Its website is a great source for information on this profession, as well as where to go for training, and the classified ads are open to all.

Scopists.com

scopists.com

This site is "dedicated to the support of the professions of the scopist and court reporter by providing reference resources, word lists, employment opportunities, and just about anything of use to court reporters and scopists all over the world!" The site includes a directory of freelance scopists, a place to post job announcements, and links to useful reference sources for scopists.

Jobs in the Humanities, Recreation, Hospitality, and Personal Services

This chapter covers occupations that provide a service to others, whether it's entertainment or assisting someone with a need. Persons searching for jobs in these areas will not usually see jobs that specify "English literature majors desired," so it's important for you to know how your skills can be used before reviewing job listings. The career-exploration resources listed in Chapter 14 will be very helpful in this regard.

Please Note: Unless indicated otherwise by the inclusion of *http://* you must add *www.* to the beginning of each URL listed here.

General Arts and Humanities Sources

H-Net Job Guide for the Humanities and Social Sciences

h-net.org/jobs

This guide covers positions in history and other fields in the humanities and social sciences, including rhetoric and communications. Most positions are in academic institutions.

The Liberal Arts Job-Search Guide

http://cohesion.rice.edu/administration/careerservices/emplibrary/liberalart.pdf

This article from the Rice University Career Services Center covers options and job-search ideas for anyone with a liberal arts (or performing arts) background. This PDF document requires Adobe's free Acrobat Reader (adobe.com) for viewing and printing.

Acting and Entertainment

BackStage

backstage.com

BackStage, the weekly magazine of the theater community, has a website that includes reviews of various productions and a performing arts directory with training and education resources. The casting calls are divided into East, West, Chicago, Florida, and Las Vegas listings and include both union and nonunion opportunities. Paying members get better access, particularly to casting calls.

EntertainmentCareers.net

entertainmentcareers.net

This site lists all kinds of jobs and internships within the entertainment industry, even news reporters and editors. Paying members have access to more listings.

Hollywood Creative Directory Online

hcdonline.com

This site offers information to help you connect to the people you want to talk to in the entertainment industry. While some portions of this site are limited to members, the job board is free.

Playbill

playbill.com

Playbill is a great source for listings of acting and theatrical support positions on and off Broadway, throughout the United States and Canada, and around the world. Check the Casting and Jobs area for job opportunities.

ShowBizjobs.com

showbizjobs.com

This site features opportunities in all occupations in the film-, television-, recording-, and attractions-industry job markets. You can search the listings by region and job field or browse them by company or date of posting.

UK Theatre Web

uktw.co.uk

The UK Theatre Web probably includes everything you could possibly want to know about the dramatic arts scene in the United Kingdom, including what kind of employment opportunities exist.

Art and Artists

Arts Deadlines List

xensei.com/users/adl

This service lists "competitions, art contests, calls for entries/papers, grants, residencies, auditions, casting calls, funding opportunities, art scholarships, fellowships, jobs, and internships in the arts or related areas (painting, drawing, photography, etc.)." There is a free list and a fee list, so if you find a lot here that interests you, a paid subscription may be to your benefit.

NYFA Interactive

nyfa.org

NYFA is the New York Foundation for the Arts, a philanthropic organization supporting the arts and artists. Their weekly newsletter, *NYFA Current*, includes jobs as well as "opportunities for artists," listings of competitions and exhibitions calling for entries.

Cartooning

National Cartoonists Society

reuben.org

Are you the next Scott Adams? Well, the National Cartoonists Society wants you to know what it's really like to work as a cartoonist. Check out how to go from doodler to professional doodler from the folks who really know what it's like, and see how they got where they are now. There are no job listings here, but there is information on how to advance in this field along with listings to related associations.

Child and Elder Care

Caregiver Jobs Clearinghouse

http://carecareers.net

This free service includes a searchable jobs database, links to employers in the United States, and an online resume database for elder- and long-term care providers. Users can search for jobs by location and keyword or browse by employer name. For the location search, you can enter your zip code and pull up all listings within a specific distance from your home. This is a joint project of the U.S. Department of Labor, the American Health Care Association, and the American Association of Homes & Services for the Aging.

LocalDayCare.com

localdaycare.com

LocalDayCare.com helps to connect parents with providers of full-time, part-time, and backup child care. The database lists day-care centers, in-home providers, and drop-in/backup caregivers. Persons interested in working in this field can use the listings to locate local employers. For a small fee, care providers can register to be added to the database. This organization partners with Babysitters.com for short-term care needs.

National Child Care Information Center

http://nccic.org

The National Child Care Information Center (NCCIC), a project of the Child Care Bureau, is a national resource that links information and people to complement, enhance, and promote the child care delivery system, working to ensure that all children and families have access to high-quality comprehensive services. Among the many resources here is information on starting your own child care business, including links to each state's agency for information on local regulations.

Culinary and Baking Arts

Bread Bakers Guild of America

bbga.org

This professional guild works to provide education in the field of artisan baking and the production of high-quality bread products. You'll find recipes, tips, information on places to buy supplies and equipment, education links, and job listings at this site.

Escoffier On Line

escoffier.com

Escoffier On Line is for all food professionals from bakers to chefs to food-service managers. This is a wonderful resource if you are looking for a job, for education and training information in food-service hospitality or culinary work, and for industry links.

FoodIndustryJobs.com

foodindustryjobs.com

This site features job listings and other information for persons interested in the food-preparation, food-service, institutional-hospitality, and related industries. You can search the job leads, review the employer or recruiter directories, or post your resume. Registration is required if you want to post your resume and activate the Career Scout's automatic search-and-notification service.

PersonalChef.com

personalchef.com

A personal chef typically serves several clients and provides multiple meals that are custom designed for the client's particular requests and requirements. These meals are packaged and stored so that clients may enjoy them at their leisure in the future. This site, a service of the American Personal Chef Association and Institute, includes information on this growing field, including how you can turn your love of cooking into a great business.

Dance

CyberDance: Ballet on the Net

cyberdance.org

CyberDance is a resource guide with thirty-five hundred links to classical ballet and modern dance resources on the Internet. This list includes dance companies, news and information (featuring events, auditions, and competitions), people, international information, and more.

Voice of Dance

voiceofdance.com

Voice of Dance is a directory of resources, news, and discussions on dance. Under Community you'll find announcements of auditions, jobs, and classes.

Fashion and Beauty

The Apparel News

apparelnews.net

This site presents news for the industry along with loads of links to the players and buyers. The classified ads are accessible for a small weekly fee.

FashionCareerCenter.com

fashioncareercenter.com

The Fashion Career Center features jobs for anyone in the fashion industry— models, sales representatives, pattern makers, and more. Look over the listings or post your resume at no cost. You'll also find links to other fashion-industry career sites and industry news sources.

Women's Wear Daily

wwd.com

Women's Wear Daily is the "Retailer's Daily Newspaper." At its website, along with the articles and conference lists, you'll find the Classifieds, which are updated every night before they go into the print edition the next morning. Scroll down the page to reach the Career Services and Help Wanted listings.

Funeral Directors

FuneralNet

funeralnet.com

FuneralNet links to extensive information on funeral homes and funeral services nationwide. This site includes employment and internship opportunities along with information on careers in this industry.

National Funeral Directors Association (NFDA)

nfda.org

The NFDA has an excellent site with good information on education and licensing requirements for this field. The site also features job announcements, information on careers in funeral services, and scholarships.

Gaming

Casino Careers Online

casinocareers.com

Casino Careers Online offers a job bank and a resume database for those in the gaming industry. Only candidates matching the required qualifications will be added to the database, and only gaming companies that are registered users of this service can search the database. Qualified job seekers can post either an open or a confidential resume, which must be updated every six months to stay active.

Casino Employment Guide

casinoemployment.com

The Casino Employment Guide includes job listings, a resume database, and some links to other sources. The job listings cover a wide variety of occupations in this industry.

Gender and Race Studies

Women's Studies Database

mith2.umd.edu/WomensStudies/Employment

This website is operated by the Maryland Institute for Technology in the Humanities (MITH) and serves people who are interested in women's studies and women's issues. The Employment section lists academic and nonacademic positions in gender and race studies and issues, while the Announcements area includes internships, fellowships, and funding opportunities.

Graphics, Multimedia, and Web Design

RitaSue Siegel Resources

ritasue.com

RitaSue Siegel Resources is a search and consulting firm dedicated to recruiting and placing professionals in graphic design, industrial design, user interface/Web design, interior design, architecture, fashion, textiles, and apparel at all employment levels from CEO to design staff. Its clients include consulting and design firms and leading academic institutions in the field of design. Interested job seekers can review job listings on the site.

Update Graphics

updategraphics.com

Update Graphics offers permanent, temporary, and freelance opportunities for graphic and design artists, including advertising folks.

You may also want to review Art and Artists earlier in this chapter as well as Computing and Technology in Chapter 8.

Hospitality

Hospitality Net Virtual Job Exchange

hospitalitynet.org

This site is a great source for jobs in hotels and restaurants as well as the food and beverage industry.

Hotel Online

hotel-online.com

Hotel Online is an information source and online directory for the hospitality industry. It includes up-to-date industry news (archived for the past four days), classified ads (employment openings, positions wanted, business opportunities, etc.), product and service catalogs, and special issue and trends reports prepared by several firms that do consulting for the industry.

Museums and Archives

American Association of Museums (AAM)

aam-us.org

AAM is the national service organization representing the American museum community. Its website features information about the association, museums, and career and employment resources.

Museum Employment Resource Center (MERC)

museum-employment.com

The Museum Employment Resource Center lists jobs for museums and other cultural resource institutions in the United States. You can also find information on museum studies courses.

MuseumJobs.com

museumjobs.com

This site lists jobs in museums and galleries all around the world and links to additional resources. The default job search covers the world, but you can choose to look at only postings from Canada, the United Kingdom, or the United States. Add your resume to the database for free.

Music and Music Education

The American Symphony Orchestra League (ASOL)

symphony.org

ASOL provides leadership and service to American orchestras while communicating to the American public the value and importance of orchestras and the music they perform. They also match qualified conductors and administrators with orchestras around the country. If you are interested in orchestra management, the Orchestra Management Fellowship Program is a must. Individual membership is encouraged for anyone interested in pursuing music or arts management as a career; it includes access to a special Career Development area of the website.

MENC: The National Association for Music Education

menc.org

MENC provides music educators, students, and musicians with information on and links to education standards, career opportunities, financial aid, festivals, suppliers, teacher's guides, and much more. Under Jobs you will find information on careers in music and music education as well as the MENC Job Center. This lists current openings for teachers ranging from early childhood to college. The listings are free for all to view.

MusicalOnline

musicalonline.com

This wonderful collection of resources for the performing arts community includes links to organizations, resources, and even job listings! The materials and resources cover all facets of music, from academic research links to orchestras, competitions, and managers, to help with your career.

Orchestralist

orchestralist.org

Orchestralist is a mailing list that provides an international forum for conductors, composers, players, and their colleagues in the orchestra business.

The mailing list covers a variety of topics, including repertory, conducting and playing techniques, auditions, and job opportunities (professional and academic). The website will give you the information needed for subscribing to the mailing list along with a catalog of links to more materials and an archive of the mailing list.

Philosophy

Jobs in Philosophy

sozialwiss.uni-hamburg.de/phil/ag/jobs/main_english.html

PhilNet in Hamburg, Germany, is to be commended for this excellent worldwide list of jobs in philosophy, which is posted in many languages.

Philosophy Jobs from The Guide to Philosophy on the Internet

earlham.edu/~peters/gpi/jobs.htm

This page links several resources for finding employment in the field of philosophy. The guide is maintained by Peter Suber, a professor of philosophy at Earlham College in Indiana. It features links to hundreds of philosophy resources. At the time of review, this unique guide was merging with two other resources and moving to a new home. You can check iacap.org/library.htm as well as The Riley Guide (rileyguide.com/arts.html) for updates.

Photography and Photojournalism

National Press Photographers Association

nppa.org

The National Press Photographers Association is dedicated to the advancement of photojournalism. The membership includes still and television photographers, editors, and representatives of the businesses that serve this industry. The public side of the website includes sections with information on careers, scholarships available from the organization, and schools and colleges offering courses in this field. The Job Info Bank is open to members only.

PPA's Photocentral

ppa.com

The Professional Photographers of America site offers certification courses for professional photographers, copyright protection assistance, and many other benefits. The website also includes information for those looking to get into this business or expand their business presence, including free classified ads.

Publishing, Printing, and Bookbinding

Bookbuilders of Boston

bbboston.org

This is a "nonprofit organization dedicated to bringing together people involved in book publishing and manufacturing throughout New England." Its website is an excellent resource for interested users, featuring information on education and training opportunities, resources for the industry, and a job bank.

PrintStaff

printstaff.com

This staffing agency specializes in the print, copy, and digital industries. To review job listings, select a regional office and then select a job area that interests you. At the time of review, it listed jobs in bindery, duplicating, large press, prepress digital, silk screen, and other areas.

Publishers Weekly

http://publishersweekly.reviewsnews.com

Publishers Weekly is the "international news source of book publishing and bookselling." In the online companion to the print publication, you'll find weekly updates on news affecting this industry along with other services and resources you can use. Under Tools and Services you'll see jobs covering the worldwide publishing industry along with links to more industry resources and associations.

Sports and Recreation

Cool Works

coolworks.com

Cool Works is the major source for jobs in our national parks, ski resorts nationwide, and other similar opportunities. Organized by state, the listings range from summer or seasonal to year-round permanent, parking attendants to the manager of the resort.

FitnessManagement.com

fitnessmanagement.com

FitnessManagement.com is the online companion of *Fitness Management* magazine. Resources here include articles, news, product listings and reviews, and classified ads. Sell your equipment, buy new equipment, or find a job here.

OnlineSports.com Career Center

onlinesports.com/pages/CareerCenter.html

OnlineSports.com is a catalog of sports memorabilia, products, and services. It also hosts a Career Center with job opportunities in all areas of the sports and recreation industry.

The Outdoor Network

outdoornetwork.com

Did you ever wish you could take your talent at fly-fishing and turn it into a job? Do you think it would be great to spend a summer leading Outward Bound seminars? If so, this may be the website for you. Check the Outdoor JobNet, the outdoor industry's free job and resume classified service for professionals, featuring positions in experiential education, outdoor recreation, and adventure travel.

SkiingtheNet

skiingthenet.com

Just what you always wanted—a real reason to spend the whole day at the ski resort! Here you'll find jobs in the ski, snow-sports, and snowboard industries. And when the season ends, you can use the End of Season listings to find something to keep you busy until the slopes reopen.

Sporting Goods Manufacturers Association (SGMA)

sgma.com

The SGMA website includes all kinds of information on the sports equipment industry. There are job listings, links to member companies and their employment listings, and links to executive recruiters for this industry.

Writing, Journalism, and Broadcast Media

Broadcast Employment Services

tvjobs.com

This is a great site with jobs and information for the entire broadcast industry. While you must pay to view the job listings and salary database, you can enter the call letters of target television and radio stations in the search box and find their websites (and locally posted job listings) for free. There are other terrific resources available here for free.

Editor & Publisher Online

editorandpublisher.com

Editorandpublisher.com is the online companion to the weekly print newsmagazine for the newspaper industry. The Career Center includes employment listings for academic, administrative, editorial, advertising, production/technology, and other facets of this industry. Paying subscribers have access to today's listings, but anyone can view the older listings (twenty-four hours old) for free. A separate list of entry-level and internship opportunities is available.

J-Jobs Journalism Job Bank

journalism.berkeley.edu/jobs

J-Jobs is a service to the journalism community provided by the University of California at Berkeley Graduate School of Journalism. Jobs are posted once a week and are removed after about thirty days. These listings are also available in a weekly list format hosted by Louisiana Tech's Journalism Department (http://eb.journ.latech.edu/jobs.html). J-Jobs includes links to additional job-search support and career resources for journalists.

Journalism and Women Symposium (JAWS) Job Bank

jaws.org/jobs.shtml

In this job bank focusing on opportunities for women journalists, no listing is more than thirty days old. Look over the list of related links for more sites on journalism.

National Diversity Newspaper Job Bank

newsjobs.com

Visit this site for jobs in all facets of the journalism industry. While the job bank is targeted to diversity populations, it is open to all users. However, you must submit your resume in order to get a free password allowing you access to the job database.

National Writers Union (NWU)

nwu.org

The NWU is a labor union that represents "freelance writers in all genres, formats, and media." All working writers are eligible to join the union. Part of the NWU's service is the Job Hotline, a list of writing, authoring, and multimedia jobs in the United States. While anyone can view the list of jobs, the contact information for each employer is available only to members. If you win a job with the help of a Hotline listing, you must agree to pay the Hotline a nominal finder's fee, which goes to help continue the service. Freelance writers will appreciate the many resources on the site, including the Alerts from the Grievance and Contracts Division.

NewsLink JobLink

http://newslink.org/joblink

This searchable database features positions of all kinds in journalism, including research and communication. It includes entry- to senior-level jobs and crosses the lines among academic, traditional, and online media.

Radio & Records

radioandrecords.com

Radio & Records is "the Radio and Record Industries Information Leader." It includes industry headlines, job announcements for general managers as well as radio personalities, and loads of directory-type listings for you to peruse under The Directory.

Society for Technical Communications

stc.org

The Society for Technical Communications is an individual membership organization dedicated to advancing the arts and sciences of the field. Its twenty-three thousand members include technical writers, editors, graphic designers, multimedia artists, and others whose work involves making technical information available and comprehensible to those who need it. Members have access to a job database, but any visitor can download and view the free guide *A Career in Technical Communication.*

SunOasis Jobs

sunoasis.com

SunOasis lists jobs and freelance opportunities for writers, editors, and copywriters. There are also links to additional sources and job sites. Be sure to check out the Writers Guide to Finding Jobs Online, a nice tutorial on how to use the Internet to help you find work.

7

Jobs in the Natural
Sciences, Health,
and Medicine

This chapter leads you through sources for the natural sciences, including agriculture and food sciences, physics, chemistry, and the earth sciences, as well as the many health and medical fields. Many of the natural science, health, and medical fields overlap, so don't limit your review of this chapter to one particular heading. You should also look at Chapter 8 for related areas of interest.

Please Note: Unless indicated otherwise by the inclusion of *http://* you must add *www.* to the beginning of each URL listed here.

General Resources

BioSpace.com

biospace.com

BioSpace is a "global hubsite for life sciences." Persons interested in biotechnology and other life sciences will find news, jobs, and career information here. The job listings can be reviewed by region, company, or job category. Avid bioscientists will want to join the GenePool, its free e-mail news list.

MedZilla

medzilla.com

MedZilla is an established recruiting site for the biological and health care industries; it's run by a recruiting firm with several years' experience. This site includes jobs and a resume database. All resumes are kept confidential (only your brief profile is displayed online), and MedZilla staff will contact you about opportunities before forwarding your information to a prospective employer.

Nature

nature.com

Nature is the weekly international journal of science. Visitors will want to check out the latest features, sign up for the daily update, and go through NatureJobs for news on career and employment issues, upcoming meetings and courses, announcements, employer listings, grants, and jobs.

New Scientist Jobs

newscientistjobs.com

This site lists the international employment listings from *New Scientist*, a major newspaper for the scientific community. You can search for jobs by area, discipline, or keyword. Users can register for this site for free if they wish to apply online, store cover letters and CVs here, or receive a tailored e-mail alert notice. The CVs and cover letters are not searchable by others.

Postdoc Jobs

post-docs.com

As you might assume from its name, Postdoc Jobs lists positions for those who hold a Ph.D. The listings are open for all to view, but posting your resume will allow you to sign up for an e-mail notification list. There are other good resources to review, including information for non-U.S. citizens interested in positions in this country. Postdocs interested in university faculty positions will want to visit Postdoc Jobs' partner University Job Bank (ujobbank.com).

Science Careers

http://recruit.sciencemag.org

Science Careers is operated by the American Association for the Advancement of Science and *Science* magazine. This site includes job and career information for those who are pursuing a career in any scientific field. The jobs can be browsed by company, position title, or date posted, or they can be searched by keyword. Users can also sign up for the free Job Alerts e-mail service.

Sciencejobs.com

sciencejobs.com

Sciencejobs.com is owned and produced by the publishers of ChemWeb.com, BioMedNet, *Cell*, and *New Scientist*. Select either the Bioscience or Chemistry job search to begin your search for industry, academic, and government jobs in a variety of fields located all over the world. You can register to receive a free job-search e-mail alert on a schedule you choose and based on your search criteria.

Agriculture, Forestry, and Landscaping

American Agricultural Economic Association (AAEA)

aaea.org

Agricultural economics is the study of the economic forces that affect the food and fiber industry. Selecting Careers & Education will give users access to the AAEA Career Center with job and internship listings, a resume database, information on careers in this field, and much more. Most areas of the site are open to all users.

American Society of Agricultural Engineers (ASAE)

asae.org

ASAE is "the society for engineering in agricultural, food, and biological systems." This is a great site for finding information and links to agricultural, biological, and environmental sources. All users can view the recent job listings from *Resource* magazine, the society's monthly publication, easily located in the Career Resources section. ASAE members have access to a resume database on the site.

ASA/CSSA/SSSA Personnel Listings

asa-cssa-sssa.org/personnel

This is a joint project of the American Society of Agronomy (ASA), the Crop Science Society of America (CSSA), and the Soil Science Society of America (SSSA). Users can browse the position announcements from *Crop Science*, *Soil Science*, and *Agronomy News (CSA News)* and from submissions received throughout the month. The listings include government, private, supervisory, international, and assistantship/fellowship opportunities.

Cyber-Sierra's Natural Resources Job Search

cyber-sierra.com/nrjobs

This is a wonderful collection of links to resources for jobs in forestry, earth sciences, and other natural resource fields. The maintainer has an excellent Read First file with tips on finding work in these fields.

Farms.com AgCareers

farms.com/careers

This site is a source for jobs in all areas of agriculture, including working with animal health, teaching, natural resources management, and administration/sales. The listings cover Canada, the United States, and other international locations. The site also offers several links to additional resources.

Tree Care Industry Association (TCIA)

natlarb.com

Established in 1938 as the National Arborist Association, TCIA "develops safety and education programs, standards of tree care practice, and management information for arboriculture firms around the world." The help-wanted announcements are updated monthly, and other career information is available from this site.

Weed Science (WeedJobs)

wssa.net/weedjobs

WeedJobs, hosted by the Weed Science Society of America, lists permanent, term, postdoctoral, graduate student, and summer positions in weed science. This site is also the official online resource for positions listed with the Canadian Weed Science Society.

Information for farm workers is included later in this chapter. You will also find related resources under "Architecture and Urban Planning" in Chapter 8.

Animal Sciences, Fisheries, and Marine Sciences

American Fisheries Society

fisheries.org

This society works "to improve the conservation and sustainability of fishery resources and aquatic ecosystems by advancing fisheries and aquatic science and promoting the development of fisheries professionals." The website includes a Job Center with employment and internship opportunities and links to additional resources for this field.

American Society of Limnology and Oceanography (ASLO)

aslo.org

ASLO is the society dedicated to "promoting the interests of limnology, oceanography, and related sciences." Its website includes job listings with openings for biologists, aquatic scientists, postdoctorates, trainers, and administrators, as well as funding opportunities, links to additional career resources, and a guide to careers in the aquatic sciences.

American Zoo and Aquarium Association (AZA)

aza.org

The AZA is a nonprofit organization "dedicated to the advancement of zoos and aquariums in the areas of conservation, education, science, and recreation." Those interested in working in zoos and aquariums in the United States will find internships and employment opportunities in the Job Listings. Please note that some non-AZA-accredited organizations will have postings here. Information on careers in zoos and aquariums is also available.

Aquatic Network

aquanet.com

Aquatic Network includes information on aquaculture, conservation, fisheries, limnology, marine science and oceanography, maritime heritage, ocean engineering, and seafood. The employment opportunities are worldwide, and the page includes links to additional resources for career and job information.

Equimax

equimax.com

Equimax's motto, "Where jobs and horse people find each other," says it all. Its website provides job listings and resume services to job seekers interested in working in the horse industry (both for a fee). You will want to look at the free hiring and career advice, including the article on "What It's Like to Work in the Horse Industry." The list of links to interesting sites includes many more resources for you to review.

HerpDigest

herpdigest.org

HerpDigest is a "free, electronic newsletter dedicated only to reptile and amphibian science and conservation." This weekly e-mail newsletter offers the latest news from the scientific general media as well as professional information. There's also information on new legislation, job notices, and related resources. Visitors can read the full text of archived articles, but herp enthusiasts will want to subscribe to the free newsletter.

You may also want to review our information on Veterinary Medicine later in this chapter.

Astronomy

American Astronomical Society (AAS)

aas.org

The AAS is the largest organization of professional astronomers in North America and it promotes the advancement of astronomy and related sciences. The association's website offers the public access to several good career resources, including the AAS Job Register and a guide to careers in astronomy.

More resources can be found under "Physics" later in this chapter.

Biology

Bio.com

bio.com

Bio.com is a resource center for the life sciences community. The Career Center includes employment listings, career forums, and great articles on bettering your career and improving your job search.

Listings for Biotechnology and Biomedical Engineering can be found in Chapter 8.

Chemistry

American Association of Cereal Chemists (AACC)

aaccnet.org

This association is an international organization of cereal science and other professionals studying the chemistry of cereal grains and their products or working in related fields. The AACC Placement Service can be found under Membership and includes job announcements as well as links to related sites of interest.

CEN-Chemjobs.org

cen-chemjobs.org

Operated by the American Chemical Society (ACS), this is a job and career information service for chemistry, biotech, and pharmaceutical professionals. It is not limited to ACS members and you do not need to register to use the Apply Now button on the job announcements. You have the option of posting your resume to the database, but it is not absolutely necessary.

Chiropractics

Chiropractic Employment Opportunities

life.edu/career/opp_in_chiro.html

This is a source for opportunities in chiropractic practice, including chiropractic associate and independent contractor positions, practices for sale, clinic space for rent/lease, and chiropractic technician and assistant positions. This site is hosted by the Career Counseling and Placement Office at Life University in Marietta, Georgia. All U.S. listings are retained for four months and the international listings are retained for five months, so be sure to note posting dates and application deadlines.

PlanetChiropractic.com

planetchiropractic.com

PlanetChiropractic.com is a community where chiropractors can share information with one another, but it also serves students of this profession and potential patients quite well. Among the many resources here are articles on a variety of topics authored by doctors and other professionals, resources for finding practitioners and equipment, and employment listings.

Dentistry

American Dental Association (ADA)

ada.org

Job seekers will find the ADA is a good source of information on all careers in dentistry, including dental hygiene, dental assisting, and dental laboratory technology. Select the Profession area from the front page to access the Education and Careers section, which has all you need on how to prepare for a career in dentistry, including job listings.

Entomology

Entomological Society of America

entsoc.org

The society hosts listings for jobs and internships in entomology along with a short list of links to additional sources for jobs and internships or graduate assistantships. If you are interested in studying bugs or just want to figure out what these people really do, you will find guides to entomology, the work of entomologists, and how to prepare for a career in this field under Education and Information.

Job Opportunities in Entomology

colostate.edu/Depts/Entomology/jobs/jobs.html

Colorado State University's entomology department posts listings for openings in this field, including internships and assistantships. They also link to other resources that may have job openings.

Environmental and Earth Sciences

Earthworks

earthworks-jobs.com

Earthworks lists jobs in geoscience, environmental science, ecology, conservation, and other related positions. It is operated by a small advertising agency based in Cambridge, England. Under Links users will find a list with hundreds of related resources to explore.

Ecological Society of America Career and Funding Opportunities

esa.org/opportunities

The Ecological Society of America posts job announcements, internships, and funding opportunities that are submitted to the site. Students will want to review the online Careers in Ecology feature for information about the field and links to related websites. There are versions available for high school students and undergraduates.

EnvironmentalCareer.com

environmentalcareer.com

This site from the Environmental Career Center in Virginia lists environmental and natural resources job listings covering all experience levels from entry-level to senior management. You are required to post your resume in order to use the online application feature, but it is not required to view the listings and the employers' contact information.

Farm Workers

Migrant and Seasonal Farm Workers Homepage

http://wdsc.doleta.gov/msfw

This site from the Employment and Training Administration, U.S. Department of Labor, includes information on several programs that assist migrant and seasonal farm workers with housing, job training, and much more.

Forensics

This field covers many disciplines and is adding new areas of study all the time.

American Academy of Forensic Sciences

aafs.org

This professional society is dedicated to the application of science to the law. Its membership includes physicians, criminologists, toxicologists, attorneys, dentists, physical anthropologists, document examiners, engineers, and others who practice and perform research in the many diverse fields relating to forensic science. You can review information on a career in forensic sciences, check the employment opportunities, look for educational institutions offering programs leading to this field, and much more.

American Society of Crime Laboratory Directors

ascld.org

This nonprofit professional society is devoted to the improvement of crime laboratory operations through sound management practices. The site includes information on meetings and accreditation of labs, links to additional forensic societies, and jobs.

Geography and Geographic Information Systems (GIS)

GIS Jobs Clearinghouse

gjc.org

This clearinghouse is a great source for jobs in geographic information systems (GIS), remote sensing (RS), image processing (IP), and global positioning systems (GPS). It also provides links to additional information and resources. You can post a resume here for free.

Internet Resources for Geographers

colorado.edu/geography/virtdept/resources/contents.htm

This is a collection of links to geography information maintained by Anita Howard and Kenneth Foote of the Department of Geography at the University of Colorado at Boulder. The collection includes journals, professional and research organizations, map collections, job and education resources, and much more for the practicing or budding geographer.

Health Care and Medicine

The resources listed here cover numerous job areas within the health care and medical fields, including medical school faculty, physicians, nurses, clinical researchers, therapists, and lab technicians. You may also want to review the many specific career areas listed in this chapter, including Chiropractics, Dentistry, Hospice Care, Midwifery, Nursing, Pharmacology and Pharmaceutics, Physical, Occupational, and Massage Therapy, and Public Health.

Academic Physician and Scientist (APS)

acphysci.com

APS is a joint effort of the Association of American Medical Colleges and Lippincott Williams & Wilkins, a publisher of professional health information for physicians, nurses, specialized clinicians, and students. This site lists open academic medical teaching positions and research fellowships for U.S. medical schools and affiliated institutions.

America's HealthCareSource

healthcaresource.com

This site brings you jobs in the health care industry along with information on continuing education units (CEUs) and seminars for these professionals.

Classified Advertising for *JAMA*, *American Medical News*, and the *Archives Journals*

ama-assn.org/cgi-bin/webad

This searchable database includes the current employment listings for many of the publications of the American Medical Association. You can select a region or state and then choose as many specialties as you wish in order to collect all relevant openings for your search.

Experimental Medicine Job Listings

medcor.mcgill.ca/EXPMED/DOCS/jobs.html

This official job board of the Canadian Society of Biochemistry and Molecular & Cellular Biologists (CSBMCB) includes jobs from all around the world. The listings are primarily for placements in academic and government research facilities. You'll also find links to fellowships and even more job resources.

MedHunters

medhunters.com

MedHunters lists jobs for all health care professionals in hospitals all around the world. Among the professions listed here are EMT/Paramedics and Social Workers, making this an interesting site for job seekers in this field. Users can browse the listings by location or profession. Registration is not necessary to apply for jobs here, but it does make it easier.

Physicians Employment

physemp.com

Job listings for physicians, nurses, and other allied health professionals make up the Physicians Employment site. The listings can be searched by specialty and location, and your visa status is needed. Military positions are also included.

Hospice Care

National Hospice and Palliative Care Organization (NHPCO)

nhpco.org

This organization's website includes information on hospice care that will be helpful to anyone interested in this line of work as well as anyone interested in utilizing these services. NHPCO maintains an excellent searchable directory of hospices as well as a Career Center with job and resume postings.

Meteorology

American Meteorological Society

ametsoc.org/ams

The American Meteorological Society (AMS) promotes the development and dissemination of information and education on the atmospheric and related oceanic and hydrologic sciences. Founded in 1919, AMS has a membership of more than eleven thousand professionals, professors, students, and weather enthusiasts. The site includes publications from the association, a career guide for the atmospheric sciences, certification information, a directory of local chapters, and employment opportunities in a variety of organizations.

Midwifery

MidwifeJobs.com from the American College of Nurse-Midwives

midwifejobs.com

This site holds employment opportunities as well as excellent information on a career as a certified nurse-midwife. Users can register to store a resume here at no cost, making it possible to use the Submit Resume feature found on each job announcement. Registration is not required to search the database, and contact information for each employer is noted.

Nursing

Nurse Week

nurseweek.com

Nurseweek includes current news and information for those in this field, continuing-education information, and a Career Center.

Nursing Spectrum

nursingspectrum.com

This is the online companion to the regional magazines. Along with career information, it features a good job database. Interested users can also sign up to be notified when the job database is updated, which usually takes place every two weeks or less.

Pharmacology and Pharmaceutics

InPharm.com

inpharm.com

InPharm.com provides "executives in the pharmaceutical and health care industries with relevant information services such as news, views, jobs, directories of services, and thousands of links out into the Net." Job seekers will appreciate being able to search this international database by location, type of business, or specific recruiting firm.

International Pharmajobs

pharmajobs.com

At this site, you can search for jobs in the worldwide pharmaceutical and chemical industry as well as biotech. Several career and industry links keep you connected and informed about your world.

Pharmacy Week

pharmacyweek.com

Pharmacy Week's website includes job postings, articles, and links to more information from the weekly print magazine. Browse the job listings by category, search the listings for those in a particular location, or view all listings at one time.

Physical, Occupational, and Massage Therapy

American Massage Therapy Association

amtamassage.org

This site from the professional association for massage therapists presents great information on what massage therapy is and how you can become a massage therapist, along with other news and information, including select articles from the association journal. It's a great resource for people considering this career option. A job-lead bank is available to members only, but if this is your career field then membership is recommended.

RehabTime.com

rehabtime.com

RehabTime is an online resources site that is focused mostly on the "rehab team," including physical therapy, occupational therapy, and speech therapy. Users will appreciate the free job listings and continuing-education information along with resources for those in this field.

Physics

American Institute of Physics: Employment and Industry

aip.org/industry.html

Jobs in academe, industry, and business are all listed here for the public to view. You can also review in-depth articles about working physicists and engineers from *The Industrial Physicist*. Registration is not necessary to apply for the jobs advertised here, but it is free and will make applications easier.

PhysicsWeb

http://physicsweb.org

PhysicsWeb, sponsored by the Institute of Physics, is a great resource for persons in this field. It covers news, product reviews, Web links, articles from *Physics World* magazine, and physics jobs. All the jobs advertised in *Physics World* and *CERN Courier* recruitment are listed here. You can quickly and easily search through the listings to view quality positions in academia, industry, and commerce.

PhysLink

physlink.com

PhysLink was founded to provide comprehensive research and education tools to physicists, engineers, astronomers, educators, students, and all other curious minds. The Job Board lists corporate, academic, graduate, and postgraduate opportunities.

Public Health

Career Espresso

sph.emory.edu/studentservice/Career.html

Career Espresso is the Career Action Center from the Rollins School of Public Health at Emory University. It is a fun and very useful resource for professionals in the field, featuring its own source of job listings and links to several other good information sources. The Featured Menu Items are open to all visitors; the House Specials are intended for students of the school and access is therefore restricted.

Public Health Resources on the Internet

lib.berkeley.edu/PUBL/internet.html

This guide to public health information is maintained by the Public Health Library at the University of California, Berkeley. It is a great source of information on the field of public health and includes links to associations and other resources for professionals.

Veterinary Medicine

Association of American Veterinary Medical Colleges

aavmc.org

The Association of American Veterinary Medical Colleges represents faculty, staff, veterinary students, and graduate students studying and working in veterinary colleges, departments of veterinary science, and noted animal medical centers in the United States and Canada. Visitors will find information on preparing for a career in veterinary medicine, applying for admission to a veterinary college, and job listings in member institutions plus similar institutions around the world.

AVMA Veterinary Career Center, American Veterinary Medical Assocation

avma.org/vcc

This career center lists jobs for veterinarians, veterinary faculty, and veterinary technicians. All users can view the jobs, which include some contact information, but only AVMA members can apply online.

VeterinaryLife.com

http://veterinarylife.com

This is a source of classified ads for veterinarians and vet techs from all over the world. These include veterinarian jobs offered or wanted, clinic jobs offered or wanted, and equipment and practices for sale.

VetQuest Classifieds

vetquest.com/Classifieds

These classified ads are directed to persons in veterinary medicine. You can review all Positions Offered posted in the past twenty-four hours, forty-eight hours, week, or month, or select a category. Anyone wanting to take over an existing practice can search through the Hospital Sale Lease Buy listings.

Jobs in Engineering, Mathematics, Technology, and Transportation

Presented here are all the fields and occupations with any relation to engineering, technology, and transportation. These include all of the engineering specialties, as well as mathematics, construction, mining, public utilities, unions, and manufacturing. You may want to review Chapter 7 for some related areas.

Please Note: Unless indicated otherwise by the inclusion of *http://* you must add *www.* to the beginning of each URL listed here.

Multiple Fields

AEJob.com

aejob.com

Hall & Company operates this site, which lists jobs nationwide for engineering, architecture, and environmental consulting firms.

ContractJobHunter

cjhunter.com

This website from *Contract Employment Weekly* specializes in job openings for contractors and consultants in engineering, IT/IS, and technical disciplines. It includes all the jobs from the print publication as well as those posted here. The job listings are open only to members, but the membership fee is quite reasonable.

Engineering Job Source

engineerjobs.com

This free site lists jobs for engineers and technical professionals. Browse the listings by state or search by keyword. The site also hosts a resume database.

Kolok Enterprises

kolok.net

This recruiter specializes in engineering, technical, and manufacturing management. A partial list of current openings is available on the website. You must contact the recruiter for more information on any that interest you.

The National Engineering Information Center (NEIC) from ASEE

asee.org/neic

The American Society for Engineering Education's NEIC is a collection of links and resources pertaining to engineering and engineering education, including general resources, societies, education information, and careers in engineering. The *ASEE Prism* magazine lists announcements for faculty and other academic positions as well as research management openings each month in all fields. These announcements are posted online for members to review thirty days prior to publication, but the listings are open for all to review on the first day of the issue month.

National Society of Professional Engineers (NSPE)

nspe.org

The NSPE website provides excellent career information for those interested in any engineering specialty. Under the Employment heading is a collection of resources from career tips and job listings to salary information and lists of NSPE member firms to contact. Other areas of the site include more information on this career field, networking opportunities, and PE (professional engineer) licensure. Membership is required to participate in some services here, but it is worth the investment.

Society of Women Engineers (SWE)

societyofwomenengineers.org

SWE's mission is to "stimulate women to achieve full potential in careers as engineers and leaders, expand the image of the engineering profession as a positive force in improving the quality of life, and demonstrate the value of diversity." The website includes tremendous information and career/employment resources for women interested in or currently pursuing engineering careers.

Aeronautics and Aerospace

American Institute of Aeronautics and Astronautics (AIAA)

aiaa.org

At this site, the association rolls out loads of good information for you to review in your career or job search. The Industry Info area pulls together much of what you'll need to target employers, plan a career, and find opportunities, but take the time to explore the entire site.

Astronaut Selection from NASA

http://nasajobs.nasa.gov/astronauts

Here's your chance to be a part of this exciting program. The National Aeronautics and Space Administration (NASA) needs pilot astronaut candidates and mission specialist astronaut candidates to support the Space Shuttle and Space Station programs. NASA is accepting applications on a continuous basis and plans to select astronaut candidates every two years, if needed. Persons from both the civilian sector and the military services will be considered. This site includes all the information you need on qualifications, applications, positions, pay, and much more.

Space Careers

spacelinks.com/SpaceCareers

Space Careers carries job listings along with links to hundreds of sources for employers, industry news, and information that spans the entire world. It is well organized and easy to review.

Space Jobs

spacejobs.com

Space Jobs connects you with employment opportunities in the aerospace industry worldwide while keeping you up-to-date with industry news. Review the list of jobs currently posted, and review information on each employer so you know who they are before you apply. Job seekers will also be interested in the list of events, which allows for easy planning of networking activities.

Architecture and Urban Planning

American Planning Association (APA)

planning.org

You will find great information on careers in planning and affiliated fields here along with jobs posted with this professional organization. APA's Jobs Online listings are open to the public and may be posted for as little as one week, so you will want to check this site weekly if it is a part of your search plan. There is also a separate *JobMart* print newsletter issued twice a month (subscription information is available on the site). Ads in Jobs Online and *JobMart* are not copied to each other's listing source, so you'll need to check both to get the full list of leads from the association.

American Society of Landscape Architects (ASLA)

asla.org

ASLA's website includes information on careers in landscape architecture, a list of landscaping firms, notices of scholarships and internships, and job openings. In other words, it's possible to learn about this career field, find an accredited program, study the industry, and get a job right here. A resume database is available for members and nonmembers, but nonmembers pay a much higher price for posting.

Architecture.com

architecture.com

This is the official home page of the Royal Institute of British Architects (RIBA). The heart of the site is an indexed collection of hundreds of annotated links to architecture resources from around the world, though it focuses mainly on Britain (search the links by keyword or browse them by category/subject). The Careers section is a wonderful exploration of the field, from how it affects society to necessary training—and where to get that training. While this is all wonderful for any reader, much of the really good stuff (for example, where to study and how to pay for it) is dedicated to the United Kingdom. Other features here include a registry of architects in the United Kingdom, information on events and competitions, and a job board (riba-jobs.com).

Cyburbia, the Planning and Architecture Internet Resource Center

cyburbia.org

Cyburbia is a terrific list of resources for jobs in planning, architecture, and some landscape architecture. It is operated by a single individual who has been operating this site since 1994 and has earned our respect for his longevity, expansive coverage of the resources in this field, and continued efforts to provide the best for this profession. The Cyburbia Forums are discussion boards where anyone can read or participate in discussions, including one where job announcements may be posted.

E-Architect, the American Institute of Architects

e-architect.com

This site includes excellent career and job information along with many resources for professional development and networking with others in the field. Anyone interested in a career in architecture will learn a lot from what is here.

Job Hunting in Planning, Architecture, and Landscape Architecture

lib.berkeley.edu/ENVI/jobs.html

Created by the Environmental Design Library at the University of California, Berkeley, this is a selectively annotated guide to help job seekers in the professions of architecture, landscape architecture, and city/regional planning. This guide is not a resource for job listings but an outline of the complete job-search process targeted to those in these career fields and listing resources and links to job-lead sources. While many annotations and resources are specific to resources available from the University of California, all that review the site will find it useful as a guide to the many resources available to assist in a job search. Almost all resources noted can be accessed in almost any public or university library.

Automotive

Society of Automotive Engineers

sae.org

The Society of Automotive Engineers includes nearly eighty thousand members in more than ninety-four countries worldwide who share a common interest in advancing mobility technology. This includes engineers, business executives, educators, and students. The website includes information on the association, its conferences and training opportunities, and job leads.

Aviation

Aviation Employee Placement Service (AEPS)

aeps.com

AEPS is a source of jobs for all occupations and fields in the aviation industry, from executives to mechanics and including both general and corporate opportunities. Access to listings of current jobs requires a paid subscription, but a free trial subscription is available so you can test the database.

AVJobs.com

avjobs.com

AVJobs.com and The Airline Employment Assistance Corps (AEAC) offer an online resource that brings together employers and employees in the aviation industry. Offerings for paying members include a job database, a resume service, and other career guidance resources. Free resources found here include excellent career information covering many specific fields within this industry.

Find a Pilot

findapilot.com

This site includes public job announcements for flight instructors, corporate and other pilots, mechanics, helicopter pilots, and others. For a fee, you can post your resume here. There's also a list of links to additional aviation sites for you to use.

Biotechnology and Biomedical Engineering

Medical Device Link

devicelink.com

This service is targeted to the people who design, manufacture, and market medical devices. The Career Center includes a salary survey, a salary estimator work sheet, and job listings, while the rest of the site includes news, events, extensive links to suppliers and consultants, and links to even more information. Registration is required to view jobs and use some other special features on this site, but it is free.

There are more resources for this field in Chapter 7.

Chemical Engineering

AIChE, the American Institute of Chemical Engineers

aiche.org

The AIChE website is designed to help those considering a career in this field, students of the field, or seasoned professionals. The Careers & Employment section includes job listings, information on managing your career, top employers of AIChE members, and much more. Other areas of the site will have more information for individuals. Some services and resources are available only to members, but many are open to the public.

Chimney Sweeps

Chimney Safety Institute of America

csia.org

This is "a nonprofit educational foundation that has established the only nationally recognized certification program for chimney sweeps in the United States." Those interested in working in this field will find training opportunities here. Visitors can check the site for consumer information on safe chimneys and how to find a certified professional.

National Chimney Sweep Guild

ncsg.org

This guild is an organization owned and managed by chimney-service professionals dedicated to making life and business better for every sweep.

Civil Engineering

American Society of Civil Engineers

asce.org

The American Society of Civil Engineers (ASCE) represents more than 123,000 members of the civil engineering profession worldwide and is America's oldest national engineering society. Under Kids and Careers users will find career information such as a description of civil engineering, how to get started in this field, and lists of colleges and universities offering degrees in the many disciplines that make up this field. The Professional Issues area includes career-development information and job leads.

For more information and resources, check out Construction and Public Works and Mining, Drilling, and Offshore in this chapter, as well as Environmental and Earth Sciences in Chapter 7.

Computing and Technology

Aquent

aquent.com

Aquent is a professional-services firm supplying companies with creative and information technology professionals. They have been rated very highly by the designers and other talented individuals who work for them. Look over some of the current opportunities, submit your resume, and review the benefits of being a part of the Aquent team—you can do it all online.

Association for Computing Machinery (ACM)

acm.org

ACM provides most of its online resources for members, but nonmembers will find several areas open for review. The chapter listings will connect you to local professionals who share your interests; many of them maintain their own websites. The career opportunities are open to the public, but the majority of these listings are for academic positions. ACM members have access to an even larger array of career services, so you may want to consider joining.

BrassRing.com

brassring.com

BrassRing is one of the larger and better employment sites for IT professionals. It includes job listings, career tips, listings of career events, and much more. They have a list of featured cities along with dedicated international areas.

ComputerJobs.com

computerjobs.com

This Internet-based advertising service posts technical job and career information for computer professionals. The site is divided into geographic and skill areas to make it easier for you to target the opportunities that interest you, but keyword searching is also possible. A nice feature here for non-U.S. citizens is a flag on opportunities posted by an employer willing to sponsor a work visa for you.

Computerwork.com

computerwork.com

This site offers job listings and a resume database for computing and technical professionals. Candidates can search for jobs by skill set, employment type, or location using the extensive Computerwork.com Family of Sites. In addition, when candidates post their resumes, they can choose to have their resumes matched with employer requirements and e-mailed to the appropriate member firms.

ComputerWorld

computerworld.com

This website accompanies and expands on the weekly print IS/IT trade publication. If you are considering a career in computing, or are an experienced professional who wants to keep up with the latest developments, this is the place to learn everything you need to know about what to expect, where to go, and what to do once you get there. Most readers will want to home in on the Careers area (with its job listings, surveys, and career-related articles), but the entire site has much to offer.

Computing Research Association (CRA)

http://cra.org

CRA is an association of more than two hundred North American academic departments of computer science and computer engineering, industrial and government laboratories engaging in basic computing research, and affiliated professional societies. The site includes public job listings for computer science, computer engineering, and computing research professionals.

Developers.Net

developers.net

Developers.net offers career information and job listings for software developers. Those wishing to apply for a listed job are sent to the employer's website, which is a nice privacy feature.

Dice.com

dice.com

If you searched only one IT site online, it should be Dice.com. This is probably the best single site for IT professionals and is consistently highly rated by recruiters looking for IT talent, which means they are using this site and liking it a lot. As a job seeker, you will appreciate the job listings, online resume database, and other good career tools. Some services will require you to fill out the free registration form.

ERP Jobs

erp-jobs.com

This is a place for enterprise resource planning (ERP), supply chain management (SCM), execution management (EM), and many other software specialties and firms to advertise their career and contract opportunities and their availability. Jobs are categorized by enterprise area (SAP R/3, JD Edwards, Enterprise Asset Management, etc.). There is also a nice list of corporate subscribers for you to review.

Techies.com

techies.com

This site lists jobs and projects for IT professionals around the United States and also offers good career and professional development information and resource links. Registration is required in order to apply for the jobs posted here, meaning you will need to store your resume in the database, but you have the option of making it available to employers searching the database. An interesting feature is the ability to research lists of employers based on a geographic region.

WITI4Hire from Women in Technology International

witi4hire.com

WITI's purpose is to encourage more women to pursue technical careers and to reach the upper administrative levels in all industries. Its job board is open to the public and features an international database of listings.

Construction and Public Works

American Public Works Association (APWA)

apwa.net

The APWA site is a tremendous resource for information on the many fields covering public works, featuring a stellar list of links to related professional and trade associations. The association also hosts a nice job board with opportunities sorted by region. Jobs are listed for eight weeks or until one week past the stated deadline, whichever comes first.

Builder Online

builderonline.com

This extensive website for construction professionals includes features such as the searchable Builder 100, a ranking of companies in the industry with profiles and contact information for each. Users will also like the product database and industry news from the print magazine and other sources. There is also a career center operated in cooperation with Monster.com. This site is highly recommended as a good resource for project managers, purchasing agents, and similar fields in this industry.

Construction Executive

constructionexecutive.com

This is "a career advancement and leadership development center for CEOs and executives in the architecture, engineering, and construction industry." There are job leads, a resume board, and other resources useful to your search.

ConstructionWebLinks.com

constructionweblinks.com

This site bills itself as "the nation's most comprehensive guide to architecture, engineering, and construction resources on the Internet," with annotated links to more than three thousand sites. Links are organized by topic under the headings of Organizations, Industry Topics, Resources, and Prior Issues. Professionals in these fields will appreciate these sources plus the extensive links to Jobs and Careers along with the Organizations. Don't miss additional career resources under Finding Personnel.

Right of Way

rightofway.com

This site, sponsored by Allen, Williford & Seale, Inc., has good information along with job listings for the industries and occupations related to this field. Jobs are posted for ninety days. If you aren't sure what "right of way" means, check the FAQ.

Electrical Engineering

IEEE (Institute of Electrical and Electronics Engineers) Job Site

http://careers.ieee.org

Here you'll find jobs, job resources, and career advice for IEEE members and others in electrical engineering. While some services are limited to members, the job listings and employer profiles are open for the public to review. There is additional Career and Employment information available from the main IEEE page (ieee.org) along with resources from individual IEEE societies and councils.

Environmental Engineering

See Environmental and Earth Sciences in Chapter 7.

Explosives Engineering

International Society of Explosives Engineers

isee.org

This professional society is dedicated to promoting the safe and controlled use of explosives in mining, quarrying, construction, manufacturing, forestry, and other commercial pursuits. Its website includes major legislative and society announcements, a calendar of events, information on training and certification, the chapter contact list, and job announcements, but we find the other resources to be more beneficial than the job announcements.

Facilities Engineering and Maintenance

Association for Facilities Engineering (AFE)

afe.org

AFE is a professional organization of nine thousand members bringing together professionals who ensure the optimal operation of plants, grounds, and offices at Fortune 500 manufacturers, universities, medical centers, government agencies, and innovative small firms around the world. The CareerNet includes new job and resume database services. It appears to be free for all users, but we could not learn much from the organization at the time of review.

Association of Higher Education Facilities Officers

appa.org

This international association is dedicated to maintaining, protecting, and promoting the quality of educational facilities and other nonprofit organizations, such as public and private schools, military installations, and city/county governments. The Job Express listings are updated weekly (several weeks are available at any time) and the resume database is available to all users for a small fee.

Finishing

Finishing.com

finishing.com

This website is dedicated to professionals of the metal finishing industry, those who coat, anodize, plate, and otherwise cover everything. There are chat rooms and links to technical resources, events, professional societies and related organizations, job shops, consultants, and suppliers, all of which are sources of potential opportunity. The site also hosts Help-Wanted and Situation-Wanted boards.

Fluid Dynamics

CFD (Computational Fluid Dynamics) Jobs Database

cfd-online.com/Jobs

The CFD Jobs Database is filled with jobs in this field. The job listings include those in industry, academe, postgraduate, Ph.D., full time, contract, and country/continent. This is a service of CFD Online, and you should examine the entire site for even more links to potential job sources and employers.

Food and Beverage Processing

FishJobs

fishjobs.com

This site lists employment opportunities in seafood, fisheries, or aquaculture companies seeking to fill sales, marketing, management, operations, or quality-control positions. Opportunities are categorized by geographic region, and postings are retained for as long as six months. Many listings include direct contact information for the employer, while others require you to submit your resume to H. M. Johnson & Associates, the recruiters who operate this site.

Food Processing Machinery Association

foodprocessingmachinery.com

The Food Processing Machinery and Supplies Association is a nonprofit trade association representing more than 350 suppliers of the machinery, equipment, supplies, and services used to prepare the world's beverages and processed foods. The Industry Jobs section has listings of openings posted by member companies, but you must look at the full listing to see the date it was posted. The Product Locator and Industry Directory areas can help you find potential employers and connect to more resources.

Professional Brewers' Page

http://probrewer.com

This site includes terrific information for people interested in the brewing industry. The Classifieds include an area for employment listings, but users should also check the Resources for lists of suppliers, events, and profiles of other registered users of the site. Registration for the Classifieds and discussion areas is free and necessary only in order to participate in the discussions. This is a handy international industry resource.

Winejobs from WineBusiness.com

winebusiness.com/services/industryjobs.cfm

This site lists wine industry jobs from big-name wineries, distributors, universities, and more. You can search the jobs by category, location, and company. Job seekers can also post job-wanted announcements on a community board. Persons interested in even more industry information will enjoy checking out the Directory.

Footwear and Apparel

The American Apparel and Footwear Association (AAFA)

apparelandfootwear.org

This is the national trade association representing apparel, footwear, and other sewn products companies in the United States. Job seekers will appreciate the free access to the AAFA membership directory and Sole Source, a directory for the footwear industry. The Industry Links provide additional resources for this industry, including CareerThreads, AAFA's career and employment information source.

Shoemaking.com

shoemaking.com

Shoemaking.com is a source for news, equipment, listings of worldwide manufacturers of footwear, and jobs.

Industrial Design

Core77 Design Magazine and Resource

core77.com

Industrial designers are the people who create toys, develop new TV sets, and even redo the entire Tupperware line! This area will fill you in on the field and the benefits, offer advice for freelancers, and connect you with education and training opportunities—and jobs. The job board, Coroflot (coroflot.com) lets you post a portfolio as well as search for employment. Core77 also gives you a frequently updated list of design firms to contact for internships, co-ops, and employment.

ISAJobs.org

isajobs.org

ISAJobs.org lists employment opportunities and resume postings for vacancies in all industries that use instrumentation, control systems, and automation equipment. The job listings are open for all to review. ISA members may post a resume in the database for free, but others may also post here for a fee. ISAJobs.org is a service of the ISA, the Instrumentation, Systems, and Automation Society (isa.org), and visitors to that website can find much more information on the field, including certification and training resources.

Logistics

JobsInLogistics.com

jobsinlogistics.com

JobsInLogistics.com lists jobs and hosts a resume database for people in logistics-related fields (customer service, distribution, inventory management, supply chain, transportation, warehousing, etc.).

Maritime

International Seafarers Exchange

jobxchange.com

Dedicated exclusively to the global cruise and maritime industry, this site sets up direct connections among cruise and maritime companies, crewing agents, maritime schools, universities, and prospective crew members. Membership, including the posting of your personal profile, will cost you a fee based on how long you want to be a member, but people who are considering work on the seas can review the many job descriptions for free. BlueSeas International operates this site.

The Seafarers International Union

seafarers.org

The Seafarers International Union (SIU), Atlantic, Gulf, Lakes, and Inland Waters District, AFL-CIO, represents unlicensed U.S. merchant mariners sailing aboard U.S.-flag vessels in the deep sea, Great Lakes, and inland trades as well as licensed U.S. mariners in the Great Lakes and inland sectors. The organization also sponsors the Paul Hall Center for Maritime Training and Education, located at Piney Point, Maryland, a vocational training facility.

Mass Spectroscopy

SpectroscopyNow.com

spectroscopynow.com

A portal from Wiley Publishing, SpectroscopyNow.com includes news, features, conferences, book releases, jobs, and directories in various subdisciplines of this field. Registration is not required to view and apply for the jobs here. More links to sources for job leads can be found under Links/Resources/MS Employment, but other areas of the Links directory will also be a good resource for job seekers.

Materials and Metallurgy

ASM International, the Materials Information Society

asminternational.org

ASM is a professional society for materials engineers and scientists. Guests to this site can review much of the online information, including journals, newsletters, directories of suppliers, and most of the resources of the Career Center.

Mathematics

American Mathematical Society

ams.org

This association website is a great resource for all mathematicians. The employment services are for Ph.D. mathematicians and include public job listings, the Academic Job Search Booklet, articles on job searching, and links to related job resources. Others in this field should look at the Career and Education page for information on pursuing or furthering a career in mathematics.

Listings for actuaries can be found in Chapter 4.

Mechanical, Electrical, and Plumbing

MEP at Work

mepatwork.com

This site serves the mechanical, electrical, and plumbing industry, including heating/ventilating/air-conditioning (HVAC), refrigeration, controls, sheet metal, and piping. Positions are for all jobs within this industry, including installers and engineers along with sales and office administration. You do not need to register to review and apply for jobs, but the free registration allows you to store a resume here and set up various customized services.

Mechanical Engineering

American Society of Mechanical Engineers (ASME)

asme.org

This website for mechanical engineers includes information on professional development, industry news, and jobs and internships. A nice feature of the job bank is the division of jobs among internships, entry-level (zero to two years' experience), and three-plus years' experience. ASME publishes several journals and newsletters that you will want to review.

Mining, Drilling, and Offshore

Drilling Research Institute

drillers.com

This site started for the purpose of marketing a CD, but the author and organizer has expanded the site to include a place for job listings as well as links to associations, recruiters, industry suppliers, and job sites. You should definitely check the information on Dayrates, a survey of highest and lowest pay rates for particular jobs in specific countries. This area also includes Warnings, information on bad employers as well as employment scams and other problems that drillers have reported.

InfoMine

infomine.com

This is probably the most informative mining site on the Internet. You'll find information on equipment, companies, education and training, events, countries, and much more. InfoMine's CareerMine includes many job listings from around the world along with a list of recruiters and a resume database. Many of the areas (including most of the job listings) are limited to subscribers, but if this is your field, then a subscription is a wise investment.

Mining USA

miningusa.com

Here you will find listings of U.S. and international mining industry jobs. All of the ads carry the date of posting. Other helpful information on the industry is also available at this site.

Thomas Mining Associates

thomasmining.com

Thomas Mining is a U.K.-based recruiter specializing in the worldwide mining and quarrying industry.

Musical Instrument Repair

National Association of Professional Band Instrument Repair Technicians (NAPBIRT)

napbirt.org

This is "a nonprofit organization that supports the activities of quality professional band instrument repair technicians." Association membership is open only to school-trained technicians (in a NAPBIRT-approved learning situation) or technicians who have been on the job for a minimum of five years on their own or have apprenticed for a period of five years. In addition, members must be presently working in a legal, licensed operating business. The website includes information on approved training programs, careers in instrument repair, and more.

Occupational Safety and Industrial Hygiene

American Industrial Hygiene Association (AIHA)

aiha.org

This association represents the people who are concerned with occupational and environmental health and safety issues. AIHA's employment services are available to the general public for a fee, but other areas of the site are open to nonmembers free of charge. Some of the local sections maintain their own job lists on their websites.

Optics and Photonics

Optics.org

http://optics.org

Optics.org is sponsored by the Institute of Physics (IOP). Within this rich resource is a great employment area with job listings and a resume database, both of which are free and open to the public.

Photonics Jobs

photonicsjobs.com

Photonics Jobs is an employment resource for persons in the laser, fiber-optic, and photonics industries. You can search job listings by location and category or keyword, or you can easily view all jobs in the database by clicking on Search by Criteria without entering any criteria. If you'd prefer, you can review the jobs by categories such as engineering, quality, technician, or pre-IPO.

Public Utilities

American Gas Association

aga.org

This trade association is composed of about three hundred natural gas distribution, transmission, gathering, and marketing companies in North America. The site gives you good industry news, a list of member websites, a searchable handbook covering the publicly traded member companies, and more. Under Marketplace you'll find the Industry Jobs, listings that are posted here and in *American Gas* magazine.

American Water Works Association (AWWA)

awwa.org

AWWA is an international nonprofit scientific and educational society dedicated to the improvement of drinking water quality and supply. Its more than fifty thousand members represent the full spectrum of the drinking water community from treatment plant operators and managers to scientists, environmentalists, and others who hold genuine interest in the water supply and public health. Membership includes more than four thousand utilities that supply water to roughly 180 million people in North America. This site is packed with job listings, links to water utility sites, links to local sections, industry and government regulation information, and much more.

Energy Jobs Network

energyjobsnetwork.com

This is a global group of energy-related sites that have joined together "to help meet the staffing needs of the energy industry." From the front page, users select either the North America or European gateway (not yet operational at the time of this review), then you select one of the many member sites to search for jobs and/or register a resume. Each site appears to access the same database of job listings, so it is not necessary to examine more than one.

Energyjobs.com

energyjobs.com

Energyjobs.com is a place where the "energy experienced" can look for opportunities in this industry. Free membership is encouraged but not required unless you want to use the fast online application process.

Platts Global Energy

platts.com

Platts is the specialist energy market reporting company of the McGraw-Hill Companies. Platts concentrates on the international energy markets but also reports on oil, petrochemicals, nonferrous metals, shipping, power, and natural gas. Under Community in the left navigation bar you will see a link to the Job Bank containing listings from *Power* magazine and *Electrical World T&D* as well a link to the Energy Jobs Network (see earlier listing).

PowerMarketers.com

powermarketers.com

Here you will find news, information, and employment opportunities for people experienced in managing and marketing power, courtesy of the Power Marketing Association. This organization represents the entire spectrum of the U.S. electric power industry, including independent power marketers and brokers, regulated utilities, unregulated utility affiliates, and providers of products and services to the industry.

Telecommunications

RCR Wireless News

rcrnews.com

Published by Crain Communications, *RCR Wireless* is updated daily with a mix of breaking news and in-depth analysis into the issues that mold today's wireless telecommunications environment. There are also terrific resources for the industry, including links to various associations and organizations. The Classifieds include employment listings, but the listings are not dated.

Telecomcareers.net

telecomcareers.net

This site lists jobs in the telecommunications industry. Search for free, and post your resume if you like. There are some advantages to registering, but it is not a necessary prerequisite to searching and applying for jobs. They also have a resource section with helpful links and a list of all the employers that use their site.

Wireless Week

wirelessweek.com

This is a companion to the weekly newspaper covering all the business, technology, and regulatory news in the cellular, personal communications services, paging, specialized mobile radio, private mobile radio, wireless data, satellite, wireless local loop, and microwave fields. The Classifieds section includes an area dedicated to Career Opportunities, but job seekers will also appreciate the many industry research resources available here.

Trucking

1800Drivers.com

http://1800drivers.com

This is a good source of job leads and job information for the trucking industry. If you are new to the industry, there are many postings from companies that are willing to train you. You will get brief information on the jobs, but registration is required to view the complete listings. No mention of fees is made on the site, but users may want to verify this. Related information at this site includes lots of useful links for truck drivers and others who might be interested in this industry.

Union Hiring Halls

IBEW Construction Jobs Board

ibew.org/jobs

This is the official job network for the construction branch of the International Brotherhood of Electrical Workers. Select the location, scale, and/or date of posting of the job, and go. Job calls are posted directly by the local unions themselves. All listings contain information on whom to contact for more information or to apply for the openings.

Union Jobs Clearinghouse

unionjobs.com

Union Jobs Clearinghouse lists union staffing and trade/apprenticeship positions across the United States. This site was set up to centralize these position announcements. You can review the staffing listings geographically or alphabetically by posting organization. There are usually many staffing positions here and few trade/apprenticeship openings, but it is always worth checking.

9

Opportunities
in Government,
Public Policy,
and Public Service

This chapter covers domestic opportunities for employment in public service, government agencies, and departments and institutions that work closely with them. International governments listing employment opportunities on the Internet are included under the appropriate heading in Chapter 12.

Please Note: Unless indicated otherwise by the inclusion of *http://* you must add *www.* to the beginning of each URL listed here.

The Defense Industry

Defense Industry

marylandcareers.org/intel.html

This guide to employment information and opportunities in the defense industry is sponsored by Maryland Careers and Tom Coates, a local career consultant. The links here include industry information, recruiters, associations, and other job sources for the defense industry, connecting to national as well as local resources and associations for the Washington, D.C., area.

Jane's Defense Section

http://defence.janes.com

This site features news and information on the defense industry, including a glossary of industry terms, picture and video galleries, and a career center operated in conjunction with Monster.com.

Federal Government

The federal government is one of the largest employers in the United States and probably the most diversified. Employment opportunities can be found in several free locations online, so it is unnecessary to pay to look at listings for government jobs. The federal government requires that resumes fit a specific format and will also ask for personal and other information not usually found on your resume. Check the application procedures at any of the sites and follow the instructions.

Federal Computer Week

fcw.com

This companion to the print magazine for information technology professionals in the U.S. government includes news and federal job opportunities as posted on FedJobs.com.

FedWorld Federal Job Search

fedworld.gov/jobs/jobsearch.html

FedWorld was established in 1992 to serve as the online gateway to information disseminated by the federal government. The jobs listed here are the same announcements you can find on the USAJobs website, and FedWorld links to those listings, but this site also allows you to add a geographic location to a quick keyword search. For more complex searches, use USAJobs.

GovExec.com

govexec.com

A service of *Government Executive* magazine, this site features news and resources of interest to federal managers and executives. Its mission is to cover the business of the government. Job seekers will appreciate the Pay and Benefits section as well as the Jobs and Career area.

The Resume Place

resume-place.com

Kathryn Kraemer Troutman, author of *The Federal Resume Guidebook* (Jist) and *Ten Steps to a Federal Job* (Resume Place), gives you great information on creating your private-sector resume as well as preparing your federal resume. She is considered the expert on the government's resume format and its new electronic resume system. If you are considering the federal government as a potential employer, then you owe it to yourself to review Troutman's information.

Studentjobs.gov

studentjobs.gov

Studentjobs.gov is designed to be a one-stop source for finding a job with the federal government. Special opportunities exist for high school, college, or graduate students that include co-ops, internships, summer employment, the Outstanding Scholars Program, volunteer opportunities, and much more. This site includes job-search and resume database services similar to those of USAJobs.

USAJobs

usajobs.opm.gov

USAJobs is the official site for federal employment information and jobs listed with the U.S. Office of Personnel Management. From here you can learn about current job openings in the government as well as pay and benefits information. You can download specific forms required for some applications and review instructions for applying for jobs with the U.S. government. USAJobs also features a resume builder you can use to create and store your resume in its system. While most government agencies post their jobs here, not all are required to do so. USAJobs will link you to those agencies for information on their openings.

In addition to these sources, individual departments and agencies may post jobs on their own pages. There are also a few departments and agencies that are not required to post their openings with USAJobs. While USAJobs will point you to many of these sites, the following resources will also help you in locating the many departments, agencies, and services that make up the U.S. government.

FirstGov   firstgov.gov

Library of Congress   loc.gov/global/executive/fed.html

Fire and Protective Services

National Directory of Emergency Services

firejobs.com

This site is a good source of information for job leads and training for people interested in careers in firefighting or police work. Access to the job leads is by paid subscription, but you can search the database of training academies for free. Persons interested in career opportunities in these areas should check out the demo database before making any decisions.

National Fire Protection Association (NFPA)

nfpa.org

NFPA's membership includes fire departments, building code regulators, emergency services, fire and safety associations, and just about anyone else you can think of who would have a part in fire protection and safety regulation in the United States and abroad. Operated by Monster.com, NFPA's Career Center lists jobs for fire protection engineers, inspectors, technicians with monitoring firms, and other professionals in this field.

Law Enforcement

The Blue Line: Police Opportunity Monitor

theblueline.com

The Blue Line is a resource for links to law enforcement resources and organizations. It offers a monthly newsletter featuring job openings in public service. A sample listing of current job openings is available, but access to the full list is available only to paying subscribers.

Lawenforcementjob.com

lawenforcementjob.com

This is a wonderful collection of employment information and job leads for those looking for work in law enforcement. This site even has online practice exams developed in cooperation with several agencies.

Security Jobs Network

http://securityjobs.net

This site features information on and jobs in security. Access to the job listings requires a paid subscription, but the site also offers links to additional security and law enforcement resources online.

You may also want to review Forensics in Chapter 7.

Public Administration

American Society for Public Administration (ASPA)

aspanet.org

This professional society represents public administration practitioners, students, and academics. The website is filled with great information on public administration, and the Careers section includes the ASPA's own job database, The Recruiter Online, featuring job openings in government and nonprofit organizations as well as at several universities.

Public Affairs and Capitol Hill

These resources include opportunities to work for members of the U.S. Congress or political action groups, lobbyists, and various nonprofit or educational institutions that work closely with the government.

Congressional Quarterly (CQ)

cq.com

One feature of the *Congressional Quarterly*'s website is Hill Jobs, a list of openings in congressional offices or organizations that work closely with the government.

Opportunities in Public Affairs

opajobs.com

This site lists public-affairs job openings in the Washington, D.C., metropolitan area spanning entry- through senior-level positions. There are some free listings on the site, but paid subscriptions will assure you the full list each week.

RCJobs

rcjobs.com

RCJobs is the free employment service from *Roll Call*, the newspaper of Capitol Hill, with news and information on what's happening "inside the Beltway." Users can search for jobs or post a resume. Registration of your resume is not required, but it is free and facilitates forwarding of your information to employers.

Public Policy and Think Tanks

NIRA's World Directory of Think Tanks

nira.go.jp/ice

The National Institute for Research Advancement (NIRA) is a policy research organization established to conduct research from an independent standpoint and contribute to the resolution of various complex issues facing contemporary society. Its directory lists think tanks and other policy research resources worldwide along with descriptive information about each.

State and Local Governments

Careers in Government

careersingovernment.com

Careers in Government is a clearinghouse of information, resources, and jobs available in public-sector organizations in the United States and abroad. Search by keyword and other criteria, or by employer and location.

Govtjob.net

govtjob.net

Sponsored by the Local Government Institute (LGI), GovtJob.net provides a centralized online source of jobs available in local governments across the United States. It also lists executive search firms that recruit in this field.

Govtjobs.com

govtjobs.com

Govtjobs.com is devoted to helping individuals find the jobs they are seeking in the public sector. In addition to job listings, the site has links to agencies, executive search firms, and resources for locating more opportunities.

JOB LISTINGS FROM THE STATE GOVERNMENTS

This is a list of the state government job pages. Unlike the state job banks noted in Chapter 11, these are jobs working for the state government. You may find other career resources for states, counties, and municipalities in Chapter 11.

Alabama	personnel.state.al.us
Alaska	state.ak.us/local/jobs.html
Arizona	hr.state.az.us/employment
Arkansas	arstatejobs.com
California	spb.ca.gov
Colorado	colorado.gov/employment.htm
Connecticut	das.state.ct.us/HR/HRhome.htm
Delaware	http://delawarepersonnel.com
District of Columbia	dc.gov
Florida	https://peoplefirst.myflorida.com
Georgia	gms.state.ga.us
Hawaii	ehawaiigov.org/dhrd/statejobs/html
Idaho	dhr.state.id.us
Illinois	state.il.us/cms/persnl/default.htm
	illinois.gov/gov/internships.cfm (internships)
Indiana	in.gov/jobs/stateemployment/jobbank.html
Iowa	iowajobs.org
Kansas	http://da.state.ks.us/ps/aaa/recruitment
Kentucky	http://personnel.ky.gov
Louisiana	dscs.state.la.us
Maine	state.me.us/statejobs
Maryland	dbm.maryland.gov

Massachusetts	mass.gov
Michigan	michigan.gov/mdcs
Minnesota	doer.state.mn.us
Mississippi	spb.state.ms.us
Missouri	oa.state.mo.us/pers/empservices.htm
Montana	http://jsd.dli.state.mt.us
Nebraska	wrk4neb.org
Nevada	http://dop.nv.gov
New Hampshire	http://admin.state.nh.us/personnel
New Jersey	state.nj.us/personnel
New Mexico	state.nm.us/spo
New York	cs.state.ny.us
North Carolina	osp.state.nc.us
North Dakota	state.nd.us/cpers
Ohio	state.oh.us/das/dhr/emprec.html
Oklahoma	opm.state.ok.us
Oregon	dashr.state.or.us
Pennsylvania	http://sites.state.pa.us/jobpost.html
	http://sites.state.pa.us/Internopp/index.html (internships)
Rhode Island	dlt.state.ri.us/webdev/JobsRI/statejobs.htm
South Carolina	state.sc.us/jobs
South Dakota	state.sd.us/applications/pr47jobs/home.htm
Tennessee	state.tn.us/personnel
Texas	twc.state.tx.us/jobs/gvjb/gvjb.html
Utah	dhrm.state.ut.us
Vermont	vermontpersonnel.org
Virginia	http://jobs.state.va.us
Washington	http://hr.dop.wa.gov
Washington, D.C.	See "District of Columbia."
West Virginia	state.wv.us/admin/personel

Wisconsin	http://wiscjobs.state.wi.us
Wyoming	http://personnel.state.wy.us

The following resources can lead you to even more information on state, local, tribal, and territorial governments.

Library of Congress: State and Local Governments	loc.gov/global/state/stategov.html
State and Local Government on the Net	statelocalgov.net

U.S. Armed Services

Connect to each service's website for more information on military service opportunities, benefits of a military career, and recruiter locations.

U.S. Air Force	airforce.com
U.S. Army	goarmy.com
U.S. Coast Guard	uscg.mil
U.S. Marines	marines.com
U.S. Navy	navyjobs.com

U.S. Military and the Department of Defense

DefenseLink

defenselink.mil

DefenseLink, the official website of the U.S. Department of Defense, was developed to serve as the starting point for finding U.S. military information online. Check the list of DoD Sites for a link to the civilian job opportunities as well as the recruiting sites for all branches of the military.

Military Career Guide Online, the Defense Manpower Data Center

militarycareers.com

If you are considering some time in the military before pursuing a career in the private sector, this site will be useful to you. It gives you details on 152 enlisted and officer occupations, and gives you the civilian counterpart for every applicable military occupation. This site also describes training, advancement, and educational opportunities within each of the major services.

10

Entry-Level
and Summer
Employment,
Internships,
and Co-ops

This chapter is targeted to college students and new graduates. Persons searching for cooperative and internship information should check with their department heads and college career centers before reviewing the leads listed here. After this, check the major job-listing sites in Chapter 3 for leads. Pay special attention to any areas set aside for college students or entry-level personnel. Then use the procedures outlined in Chapter 1 to identify other organizations in your major field, and contact them about possible work. Go to the search engines and search using the keywords *intern, internship, co-op, cooperative education, summer employment,* and *temporary employment* for some other possibilities. Check college and university Web servers in the region where you would like to work to see if they have any possible leads from local organizations, as well as the local resources listed in Chapter 11. There are a lot of ways to find these opportunities, but it will take some ingenuity on your part.

Please Note: Unless indicated otherwise by the inclusion of *http://* you must add *www.* to the beginning of each URL listed here.

General Internships, Co-ops, and Student Exchange Opportunities

Best Bets for Student Work Exchange

cie.uci.edu/iop/work.html

Put together by the Center for International Education at the University of California, Irvine, this page contains links to work-abroad websites, as well as "listings of some of the better-known programs that exist." It is intended to "assist students to find these exchange programs, as opposed to permanent career positions abroad."

California Polytechnic State University

careerservices.calpoly.edu

California Polytechnic's Career Services page has information about part-time, summer, and cooperative education positions along with good career resources. Some sections and resources are limited to registered students, but they have lists of and links to resources all users can review.

College Grad Job Hunter

collegegrad.com

Search the entry-level job or internship databases by keyword, or review the entire list of openings. You can also limit your search by state and look for selected opportunities only, or you can ask the Career Specialist a question.

Council on International Education Exchange

ciee.org

If you are considering international studies or internships, check out the programs and services offered by this organization. They offer information on summer employment and internship opportunities throughout the world, including listings of opportunities you can search, and they will help you with the legal paperwork necessary to get the proper work documents. There is a fee for participating in these programs, but the support they provide you is worth every cent.

GoAbroad.com

goabroad.com

GoAbroad.com is filled with information geared to college students, but it covers almost anything you might want to find out about going overseas. Search for internships, volunteer opportunities, teaching opportunities, study opportunities, travel information, and much more. The site has featured programs under each area, but it also offers a full directory search starting with a target country. High school students can also find opportunities here.

Idealist.org from Action Without Borders

idealist.org

This site matches idealistic job seekers with nonprofit and public-service organizations. You can search for jobs, internships, and volunteer opportunities by country or specialty.

InternshipPrograms.com

http://internships.wetfeet.com

This site, sponsored by WetFeet, offers listings with thousands of internship opportunities from around the world. You can search the database by location and/or job category, or you can browse the lists for U.S city/state, international opportunities, or company name. Registration is not required to review the listings, but submitting your resume will make your application process easier and will enable employers to find you.

Jobs, Internships, and Volunteer Positions from the Career and Community Learning Center

http://www.cclc.umn.edu/students/irjobint.html

The Career and Community Learning Center provides experiential learning opportunities for students at the University of Minnesota through its internship, career services, and field learning and community service programs. This list of links will help you find resources for internships and summer opportunities.

MonsterTRAK

monstertrak.com

Formerly known as JobTrak, this Monster zone is dedicated to college students and college graduates. All users can review the career advice, but your college must be a registered participant for you to search for jobs and internships. Check with your college career center and ask for the login and password. If the school isn't registered, you can request that it join.

New England Board of Higher Education (NEBHE)

nebhe.org

The NEBHE website has a nice collection of resources for high school students, college students, and beyond. Search the links of interest to you.

Russian and Eastern European Internship Opportunities from REEIWeb

indiana.edu/~reeiweb/indemp.html

The REEIWeb lists internships available in Eastern European countries, along with academic and nonacademic positions. Check this site for information on funding of related studies and additional links. This site is sponsored by the Russian and East European Institute at Indiana University, Bloomington.

Sistahs in Science

mtholyoke.edu/courses/sbrowne/sistahs/final

Sistahs in Science is a Mount Holyoke student organization for minority women in the sciences, founded four years ago by Professor Sheila Browne and one of her students, LeAnn Williams. This site is designed to help science students to locate and obtain research internships in science. It offers information on resume preparation, career development, and links to resources for internship opportunities.

Studyabroad.com

studyabroad.com

Studyabroad provides links and contact information for thousands of opportunities in dozens of countries. Search by country, or use the menu for language programs, internships, or summer jobs. Consult the StudyAbroad.com Handbook for tips on living abroad, including the section entitled "Before You Leave Home." Contact the specific sites for more information about their programs.

Youth Employment Information from the Youth Employment Strategy (YES)

youth.gc.ca

Created to help prepare young people for the workplace and the job hunt, Canada's YES is a partnership among several agencies of the Canadian government and the private sector. Visitors to this website will find self-assessment tools and career resources, along with job opportunities and resources for starting your own business. This site is available in both English and French.

Government-Sponsored Student Work Opportunities and Internships

The Corporation for National & Community Service

nationalservice.org

Established in 1993, the Corporation for National & Community Service engages more than a million Americans each year in service to their communities—helping to solve community problems. The Corporation's three major service initiatives are AmeriCorps, Learn and Serve America, and the National Senior Service Corps. The corporation offers its own opportunities for fellowships and internships in its offices across the United States, and anyone interested in any of the AmeriCorps programs can learn about them and apply through that section of the website.

Peace Corps

peacecorps.gov

You'll find background information on the organization and access to a transition service for RPCVs (returned Peace Corps volunteers) at this site provided by the Peace Corps. Check out the database for current positions, and then send in your application using the guidelines outlined on the Web page. The College Students Guide lists opportunities in the Masters International Program.

Studentjobs.gov

studentjobs.gov

Studentjobs.gov is a site from the U.S. Office of Personnel Management and the U.S. Department of Education's Student Financial Assistance Office. As they say, "this website is designed to be your one stop for information you need to find the job you want in the federal government. Whether you're in high school, college, or graduate school, you could be eligible for a variety of special opportunities for students in the federal government." Most federal agencies are required to post vacancies in this database, but Studentjobs.gov has gathered information on the agencies that aren't under Other Job Opportunities, which provides "the most comprehensive access to federal job opportunities available. Learn about co-ops, internships, summer employment, the Outstanding Scholars Program, volunteer opportunities, and plenty of temporary and permanent part-time and full-time jobs." You can search for jobs, post a profile to allow auto-matching with posted jobs, store your resume, and learn about the many government agencies and departments.

The White House Fellowships

whitehouse.gov/fellows

The White House Fellows program spans multiple fields and provides gifted young Americans firsthand experience in the process of government, either in the Office of the President or in one of the cabinet-level agencies. You'll find information about applying here.

Seasonal and Other Work Opportunities

Back Door Jobs—Exciting Career Adventures

backdoorjobs.com

This is a companion to the book *The Back Door Guide to Short-Term Job Adventures* by Michael Landes (Ten Speed Press). Landes uses this site to keep his material current. For a younger person, this could open some interesting doors. For an older person, it could be an interesting break from the suit and tie and give you that chance to follow your childhood dream of riding the range.

CollegePro Painters

collegepro.com

You've seen the signs—these people are painting houses all over the United States and Canada! Job and internship descriptions plus information about the availability of local franchises are here online.

Cool Works

coolworks.com

Check out the loads of seasonal jobs at this website. Ranch jobs, ski jobs, and cruise jobs are a click away! Search by state, or use the menu of job categories. Cool Works links you to information about the job and the organization's Web page, if available, along with contact information so you can follow up on the lead.

My Summers

mysummers.com

This is a source for summer jobs; most of the opportunities are at summer camps. The free registration is required, and you must be eighteen or older and a high school graduate to participate. Once you are registered (which entails filling out an application), your information will be forwarded to all of the camps that subscribe to this service (pretty much the same list you see advertised in Campfinders.com). You can also search the job postings and apply for any jobs that look interesting.

Seasonal Employment

seasonalemployment.com

Seasonal Employment lists jobs for specific times of the year, which means they are usually in or about various recreational facilities. Pick a season (summer or winter), a location (by state or choose Canada), or employer, and review the information on available job openings.

Summer Jobs

summerjobs.com

Search these summer jobs by keyword or geographic location, or link to other job sites and career or training resources. There are listings for all over the world, and you'll find many opportunities to exchange your skills for several weeks in locations such as the Caribbean.

Volunteer Opportunities

Missions Opportunities from The WEA Mission Commission

globalmission.org

Are you looking for an opportunity to serve others throughout the world in a variety of ways? The World Evangelical Alliance Mission Commission offers databases with hundreds of short- and long-term openings in countries and areas where help is needed. Many assignments are unpaid voluntary positions, but some provide a small salary or stipend. Visually impaired persons may have trouble navigating this site due to the design.

VolunteerMatch

volunteermatch.org

If you are looking for something to do with your time and talent that can benefit your community and yourself, then plug in your zip code and get a list of organizations nearby that need you. You can even specify how far you can travel, when you can start, and whether you want a one-time or ongoing opportunity. Each listing includes a profile of the organization plus a rundown of all activities associated with the group. You can even "Express interest in this activity" online by filling out the form provided, which will then be forwarded to the sponsoring organization.

11

State and Local Resources for the United States

Focused niche and geography-specific resources can be the most helpful during the job search. Cities, states, regions, and dependencies of the United States such as Guam and Puerto Rico have developed and maintain websites of interest to their local job seekers and career changers. Many of these sites go beyond the provision of employment information to offer child care assistance, transportation, and other resources that empower today's workers as never before.

In this chapter, we have provided the URLs for all of the state-sponsored job-service sites and some of the larger county or municipal job sites. Due to space considerations and the large numbers of local resources that are available, we offer a relatively brief sampling of the other initiatives developed by individual jurisdictions, grassroots organizations, or other local institutions. We have not included U.S. colleges and universities in this list, except for noting a few of the best career-service centers maintained by these institutions. You can easily find colleges and universities by using an online directory or search engine, or by using any of the directories listed in Chapter 14. Colleges and universities usually collect information pertinent to their local communities and list their own employment opportunities on their websites.

Community information networks frequently carry local job listings and provide all kinds of information for a region, including available housing and lists of local businesses. Although each community net is organized differently, you can generally find helpful career information in the listings of government resources and services, community centers, libraries, or business resources. The business or commercial resources may also cite the names of companies or people to contact about potential work opportunities.

Remember that local newspapers are a very important component in your search for employment. These will help you learn about a community, learn about the employers present, find potential contacts within those organizations, and even connect you with local job listings. Most newspapers in the United States are now represented on the Web, which makes it easy for you to find and review the newspapers for your target location. Rather than list each newspaper available for each state, we have provided a link to the specific section of NewsLink that lists the newspapers for each state. Because one source cannot list everything, we also suggest you use the other online newspaper collections listed in Chapter 3.

New to this edition is the arrangement of states into regions. We encourage you to check resources for neighboring states, as they may frequently cover your area too. This is particularly important for anyone living near a state line, but it could also apply to other areas where employers must work to attract new workers to the area to help fill openings. Each region begins with any regional job resources that cover multiple states within the area. The states then follow in alphabetical order, with each state's job bank listed first and the newspaper link second. All other resources within the state are listed alphabetically after that. For those of you interested in jobs with the various state governments, that list can be found in Chapter 9.

Business directories are another helpful resource for finding a business in your industry or one that could use your skills. SuperPages (http://superpages.com) and other online telephone directories offer searches by category and by location. You can also explore an online directory such as Business.com (business.com) or Yahoo! (yahoo.com). If you have a specific business you're looking for, try putting the name of the business in quotes in the Google (google.com) search box.

And don't forget the library! It's generally a good first stop when you're conducting a job search. You'll find some good local job links plus a bit of help in fine-tuning your job search, creating a resume, and developing your interview skills. Your library also has business directories and databases, directories of libraries and chambers of commerce, and knowledgeable librarians who can help you find what you need. Libdex (libdex.com), a worldwide directory of libraries, can help you connect to a distant library in your target area.

While we have a lot of information here, it's possible that we still don't have exactly what you need. In that case, use the resources and strategies in Chapter 1 to help you find more local sources for employment. Keep in mind that many of the job sites featured in other chapters of this guide are also searchable by location. The general resources featured at the beginning of this chapter will also serve you well. And The Riley Guide will have additional listings for the states as well as updates for these listings, so you may want to check there for more information (rileyguide.com/local.html).

Please Note: Unless indicated otherwise by the inclusion of *http://* you must add *www.* to the beginning of each URL listed here.

General Resources

America's Career InfoNet

acinet.org

America's Job Bank (AJB)

ajb.org or jobsearch.org

America's Service Locator

servicelocator.org

CareerOneStop

careeronestop.org

America's Career InfoNet provides a library of information to assist you in finding or building your career. America's Job Bank includes the job listings for all of the state employment services (and those of Guam, Puerto Rico, and other U.S. territories). It is simple to use and offers several ways for you to search, including military specialty codes so that people leaving the military can match their skills to jobs in the nonmilitary marketplace. America's Service Locator can help you find the support services you need, and CareerOneStop attempts to pull it all together for employees and employers alike. Can't find what you need? Dial 877-US2-JOBS for direct assistance.

AnyWho

anywho.com

SMARTpages.com

smartpages.com

SuperPages.com

superpages.com

These three sites offer online telephone directories, including yellow and white pages, and are searchable by business categories as well as name. AnyWho is provided by AT&T, SMARTpages.com is provided by SBC, and SuperPages.com is provided by Verizon. We suggest using all three as they are provided by different vendors, and each specializes in the calling areas covered by that vendor.

Internet Job Source

statejobs.com

The Internet Job Source brings together career resources, newspapers, colleges, and major employers for most of the United States. Click on the map or scroll down the page to the state that interests you.

LibDex

libdex.com

LibDex is a worldwide directory of library websites, online public-access catalogs, and other library-related organizations. You can browse the listings by location (country, then state) or search using a keyword (the city you are targeting).

NewsChoice Online Newspaper Network

newschoice.com

NewsChoice offers easy access to the job ads of many newspapers simultaneously. Click on the wizard to access the Job Finder. Search by state, region, or newspaper.

State and Local Government on the Net

statelocalgov.net

Dana Noonan's outstanding collection of links provides a convenient gateway to state and local government resources. These government websites can be fantastic sources of information! Beyond providing information about themselves, they often list businesses, educational institutions, and other bits of helpful information for job hunters.

Tech Corps

techcorps.org

techcorps.org/about/stateprogs.html

Tech Corps was created to take advantage of the technical expertise available within most communities. Volunteers from the Tech Corps use their skills to work with public schools, helping to teach young folks about technology or working on projects to enhance technology in the classrooms. More volunteers are needed, and this could be a great way to get that much-needed hands-on experience, develop your network, or keep active by sharing what you know with others. The second URL goes to the menu organized alphabetically by state.

The Midwest and the Great Lakes

This region includes Illinois, Indiana, Iowa, Kansas, Michigan, Minnesota, Missouri, Nebraska, Ohio, Oklahoma, and Wisconsin.

ILLINOIS

Illinois's Job Bank

ajb.org/il

This is the job bank for the state employment service of Illinois.

Illinois Newspapers

newslink.org/ilnews.html

This gateway from Newslink.org will link you to many of the newspapers for this state.

Chicago Public Schools

cps-humanresources.org

CPS is actively recruiting elementary and secondary schoolteachers. The site features information about Alternative Certification Programs and other resources of interest to teachers. Interested individuals can apply online.

Chicago Tribune

chicagotribune.com

Since the debut of the Web, the *Chicago Tribune* has been a leader in providing online job and career content. One of its best features is "Career Coach," a column by Carol Kleiman that appears several times a week.

ChicagoJobs.org: The Definitive Chicago Area Job and Career Guide

chicagojobs.org

ChicagoJobs serves as a gateway to resources for local job seekers and career changers. Job postings, salary surveys, recruiters, networking opportunities, and career advice are easily accessible here. ChicagoJobs is maintained by librarians at Skokie Public Library and is part of NorthStarNet (northstarnet.org), the comprehensive community information network for the northern suburbs of Illinois.

City of Chicago

egov.cityofchicago.org

Click on Your Government, then select Local Government to reach the link to municipal employment opportunities. You may also call the twenty-four-hour job hotline at 312-744-1369. New to this edition is the online application process that is now available. You may also apply at the Application Service Center at City Hall, 121 North LaSalle, Room 100, Chicago, Illinois 60602.

One Source: Your Gateway to Workforce and Career Information

ilworkinfo.com

The Illinois Department of Employment Security continues to improve its services and the resources it offers the citizens of Illinois, and this URL takes you to all of them. IDES, with the well-regarded Illinois Occupational Information Coordinating Committee (IOICC), created Countdown 9,8,7 for middle school students, Career Clicks for both high school students and adults, and the Career Information System, a self-service interactive source of information about careers, training, and more.

Illinois Department of Commerce and Economic Opportunity (DCEO)

illinoisbiz.biz

The DCEO site provides loads of information about starting a new business and managing it successfully, plus up-to-date community profiles and fact sheets about doing business in Illinois.

Illinois Skills Match (ISM)

illinoisskillsmatch.com

Illinois Skills Match automatically connects your skills and requirements to thousands of jobs in the state. This is another service of the Illinois Department of Employment Security (IDES).

INDIANA

Indiana's Job Bank

ajb.org/in

This is the job bank for Indiana's state employment service.

Indiana Newspapers

newslink.org/innews.html

This gateway from Newslink.org will link you to many of the newspapers for this state.

Access Indiana: Linking Hoosiers to Government

ai.org

state.in.us

Indiana's official website provides convenient access to loads of good information. Either URL will take you to the main page from which state agencies, educational resources (including educational requirements for specific vocations), social services, and business information are all easily accessible. Click on the Labor and Employment link to access the job leads and career information.

HoosierNet

bloomington.in.us

HoosierNet's mission is "to develop and maintain a quality information infrastructure" for its community. It accomplishes just that by offering a wealth of community information for the Bloomington area in a simple, easy-to-use format. You'll find links to educational and business resources, libraries, and IRIS, the searchable database of local social service organizations. Click on the Employment link to reach the career resources.

Indiana Career and Postsecondary Advancement Center (ICPAC)

icpac.indiana.edu

The ICPAC website provides timely, useful education, financial aid, and career information. Complete the interactive Career Interest Checklist to see what careers fit your interests. Use the Financial Aid–Scholarship Search or check out the profiles of more than 2,800 colleges and universities nationwide.

Indiana Department of Workforce Development (DWD)

in.gov/dwd

The DWD website offers access to career-planning assistance, unemployment assistance, a calendar of career fairs, and more. From the main page, select Job Seekers and then Job Listings to access several Indiana job databases as well as DWD's Customer Self-Service System (CS3), an interactive service that provides access to job-matching and labor market information.

Indianapolis Online (IO)

indianapolis.in.us

This site provides simple access to lots of good resources—housing and relocation information, government agencies, educational institutions, business directories and assistance, plus several local and state job links.

IOWA

Iowa's Job Bank

ajb.org/ia

This is the job bank for Iowa's state employment service.

Iowa Newspapers

newslink.org/ianews.html

This gateway from Newslink.org will link you to many of the newspapers for this state.

Iowa Workforce Development (IWD)

iowaworkforce.org

iowajobs.org

The organization whose motto is "Putting Iowa to Work" offers easy-to-navigate access to job placement, skill development, and lifelong learning through programs and services created for workers, job seekers, and employers. The second URL leads directly to the Iowa Jobs site. Browse or search for full-time or part-time work in the public or private sector. To see the newest jobs available, click on the Recent Jobs link.

KANSAS

Kansas's Job Bank

ajb.org/ks

This is the job bank for Kansas's state employment service.

Kansas Newspapers

newslink.org/ksnews.html

This gateway from Newslink.org will link you to many of the newspapers for this state.

AccessKansas.org

accesskansas.org

The official website for the state of Kansas offers simple access to government and community information, assistance in doing business in Kansas, and links to educational institutions. Click on Working in Kansas to open a helpful page of links to government jobs, resources organized by profession, and more.

Kansas Department of Human Resources (KDHR)

hr.state.ks.us

kansasjoblink.com

The KDHR offers a full range of training and career resources, along with information about the employment services offered to Kansans. Click on the Employment and Training link to access information about Apprenticeship Programs, the Wheat Harvest Matching Service, and the Kansas Job Link (KJL). You can also use the second URL to access KJL directly. Scroll down the page to start your job search by location and keyword. Sort the results by title, date, or location.

Kansas Educational Employment Board (KEEB)

kansasteachingjobs.com

Looking for a job teaching in Kansas? Use this site's online form to apply for various teaching positions in Kansas school districts simultaneously.

Wichita Area Chamber of Commerce

wichitakansas.org

The newly reorganized Chamber of Commerce site offers a variety of helpful resources. You'll find a searchable membership directory and several helpful resources under Small Business Development. Click on Quality Living, then on Jobs to access CareerCentral at Wichita Network.com and the Wichita NationJob Network, which is updated daily. You can search or view all current job leads or browse by company name.

MICHIGAN

MichiganWORKS!

michiganworks.org

This is the job bank for the state of Michigan. The Michigan Department of Career Development (MDCD) and Michigan Works! maintain this customer-driven Talent Bank, supplying job seekers and employers with the help they need via a statewide system of service centers. Users have access to training opportunities, employment support services, selected Web resources, and job leads. Register your skills and post your resume. Click on Job Seeker to start your search.

Michigan Newspapers

newslink.org/minews.html

This gateway from Newslink.org will link you to many of the newspapers for this state.

Michigan Department of Career Development (MDCD)

michigan.gov/mdcd

The MDCD website reflects the department's mission to provide resources and support services that increase the skill levels of Michigan workers. These services include Michigan Works!, the Michigan Talent Bank, and other workforce-development initiatives. MDCD offers career exploration and planning tools for youth, retirees, college-age job seekers, and others navigating the world of work.

Michigan Electronic Library Internet Collection (MEL)

mel.org/melindex.html

mel.org/michigan/employment

A joint project of the state's libraries, MEL is an excellent one-stop answer for your Michigan information needs, including businesses (potential employers) and job links. Click on Michigan to access the alphabetical listing of resources. Use the second URL to go directly to the Michigan Employment page.

MINNESOTA

Minnesota's Job Banks

ajb.org/mn

mnworks.org

Those living in the state of Minnesota have two job banks! The first URL leads to the usual menu of options from America's Job Bank. The second URL links to Minnesota's Job Bank, a self-service job-matching system where job seekers and employers can find one another. You'll find apprenticeships, internships, and volunteer positions along with job opportunities. To take advantage of the full range of services, you must register (free).

Minnesota Newspapers

newslink.org/mnnews.html

This gateway from Newslink.org will link you to many of the newspapers for this state.

METRONET

metronet.lib.mn.us/mn/mn-bizb.html

METRONET is an organization serving libraries in the Twin Cities (Minneapolis and St. Paul). The link provided here takes you directly to the business-to-business resources, including employment information. Other links in the Minnesota Web Directory are easily accessible from the contents on the left. These include education, government, association, and business resources that could prove helpful in navigating the hidden job market.

Minnesota Workforce Center System

mnwfc.org

iseek.org

mnwfc.org/cjs/cjsbook/contents.htm

Minnesota continues to deliver cutting-edge service to its job seekers and career changers! The first URL leads to the full range of career-related resources provided by the state of Minnesota. You can reach the Creative Job Search or access the Internet System for Education and Employment Knowledge, among other quality offerings, or use the second URL to access ISEEK directly. ISEEK offers assessment tools, educational opportunities, training programs, occupations, skill requirements, and job openings. Use the third URL to access the Creative Job Search manual for ideas that will assist you in developing a job-search strategy and career plan. You can order a paper copy to read and work on at your leisure. These are wonderful resources!

MISSOURI

Missouri's Job Bank

ajb.org/mo

This is the job bank for Missouri's state employment service.

Missouri Newspapers

newslink.org/monews.html

This gateway from Newslink.org will link you to many of the newspapers for this state.

KChasJobs.com

kchasjobs.com

Brought to you by the Kansas City Chamber of Commerce, KChasJobs.com is a collection of helpful resources designed to help you find work. Click on the Chamber link to access the directory of chamber members, searchable by keyword or company name, or use the handy relocation guide. Click on Jobs to browse current job listings by occupation, or browse the employer links.

Missouri State Government Web

state.mo.us

The state website links to the usual government agencies and services. Click on Working to go to a nice assortment of Missouri job links, including the State Park Rangers page, jobs for Missouri teachers, and Missouri WORKS!

Missouri WORKS!

works.state.mo.us

Missouri WORKS! is devoted to employment, job-development, and training opportunities. Job seekers can register and post their resumes online. The Resource Center offers child care providers, college and university websites, information on veterans' benefits, details of federal training programs, and more. Start your search for employment opportunities by selecting Job Seekers. New to this edition is the Career Information Hotline, which is reachable during the day. Call 800-392-2949 for information about education, training, or job hunting.

St. Louis, Missouri, Community Information Network (CIN)

http://stlouis.missouri.org

http://stlcin.missouri.org/citypers

The St. Louis CIN features information about housing, business development, the neighborhoods of St. Louis, and local and state governments. Click on Resources & Links to access the Community Resources database. It includes more than thirty organizations that offer employment assistance along with many other useful links. Use the second URL to go directly to the current city job opportunities.

StLouisatwork.com

stlouisatwork.com

This site represents a public-private partnership that matches candidates to jobs. You'll find profiles of leading employers as well as training and educational opportunities. View all jobs or search by category, job title, or salary.

STLToday.com

stltoday.com/jobs

The *St. Louis Post-Dispatch* and suburban journals job listings are all accessible here in one easy search.

NEBRASKA

Nebraska's Job Bank

ajb.org/ne

This is the job bank for Nebraska's state employment service.

Nebraska Newspapers

newslink.org/nenews.html

This gateway from Newslink.org will link you to many of the newspapers for this state.

Career Link

careerlink.org

The Applied Information Management (AIM) Institute maintains this database of Nebraska career opportunities organized by field. Most jobs are in the information technology, education, engineering, and health care fields.

LincolnJobs.com

lincolnjobs.com

Maintained by the Lincoln Partnership for Economic Development, lincolnjobs.com offers a bit of career advice, links to several local employers, and a place to create and store your resume. This site is simple to navigate and offers loads of information about Lincoln, Nebraska.

Nebraska Works

http://nebworks.neded.org

"Nebraska wants you!" The Nebraska Department of Economic Development offers this page of links to many of the online job resources available for Nebraska and its larger communities. Select Job Seekers on the front page to access a variety of resources, including services from the state's Department of Labor, the Nebraska JobLink, and much more.

Nebrask@Online

nol.org

Nebraska's official state website offers links to libraries, government agencies, and more. Use the Business Portal to access the handy Business Toolkit, find assistance for business start-up and information about specific industries. Nebrask@Online also includes links to state educational resources and child care alternatives. Click on Moving to Nebraska to access the employment information.

Omaha: Where Intellectual Capital Goes to Work

omahachamber.net

The local chamber of commerce maintains this website featuring a business directory searchable by company name or industry. Click on Area Jobs or use the pull-down menu to reach the employment resources and Web links. These include hotlines, employer information, career fair schedules, and job leads.

University of Nebraska (UNL) Career Services

unl.edu/careers

UNL Career Services offers tons of helpful information, including information about internships and specific career paths and advice about resumes, cover letters, and interview presentation. The Husker Hire Link is available to students and alumni only; it matches job candidates with potential employers.

OHIO

Ohio's Job Bank

ajb.org/oh

This is the job bank for Ohio's state employment service.

Ohio Newspapers

newslink.org/ohnews.html

This gateway from Newslink.org will link you to many of the newspapers for this state.

CareerBoard

careerboard.com

CareerBoard covers most of Ohio's metropolitan areas. To start your job search, select a section of the state. Browse the job database by category, or search by keyword, type of employment (full- or part-time), shift preference, or date of job posting. Register (free) to create and post your resume or to have job postings sent to you via e-mail.

City of Cincinnati Home Page/Hamilton County Home Page

cincinnati-oh.gov

hamilton-co.org

Looking for work with local government in the Cincinnati–Hamilton County area? Both the city and the county post their current openings on their website. The Hamilton County jobs are updated every Wednesday (click on Jobs to learn more). To access current Cincinnati Police Department and other city jobs, click on the Live & Work link on the City of Cincinnati website and scroll down to the Jobs section of the page.

ConnectOhio

connectohio.com

Connect Ohio offers an events calendar and links to eCorridor and other business resources. Developed by the Ohio Department of Development, Connect Ohio brings you companies on the leading edge of technology. Click on Ohio Jobs to browse the area businesses.

Ohio Department of Job and Family Services (ODJFS)

jfs.ohio.gov

The agency whose credo is "Helping Ohioans" certainly does just that. ODJFS offers one-stop shopping for all your health and human services needs. Information on child care referrals, transportation, and more are just a click away. You'll find career counseling, education and training, labor market information, and assistance in creating a resume and conducting your job search. Click on Ohio Job Net Online to go to the job leads.

OKLAHOMA

Oklahoma's Job Bank

ajb.org/ok

This is the job bank for Oklahoma's state employment service.

Oklahoma Newspapers

newslink.org/oknews.html

This gateway from Newslink.org will link you to many of the newspapers for this state.

Oklahoma Employment Security Commission (OESC) and OklahomaJobLink

oesc.state.ok.us

http://servicelink.oesc.state.ok.us/ada

The OESC provides programs and services for job seekers and employers throughout the state. Use the second URL to access the OklahomaJobLink, the state skills-matching service. At the time of review, many of the links were out of date. The Quick Search is available from the opening page, and we encourage individuals to use the site for the job search and local links only.

Your Oklahoma

youroklahoma.com

This state portal provides you with the easiest access to the full range of educational and job opportunities available in Oklahoma. You'll find business start-up information, a business directory, and the state's libraries and schools, all easily accessible. Click on Working to view the employment links and a handy listing of professional associations.

WISCONSIN

Wisconsin's Job Bank

ajb.org/wi

This is the job bank for Wisconsin's state employment service.

Wisconsin Newspapers

newslink.org/winews.html

This gateway from Newslink.org will link you to many of the newspapers for this state.

City of Madison

ci.madison.wi.us

ci.madison.wi.us/jobs.html

If you'd like to live in the "City of Lakes," click on City Agencies, then scroll down to the Human Resources link, or use the second URL to go directly. New job listings are posted weekly. You'll find additional links to other area job sites. Employment applications must be completed for all jobs and will not be accepted via e-mail.

State of Wisconsin Information Server

wisconsin.gov

You'll find links to information about the state and to all aspects of state government, including its employment services. This server also offers start-up assistance (via the Business Wizard) and links to the University of Wisconsin and other educational resources.

Wisconsin Job Center and JobNet

wisconsinjobcenter.org

dwd.state.wi.us/jobnet

Wisconsin's Department of Workforce Development (DWD) provides access to all of the services and programs available to Wisconsin job seekers and career changers via these websites. These include job hotlines, child care referrals, labor market data, and guidance for job seekers. Click on JobNet or use the second URL to go directly to the database of job leads. You'll find it easy to get to the information you need.

New England and the Mid-Atlantic States

This region includes Connecticut, Delaware, District of Columbia (Washington, D.C.), Maine, Maryland, Massachusetts, New Hampshire, New Jersey, New York, Pennsylvania, Rhode Island, Vermont, Virginia, and West Virginia.

REGIONAL RESOURCES

JobCircle.com

jobcircle.com

The award-winning JobCircle offers all kinds of job and career information for IT and engineering professionals, primarily on the eastern seaboard. Read the articles and locate IT user groups or JobCircle discussion forums. Browse the directory of Information Technology employers. Enter a keyword into the handy radius search to locate a job.

Jobfind.com

jobfind.com

This is a good resource for New England jobs. Check out the handy calendar of events, research company profiles, or register (free) to post your resume. To find a job, click on Search Jobs, then select specific New England locations, add keywords if you wish, and click on Search to view the results.

CONNECTICUT

Connecticut's Job Bank

ajb.org/ct

This is the job bank for Connecticut's state employment service.

Connecticut Newspapers

newslink.org/ctnews.html

This gateway from Newslink.org will link you to many of the newspapers for this state.

CT.gov: State of Connecticut Portal Site

ct.gov

ctdol.state.ct.us

Click on Working to access help for working families, including child care and assistance for special populations. Career resources, education and training opportunities, and job leads are at your fingertips. The second URL goes directly to the Connecticut Department of Labor and information about the labor market, unemployment, and links to job and career information.

DELAWARE

Delaware's Job Bank

ajb.org/de

This is the job bank for Delaware's state employment service.

Delaware Newspapers

newslink.org/denews.html

This gateway from Newslink.org will link you to many of the newspapers for this state.

Delaware Online

delawareonline.com

This site, a service of the *Wilmington News Journal*, presents all of the usual features of a daily newspaper, plus yellow pages for Delaware businesses. Click on the Jobs link to access the career resources.

DelawareWorks.com

delawareworks.com

Operated by the Delaware Department of Labor, DelawareWorks.com is "Delaware's ultimate job and workforce network." From this one-stop employment information center you can review labor market information, file for unemployment benefits, and access the Virtual Career Network (vcnet.net), the state's one-stop employment and training service system.

MBNA Career Services Center (CSC), University of Delaware

udel.edu/CSC

The University of Delaware's CSC has developed this wonderful resource for students and alumni of the school. Explore career opportunities or get sound advice for interviewing or developing your resume. The CSC also has a wonderful collection of Major Resource Kits designed to connect academic majors to career alternatives and information on developing a career path. Under Students, the section on Developing Job Seeking Skills includes Web presentations that feature lectures on a variety of topics. Downloading these requires the RealOne Player (real.com), and the files are quite large, so be sure that your network connection can handle them and that you have the proper audio equipment hooked up to the computer you are using.

DISTRICT OF COLUMBIA (WASHINGTON, D.C.)

District of Columbia's Job Bank

ajb.org/dc

This is the job bank for the employment service of the District of Columbia.

District of Columbia Newspapers

newslink.org/dcnews.html

This gateway from Newslink.org will link you to many of the newspapers for the District of Columbia.

MAINE

Maine's Job Bank

ajb.org/me

This is the job bank for Maine's state employment service.

Maine Newspapers

newslink.org/menews.html

This gateway from Newslink.org will link you to many of the newspapers for this state.

Maine Career Center

mainecareercenter.com

This site links together the Career Centers of the Maine Employment Service. Job seekers can search for the nearest career center, then check that office's schedule of events for interesting job-search workshops and recruiting events. Other services and technologies, including photocopiers, computers, phones, and fax machines, are available at the centers.

State of Maine Official Web Site

maine.gov

The state of Maine offers a great deal of information through its server. From here you can easily link to communities across the state, visit libraries and educational institutions, or find information about starting or growing a business. Click on Working to reach a listing of career resources.

MARYLAND

Maryland's Job Bank

ajb.org/md

This is the job bank for Maryland's state employment service.

Maryland Newspapers

newslink.org/mdnews.html

This gateway from Newslink.org will link you to many of the newspapers for this state.

Enoch Pratt Public Library Job Center

pratt.lib.md.us/slrc/job

The librarians at the Enoch Pratt Free Library in Baltimore have done a good job of pulling it all together for you. If you're in the vicinity, stop by and use the facilities in the Job Center itself. If not, use the website to access business information, job and career resources, and job leads from area newspapers. This is a good starting point for any Maryland job hunter.

Maryland Careers

marylandcareers.org

Maryland Careers offers loads of information in a simple, easy-to-navigate website for job seekers and career changers! You'll find association and business links, a handy page of job hotlines, career resources, and job leads.

Maryland's CareerNet

careernet.state.md.us

Maryland's CareerNet is a nicely organized page of links accessible by county or by topic. Self-assessment tools, career exploration and planning resources, and job leads are all available here. The Professional Outplacement Assistance Center (POAC) provides information and services for individuals in the professional, technical, and managerial occupations. Use the POAC Meta List to access all kinds of helpful resources.

Sailor: Maryland's Online Public Information Network

sailor.lib.md.us

Developed by the libraries of Maryland, Sailor connects its communities with state and local information and library databases. It also links to select Internet sites. To access the career resources, select the Business/Employment link or choose E (for Employment) in the Maryland A to Z section. You'll also find education, government, and community information and more!

MASSACHUSETTS

Massachusetts's Job Bank

ajb.org/ma

This is the job bank for the Massachusetts state employment service.

Massachusetts Newspapers

newslink.org/manews.html

This gateway from Newslink.org will link you to many of the newspapers for this state.

Boston Online Employment Links

boston-online.com/Employment

Boston Online maintains this collection of links that include the tongue-in-cheek Wicked Good Guides to Boston English, coffee, and public restrooms. Click on the Boston Links to reach the business and educational resources, housing, communities, libraries, and more.

BostonSearch.com

bostonsearch.com

Search for jobs, look up employers, and post your resume on this site, which is specific to the Boston area. When you find a position, you can apply online without having to register.

BostonWorks.com

http://bostonworks.boston.com

On this multipurpose site you can read the latest about area businesses or find an apartment. Check out the employer profiles, post your resume, or access a job-fair schedule. BostonWorks.com claims to have the largest database of jobs in the New England region. Scroll down the page to the Research tools to access the latest job news or participate in the Job Blog. Browse jobs by location, employer, or job title, or use the search box. BostonWorks.com is a subsidiary of Boston.com, a service of the *Boston Globe*.

Commonwealth of Massachusetts Home Page

mass.gov

Mass.gov offers a variety of services online—you can download forms or pay or apply for many services via the website. You'll find links to community profiles, information of interest to experienced entrepreneurs and new business owners alike, and health resources. Click on Resident, then Labor/Employment to access JobQuest, the Massachusetts job-search database. Browse or search by keyword or location.

WorcesterWorks.com

http://bostonworks.boston.com/worcesterworks

The *Telegram & Gazette* in partnership with BostonWorks offers this career resource for central Massachusetts. Browse jobs by community or category, or view all jobs. Career events, job leads, and more are all easily accessible from the opening page.

NEW HAMPSHIRE

New Hampshire Works

nhworks.org

http://nhetwork.nhes.state.nh.us/nhjs

New Hampshire Works features career resources, regional economic and labor market information, links to other New Hampshire resources, and job leads. Click on Job Seekers to access the newspaper links, government jobs, and the New Hampshire Employment Security Job Match System (NH Job Bank). The second URL goes to NHetwork, the New Hampshire career tool designed for individuals in need of more detailed information about careers and the world of work.

New Hampshire Newspapers

newslink.org/nhnews.html

This gateway from Newslink.org will link you to many of the newspapers for this state.

New Hampshire: Your Online Portal to State Government (NH.gov)

nh.gov

The official website for the state of New Hampshire offers community profiles for the cities and towns of the state, plus resources for living, working, and doing business there. You'll find additional links to the state's schools and colleges as well as other resources of interest. Use the Working link to access the list of job resources.

NEW JERSEY

New Jersey's Job Bank

ajb.org/nj

This is the job bank for New Jersey's state employment service.

New Jersey Newspapers

newslink.org/njnews.html

This gateway from Newslink.org will link you to many of the newspapers for this state.

New Jersey: The Official State of New Jersey Website

state.nj.us

New Jersey's official website provides information about the state, its agencies, and its communities. You'll also find links to business resources, child care, and education websites. Although the Employment link has some helpful resources, it also provides much the same information that the Workforce New Jersey site provides. So by all means look to this site for quality information, but visit WNJPIN for the job links you need.

NJ.com: Everything New Jersey Find a Job Page

nj.com/jobs

"Everything New Jersey" offers yellow pages and some community information, along with access to several of the state's newspapers. This URL goes directly to the employment page where you can easily search the classifieds of the *Express Times*, *Jersey Journal*, *Star Ledger*, or other area newspapers either separately or simultaneously. Register (free) to create a profile and post your resume.

Workforce New Jersey Public Information Network (WNJPIN)

wnjpin.net

Workforce New Jersey offers this one-stop center featuring career resources and employer information. New to this edition is the enhanced Job Search. Use this handy radius search to locate jobs in the vicinity of your home. You can decide how far you are willing to travel to get to a job. You'll also find help for students and others exploring the world of work. At the time of review, a few of these links were out of date.

NEW YORK

New York's Job Bank

ajb.org/ny

This is the job bank for New York's state employment service.

New York Newspapers

newslink.org/nynews.html

This gateway from Newslink.org will link you to many of the newspapers for this state.

DaVinci Jobs

davincitimes.org

DaVinci Jobs represents a collaboration of local community, area businesses, and educational institutions in central and upstate New York. It offers science and engineering news, plus links to internship opportunities and local technical schools. Click on a specialty to locate companies that typically need those skills. At the time of review, there were more than two hundred jobs listed, although a few of the links to other resources were out of date.

New York CareerZone

nycareerzone.org

New York State's interactive career exploration system was developed primarily for its students. Select the flash, graphics, or text version to start your session. Choose a broad category, then a job title within that. CareerZone provides information about the skills and education required, the tasks involved, and the job outlook and expected wages for each career. You can then link from the job title to current job offerings in the New York Job Bank.

New York State Department of Labor

labor.state.ny.us

The URL takes you directly to the Department of Labor home page, whose mission is "Putting New Yorkers to Work." It's an outstanding resource for job seekers and career changers (and for the next generation entering the world of work). You'll find the Job Bank and labor statistics, plus links to other career resources. If you're looking for a job in IT, you can access hightechNY.com, a collection of high-technology jobs available in the state. Find information for the kids at the Youth Careers page, visit the CareerZone, or tour NYMentor, the Web resource that helps students and their families find a college, go through the application process, and figure out how to pay for it!

New York Times on the Web

nytimes.com

Although access to the *Times* is free, the publisher of "all the news that's fit to print" asks that you register before you use the paper. You do not have to register to access the job listings, although you must register to post your resume or use the e-mail job alert system. Click on Job Market to start your job search. Enter a keyword into the search box and click Go to view the results. If the employer lists a fax number, you can fax your resume directly. Access the listing of continuing education opportunities that would be helpful in obtaining the skills necessary for a particular job. The *Times* continues to offer the best newspaper classified job-search system.

NYC.gov: The Official New York City Website

nyc.gov

Whether it's about transportation, child care referrals, housing, or jobs, you can get to the information you need from the opening page of this award-winning website. You'll find information about starting and growing a business in New York City, and anything else you could want to know about the "Big Apple." The Job Opportunities link offers an examination schedule, application procedures, job leads, and more.

Western New York JOBS (WNYJOBS)

wnyjobs.com

"Your Source for Employment in Buffalo and Rochester" updates its job leads daily. Western New York JOBS is published in conjunction with the free print version, *WNY JOBS Weekly*, which is widely available in the community. Register (free) to have job listings sent to you via e-mail or to post your resume.

PENNSYLVANIA

Pennsylvania's Job Bank

ajb.org/pa

This is the job bank for Pennsylvania's state employment service.

Pennsylvania Newspapers

newslink.org/panews.html

This gateway from Newslink.org will link you to many of the newspapers for this state.

Carnegie Library of Pittsburgh Job & Career Education Center (JCEC)

clpgh.org/clp/JCEC

Drop by the highly regarded Job and Career Education Center if you're in the neighborhood—it could be just the boost you need to jump-start your career. If you don't have the time, or don't live near the library, use the URL to visit the JCEC home page via the Internet. You'll find a great deal of assistance, including interview and resume tips, links to financial aid information, other career resources, and, yes, job leads!

JobNet.com

jobnet.com

"Greater Philadelphia's premier recruiting site" offers a simple search by job category or keyword on its opening page. View only the most recent jobs, or browse the listings by company. Register (free) to post your resume to the database.

Phila.gov

phila.gov

The home page of the City of Brotherly Love offers online access to all of its departments and services. Browse social services and agencies or search by keyword in Philly's Search Online for Services (SOS). Click on Business to access directories and helpful resources for starting and growing a business. You can access the Employment Information from either the Business or Residents areas. This includes federal, state, and city job leads along with education and training resources.

PhillyJobs.com

phillyjobs.com

This site serves as a gateway connecting companies and recruiters with the qualified talent they need. Look here for permanent jobs or independent contractor positions. You must register to apply for job listings.

Team Pennsylvania

teampa.com

pacareerlink.state.pa.us

Team Pennsylvania represents a partnership of the public and private sectors whose mission is to create and retain jobs within the state. You'll find a business directory and other information for entrepreneurs. Use the pull-down menu or the second URL to access CareerLink, Pennsylvania's online one-stop site offering services for job seekers and employers. Get help in preparing your resume, locate support services, and find training programs or career-related events. Click on Job Seeker Services to start your job search.

RHODE ISLAND

Rhode Island's Job Bank

ajb.org/ri

This is the job bank for Rhode Island's state employment service.

Rhode Island Newspapers

newslink.org/rinews.html

This gateway from Newslink.org will link you to many of the newspapers for this state.

JobsinRI: Where Employers and Job Seekers Click!

jobsinri.com

Browse the company profiles or read the helpful articles on the Career Central Advice page. You can browse all the new jobs, or only those few listed as temporary. Click on Search Jobs to start your search through all available jobs.

Rhode Island Department of Labor and Training (RIDLT)

dlt.state.ri.us

networkri.org

Here you'll find jobs in state government and a link to the Professional Regulation Division. Don't overlook the Career Resource Network and the collection of Outstanding Links to quality career resources. Use the second URL to access netWORKri, the state's recruitment home page along with employment resources and a job bank.

Swearer Center for Public Service, Brown University

brown.edu/Departments/Swearer_Center

The Swearer Center views service as an important component of a liberal education. The Center's website offers sound advice for those seeking "Careers in the Common Good." Check out the Community Work page featuring programs, networking opportunities, and job leads.

VERMONT

Vermont's Job Bank

ajb.org/vt

This is the job bank for Vermont's state employment service.

Vermont Newspapers

newslink.org/vtnews.html

This gateway from Newslink.org will link you to many of the newspapers for this state.

Department of Employment and Training

det.state.vt.us

The Vermont DET offers users an easy-to-navigate employment page with links to the state's Job and Talent Banks, training and education information, and other employment resources and agencies. Click on Identify Your Skills to learn about the assessment and career-development tools offered via the Vermont Career Resource Network. New this edition is Vermont Jobline, a twenty-four-hour telephone job-match service (800-414-5748).

State of Vermont Home Page

vermont.gov

Your entrée to the Green Mountain State features detailed community profiles and the ServiceNet guide to community services. You'll also find maps, agency links, and business, education, and relocation information. Link to the great career resources at the Department of Employment and Training, or check out the job possibilities within state government.

VIRGINIA

Virginia's Job Bank

ajb.org/va

This is the job bank for Virginia's state employment service.

Virginia Newspapers

newslink.org/vanews.html

This gateway from Newslink.org will link you to many of the newspapers for this state.

CareerConnect

careerconnect.state.va.us

Virginia's electronic one-stop workforce-development system offers training and education opportunities, apprenticeships, financial aid information, career-preparation assistance, and job listings from the Virginia Employment Commission job bank. Try Virginia's Automated Labor EXchange (ALEX) self-directed job search. Or locate child and elder care support, transportation, housing, and other community services.

Gateway Virginia

gatewayva.com

This gateway from the *Richmond Times-Dispatch* offers links to cities, universities, government information, and more. Easily accessible from the opening page are links to other Virginia newspapers. Click on the Classified link to access the employment opportunities.

Virginia Career Resource Network

vacrn.net

The network is a central access point to a variety of career tools for different stages of life, but each resource can be accessed individually too. The site r u ready?: Life After High School (readyva.com) addresses issues common to high school students trying to make decisions about their future, and assists with information for choosing a career or paying for an education. Virginia VIEW (vaview.vt.edu) provides career and education information for all citizens from kindergarten through adult. Informative and fun to use, VIEW is a great career-exploration resource with college and financial aid information, a list of Virginia job hotlines, and much more. The Guide to Career Prospects in Virginia (ccps.virginia.edu/career_prospects) provides users with detailed information about careers that are important to Virginia. For each career, you'll find a written analysis that includes required educational level, skills required, projected earnings, job outlook, and links to more information about careers and job opportunities. This is a wonderful resource for current and prospective residents of the commonwealth. At the time of review additional resources were under development.

WASHINGTON, D.C.

See "District of Columbia."

WEST VIRGINIA

West Virginia's Job Bank

ajb.org/wv

This is the job bank for West Virginia's state employment service.

West Virginia Newspapers

newslink.org/wvnews.html

This gateway from Newslink.org will link you to many of the newspapers for this state.

Welcome to Wild, Wonderful West Virginia

wv.gov

The official website of West Virginia offers simple access to all of the state's agencies and services. The links to cities, counties, colleges, and job-training resources can be particularly helpful for job seekers and career changers. Click on Working in WV to access the employment links. They include West Virginia teaching jobs, state government jobs, plus a link to the Employment Service website.

West Virginia Jobs

wvjobs.org

Use the tabs at the top of the page to go from one section to the others. Browse or search for a specific company profile. Browse all of the job listings or select a specific job category to view. You must register (free) to post your resume.

The South and the Caribbean Islands

This region includes Alabama, Arkansas, Florida, Georgia, Kentucky, Louisiana, Mississippi, North Carolina, Puerto Rico, South Carolina, Tennessee, Texas, and the U.S. Virgin Islands.

ALABAMA

Alabama's Job Bank

ajb.org/al

This is the job bank for Alabama's state employment service.

Alabama Newspapers

newslink.org/alnews.html

This gateway from Newslink.org will link you to many of the newspapers for this state.

Alabama Career Information Network System (ACINS)

adeca.state.al.us

ACINS offers information about specific careers, links to job leads, financial aid resources, and educational institutions, including a listing of Alabama colleges. ACINS is operated by the Workforce Development division of the Alabama Department of Economic and Community Affairs (ADECA), and fastest access to this great service is from the ADECA front page. Click on Services, then choose Find It Quick! and select Alabama Career Information Network System from the alphabetical listing. You might want to bookmark it to make it easier to find next time.

Alabama Department of Industrial Relations (DIR)

dir.alabama.gov

Alabama's DIR is here to help you with all aspects of your career. Under Citizens you'll find easy access to unemployment assistance, labor statistics, and workers' compensation information. Click on Job Seekers to reach the Alabama State Employment Service, which offers job leads, a listing of job fairs, and other resources for Alabama job hunters.

Everything Alabama

al.com

al.com/jobs

Everything Alabama is a comprehensive electronic source for news, business information, and classified ads. It is developed in cooperation with three Alabama newspapers—the *Birmingham News*, the *Mobile Register*, and the *Huntsville Times*. Use the second URL to access the job page and search for leads, register to post your resume and/or receive job listings via e-mail, and review career tips.

Jefferson County Personnel Board (Birmingham)

bham.net/pbjc

Click on a job title to view more detailed information about the position. Applications for these county government jobs are accepted on official forms only. Call 205-325-5515, or request an application via e-mail.

ARKANSAS

Arkansas's Job Bank

ajb.org/ar

This is the job bank for Arkansas' state employment service.

Arkansas Newspapers

newslink.org/arnews.html

This gateway from Newslink.org will link you to many of the newspapers for this state.

AccessArkansas.org

accessarkansas.org

accessarkansas.org/esd

"Your Bridge to State and Local Government" offers a single point of contact for information about Arkansas and its local communities. Click on Working or the Business and Employment link to access agencies and resources that can be of assistance. The education links include state-sponsored programs, four-year schools, and more. Use the second URL to reach the Arkansas Employment Security Department (AESD) and its services, training opportunities, and job leads. Access WhatajobMatch, which brings together registered job seekers whose skills match those the listed employers need.

Arkansas Business

arkansasbusiness.com

The site of the business weekly features up-to-date news about the state's business community and industries, small-business resources, and listings of the hottest jobs and careers in Arkansas. A downloadable business directory is available for a fee.

Arkansas Employment Register

arjobs.com

The *Arkansas Employment Register* is a free biweekly newspaper devoted solely to employment. From its website you can search for a job, visit the Reading Room, or link to other career resources.

Arkansas Next: A Guide to Life After High School

arkansasnext.com

Arkansas Next offers life and career advice for teens entering the world of work or contemplating additional schooling. The links include Arkansas schools and businesses, associations, government agencies, scholarship and financial aid information, and more.

ArkansasJobs.net

arkansasjobs.net

Developed by arkansasbusiness.com in collaboration with dozens of statewide partners, ArkansasJobs.net offers access to internships, information about colleges and financial aid, relocation and community information, and links to job opportunities.

FLORIDA

Florida's Job Bank

ajb.org/fl

This is the job bank for Florida's state employment service.

Florida Newspapers

newslink.org/flnews.html

This gateway from Newslink.org will link you to many of the newspapers for this state.

Florida Agency for Workforce Innovation (AWI)

floridajobs.org

AWI offers interviewing and resume-writing tips, along with employment links and Florida job leads.

Position Vacancies, Florida Department of Education

fldcu.org/employmentops

The Department of Education connects you to open positions for the public universities, independent colleges and universities, and community colleges in Florida. Listings are for faculty, administration, and support personnel. Select a school to access the job information. You'll also find salary information and application details.

Tallahassee Free-net

tfn.net

Tallahassee's network offers links to business information and directories, government agencies, and community and educational resources. New to this edition is a community yellow pages. Click on Employment to access the job and career links. Unfortunately, at the time of review, many links were out of date.

GEORGIA

Georgia's Job Bank

ajb.org/ga

This is the job bank for Georgia's state employment service.

Georgia Newspapers

newslink.org/ganews.html

This gateway from Newslink.org will link you to many of the newspapers for this state.

City of Atlanta Employment Opportunities

ci.atlanta.ga.us/employment

Work for the city of Atlanta! Scroll down the page for a list of current job opportunities and instructions for applying for a position.

Fulton County Employment

co.fulton.ga.us/employment/employment_home.html

New job opportunities with the county are posted at this site as they become available, along with information about applying for the positions.

Galileo: Georgia's Virtual Library

io.gsu.edu

Galileo is a great research tool for the citizens of Georgia. While providing access to numerous article databases and library resources, Galileo also offers a selection of helpful Web links. Click on Internet Resources to reach them. The Career and Job Information page includes a quick link to jobs in Georgia. You'll also find a handy collection of jobs by field, resume tips, and other good links.

Georgia One-Stop Career Network

g1careernet.com

The One-Stop offers easy access to the information you need to find a job in Georgia. Job fair schedules and detailed online workshops that cover job searching, resume writing, and other aspects of career building and job hunting are all accessible here. The One-Stop also provides support services, job information, and career resources—all in one handy location.

TeachGeorgia

teachgeorgia.org

TeachGeorgia serves as the official teacher recruitment website for public schools in Georgia. You'll find alternative education requirements, a job fair calendar, and other helpful resources. Browse the listings of jobs statewide by location or by subject, position, or system. You must register (free) to apply online or to take part in the Resume Expo.

KENTUCKY

Kentucky's Job Bank

ajb.org/ky

This is the job bank for Kentucky's state employment service.

Kentucky Newspapers

newslink.org/kynews.html

This gateway from Newslink.org will link you to many of the newspapers for this state.

Kentucky Cabinet for Workforce Development

kycwd.org

"Kentucky's Key to Employment" offers education, training, and workforce information for job seekers and employers. Take a virtual career workshop, find current labor market information, locate the nearest service center, or search for job leads.

LOUISIANA

Louisiana's Job Bank

ajb.org/la

This is the job bank for Louisiana's state employment service.

Louisiana Newspapers

newslink.org/lanews.html

This gateway from Newslink.org will link you to many of the newspapers for this state.

Louisiana Works Virtual OneStop

http://lavos.laworks.net

laworks.net/forms/er/FindRightJob.pdf

Downloadable forms, career resources, and job services are all at your fingertips! Users can access occupation and labor information, statistics, and more from the Louisiana Occupational Information System (LOIS). Click on Jobs to start your search. Or scroll through the full range of career, community, and job-search resources available via the simple menu structure. The second URL takes you to the LAWorks Career Compass *Finding the Right Job Handbook*. This is a PDF document that requires the free Adobe Acrobat Reader to view and print (adobe.com).

MISSISSIPPI

Mississippi's Job Bank

ajb.org/ms

This is the job bank for Mississippi's state employment service.

Mississippi Newspapers

newslink.org/msnews.html

This gateway from Newslink.org will link you to many of the newspapers for this state.

State of Mississippi

state.ms.us

The state of Mississippi home page serves as a gateway to resources throughout the state. Click on Working in Mississippi to view the employment links, jobs in state government, and information about the business community. You'll also find links to Mississippi's schools and colleges and to local, state, and federal government information.

NORTH CAROLINA

North Carolina's Job Bank

ajb.org/nc

This is the job bank for North Carolina's state employment service.

North Carolina Newspapers

newslink.org/ncnews.html

This gateway from Newslink.org will link you to many of the newspapers for this state.

BizLink: Your Online Business Resource

bizlink.org

Whether it's researching a company or starting a new business, you'll find plenty of information at this business website sponsored by the Public Library of Charlotte and Mecklenburg County. Select the Career Corner link from the opening page to access career-exploration tools along with local and regional job postings.

City of Raleigh Job Postings

raleigh-nc.org/mis/employ.htm

If you are interested in working for Raleigh, you can view current offerings on the city's website or call the twenty-four-hour Job Line at 919-890-3305. Download an application (PDF file), fill out the form, and send it to City of Raleigh Personnel Dept., P.O. Box 590, Raleigh, North Carolina 27602.

Employment Security Commission (ESC) of North Carolina

ncesc.com

Here you'll find easy access to labor statistics, a Job Bank, and other employment-related resources. In addition to providing job information, ESC serves as a gateway to social services, transportation, child care, and other resources available to the citizens of North Carolina.

NCCareers

nccareers.org

North Carolina's Career Information System offers a nicely organized collection of self-assessment tools and occupational information. Developed by the State Occupational Information Coordinating Committee (SOICC), NCCareers offers a good start for career assessment. Explore occupations, find career and education information, and climb the Career Planning Steps to pull it all together!

Teach4NC

teach4nc.org

If you would like to be a teacher but you lack the credentials, you should know about Teach4NC. North Carolina is actively recruiting teachers via this website that features certification alternatives for individuals who have had military or other nonteaching career experience.

PUERTO RICO

El Nueva Dia Interactivo

endi.com

The newspaper for San Juan offers this portal featuring news, lifestyle information, and more for residents of Puerto Rico. Click on Empleos to access the job listings.

Puerto Rico Clasificados Online

clasificadosonline.com

Look here for business yellow pages and real estate offerings in Puerto Rico. Click on Empleos to access the job opportunities. Job listings are retained for only twenty-eight days. Most areas of this site are in English and Spanish, but the job listings may be in Spanish.

Yellow Pages of Puerto Rico

yellowpagespr.com

Search by keyword and city, or browse the listings by category. This is a good way to find out what businesses are here and how to contact them about opportunities. The site is available in English and Spanish.

SOUTH CAROLINA

South Carolina's Job Bank

ajb.org/sc

This is the job bank for South Carolina's state employment service.

South Carolina Newspapers

newslink.org/scnews.html

This gateway from Newslink.org will link you to many of the newspapers for this state.

SCIway . . . the South Carolina Information Highway

sciway.net

"South Carolina's Front Door" offers loads of helpful information about the state and its communities. Use the simple menu structure to find exactly what you need. The home page leads to libraries, newspapers, and government and education sites. The Directories link takes you to an assortment of yellow pages for the state, organized by topic. To get to the employment links, click on Jobs. Unfortunately, at the time of review, many of the jobs were several months old, and some of the other resources were out of date as well. *Editor's Note:* SCIway has long been a leader in providing nicely organized, up-to-date information about its community. We hope that tradition will continue.

South Carolina Employment Security Commission

sces.org

scois.org

Visit this site to check out the job-related services provided by the state. Locate the closest employment office, or gather current labor market information. Link to jobs in state and federal government, or access South Carolina's Job Bank. The second URL takes you to the South Carolina Occupational Information System (SCOIS) with up-to-date career and labor market information.

TENNESSEE

Tennessee's Job Bank

ajb.org/tn

This is the job bank for Tennessee's state employment service.

Tennessee Newspapers

newslink.org/tnnews.html

This gateway from Newslink.org will link you to many of the newspapers for this state.

Nashville Area Chamber of Commerce

nashvillechamber.com

nashvillejobslink.com

The chamber of commerce maintains a searchable database of local businesses. You'll also find information about starting and growing a business in Nashville and helpful information about the community. The chamber also sponsors Nashville JobLink with job listings and employer information for the area. Browse the employer links, post your resume, or find a job. You can easily access the JobLink from the chamber's front page, but you can also use the second URL to get there faster.

Nashville.gov: Metropolitan Government of Nashville and Davidson County

nashville.org

Nashville's city and county governments maintain this website featuring links to local agencies and services. You'll find information about business start-up, downloadable forms, and a link to the chamber of commerce. If you're interested in working for county government, click on the Employment link, visit the Job Opportunities Web page, or call the job line at 615-862-6660.

The Source

state.tn.us/labor-wfd/source

tcids.utk.edu

The Source, a service of the Tennessee Department of Labor and Workforce Development, features career, demographic, and labor market information in an easily accessible format. Click on Services for Individuals to access the career resources. From there, you can link to the Job Bank or check out the other services provided for citizens of the state. The second URL will take you to the Tennessee Career Information Delivery System to explore the world of work and individual careers.

Tennessee.gov

tennessee.gov

The portal for the state of Tennessee offers easy access to some good information. Click on Residents to access the health and human services pages or visit the business or education links. When you click on Employment, you'll find links to all the state agencies so that you can find information about the jobs they offer, or access the state teaching jobs.

TEXAS

Texas's Job Bank

ajb.org/tx

This is the job bank for the state employment service of Texas.

Texas Newspapers

newslink.org/txnews.html

This gateway from Newslink.org will link you to many of the newspapers for this state.

Austin City Connections

ci.austin.tx.us

Select from the many services accessible via this page, or choose a map from the collection that includes a bike map and area guides. Choose HR from the menu on the left to search for job opportunities with Austin's city government. Browse by department or search by job title.

Everything Austin

ci.austin.tx.us/library/ea_index.htm

Part of the city of Austin website, Everything Austin includes helpful business links, information about neighborhoods, access to local government resources, and job links. Click on Jobs to access the classified ads and government and private-sector jobs in the community. Everything Austin is a service of the Austin Public Library (ci.austin.tx.us/library).

Texas Workforce Network

twc.state.tx.us

Brought to you by the Texas Workforce Commission, the Network offers services for businesses, service providers, and job hunters. Click on Job Seekers & Employees to access a full range of support services, including child care, transportation, and links to selected career resources. Select Search for Jobs to view HIRE TEXAS, the searchable job skills–matching system, the Governor's Job Bank of state government jobs, and TWC Express, which includes private-sector jobs listed with the commission.

TexasOnline: State of Texas Home Page

texas.gov

"Texas at Your Fingertips" offers links to state and local agencies along with loads of information about the state. You'll find the information you need to start your business, training and educational resources, and information about the communities of the state. The Employment and Labor link is prominently displayed in the menu on the left of the opening page. This site is easy to navigate and offers plenty of helpful information.

U.S. VIRGIN ISLANDS

The *Virgin Islands Daily News*

virginislandsdailynews.com

This website from the Pulitzer Prize–winning newspaper covers news and information from the U.S. Virgin Islands along with Tortola, British Virgin Island. Job seekers for this region will find a small area for classified advertisements here, and the Local Calendar includes meeting announcements for local business, social, and professional associations. The Business section offers many possibilities for connecting with employers, including a local Business Directory you can search by business name, browse by business category, or review by location (island).

St. Croix Source

http://new.onepaper.com/stcroixvi

This online news service is a nice source for local news and information for St. Croix. Along with its sister publications covering St. Thomas (http://new.onepaper.com/stthomasvi), St. John (http://new.onepaper.com/stjohnvi), and the British Virgin Islands (http://new.onepaper.com/bvireview), the St. Croix Source covers business, community, art, and lifestyle news and information. Job seekers will find some classifieds on each site along with an Island Directory you can use to find potential employers.

USVIYellowPages.com

usviyellowpages.com

This online telephone directory allows you to search for businesses by keyword or browse the many business categories. You can also choose to limit the directory to specific cities or islands.

Southwest, Mountain Region, Pacific Northwest, and the Pacific Islands

This region includes Alaska, Arizona, California, Colorado, Guam, Hawaii, Idaho, Montana, Nevada, New Mexico, North Dakota, Oregon, South Dakota, Utah, Washington, and Wyoming.

REGIONAL RESOURCES

CascadeLink

cascadelink.org

CascadeLink provides access to helpful local and regional information for the Portland (Oregon) and Vancouver (Washington) areas. Housing, transportation, business information, libraries, and government information are all easily accessible here. To view the Community Organizations OnLine (COOL) database of organizations, click on the IPAC link and select Online Resources. To access the employment information, click on the Jobs link.

ALASKA

Alaska Job Center Network

jobs.state.ak.us

The Alaska Job Center Network, "where people and jobs connect," brings together all of the state's resources for job hunters. The Job Seeker Resources include a job fair calendar, Alaska newspapers, and resume tips. You'll also find apprenticeships, training and continuing education, jobs in local government, and a link to Workplace Alaska, the state's online recruitment system. Select Alaska's Job Bank from the front page or just click on the map. The job bank allows you to select a region to view all jobs currently listed in that area, or you can select a region and job title from the menus to limit your search.

Alaska Newspapers

newslink.org/aknews.html

This gateway from Newslink.org will link you to many of the newspapers for this state.

Alaska Department of Labor and Workforce Development

labor.state.ak.us

The Department of Labor maintains this page for job seekers, workers, and employers. You'll find employment and unemployment services, labor statistics, information about the laws and regulations dealing with the workplace, and job leads. If you are thinking of relocating to Alaska, be sure to read the department's guide to finding work in the state.

Alaska State Troopers

alaskastatetrooper.com

The state troopers are always looking for law enforcement officers, as well as candidates for rescue operations and fish and wildlife protection programs.

Capitol City Home Page

juneau.lib.ak.us

The official page for the city and borough of Juneau offers business information, links to government and community websites, and jobs in city and borough government.

Fairbanks Alaska Internet Resources Network for Education and Training (FairNet)

fairnet.org

Fairbanks's electronic community network features links to agencies and organizations, educational resources, training programs, and government information. Click on Employment to access the career resources.

I Love Alaska

ilovealaska.com

At the time of review, we found very few job postings under Alaska Jobs on this site's front page. But when we selected the Alaska Links Encyclopedia and looked at the Jobs category here, we found major employers, business and organization websites, newspapers, educational institutions, government agencies, and seasonal job opportunities. The detailed community profiles are a nice addition.

SLED: Alaska's Statewide Library Electronic Doorway

sled.alaska.edu

Since 1994, SLED has provided straightforward and well-organized access to electronic information. The Alaska Communities link offers all kinds of information about the state and its local communities, and the business links could be helpful to you in your job search. Click on Job & Employment Resources to go directly to a comprehensive page of career information.

ARIZONA

Arizona's Job Bank

ajb.org/az

This is the job bank for Arizona's state employment service.

Arizona Newspapers

newslink.org/aznews.html

This gateway from Newslink.org will link you to many of the newspapers for this state.

CALIFORNIA

California's Job Bank

ajb.org/ca

This is the job bank for California's state employment service.

California Newspapers

newslink.org/canews.html

This gateway from Newslink.org will link you to many of the newspapers for this state.

BayAreaCareers.com

bayareacareers.com

BayAreaCareers.com connects candidates directly to employers in the greater San Francisco area. At the time of review, there were hundreds of employers and few jobs listed. The same company also offers local career pages for California, including:

East Bay	eastbaycareers.com
Los Angeles	lacareers.com

North Bay	northbaycareers.com
Orange County	orangecountycareers.com
Sacramento	sacramentocareers.com
San Diego	sandiegocareers.com
San Francisco	sanfranciscocareers.com
Santa Cruz	santacruzcareers.com
Silicon Valley	siliconvalleycareers.com
680 Corridor	680careers.com

California Online Job Network (COJN)

cajobs.com

Click on the community icons to access the job leads. Register to post your resume online and have job postings sent to you via e-mail. The network includes these sites:

Los Angeles	losangelesjobs.com
Oakland	oaklandjobs.com
Orange County	orangecountyjobs.com
Riverside	riversidejobs.com
Sacramento	sacramentojobs.com
San Diego	sandiegojobs.com
San Francisco	sanfranciscojobs.com
San Jose	sanjosejobs.com

California State Government

ca.gov

California continues to lead in bringing information to its citizens. You'll find education and training resources, business start-up and company information, government agencies, and more. Click on Labor and Employment to reach dozens of helpful links.

California State University Employment Board

http://csueb.calstate.edu

The Employment Board maintains a list of all available faculty and administrative positions for the twenty-three campuses of California State University, searchable by campus and discipline.

Employment Development Department (EDD)

edd.ca.gov

caljobs.ca.gov

worksmart.ca.gov

For more than sixty years, the EDD has been linking Californians with jobs. At this site, you'll find labor market information, links to training resources and the One-Stop Career Center service system, assistance for youth entering the world of work and for other special groups, and job clubs. Use the second URL to go directly to the CalJOBS skills matching database where job seekers can enter their skills into the database to match with job openings posted by employers. Use the third URL to access WorkSmart and explore careers, get help with the job search, review interviewing tips, and much more.

JobStar Central

jobstar.org

JobStar remains one of the best career offerings on the Web! Cybrarian Mary-Ellen Mort, a.k.a. Electra, brings you the most comprehensive listing of salary surveys available, along with resume-writing tips and a guide to the hidden job market. Search for jobs in specific California regions, use the Ask Electra function for career advice, or find additional assistance with national and international job searching.

San Bernardino County Employment Opportunities

jobaps.com/sbr

At this site, you'll find all the information you need to apply for a job in San Bernardino County. For the latest job information, call the twenty-four-hour Job Line at 909-387-5611.

San Francisco Bay Area Volunteer Information Center

volunteerinfo.org

Don't overlook this site if you're interested in working in the nonprofit sector—where there are volunteer positions, there might be job possibilities as well! Many organizations also make the information available via telephone at 800-CARE123.

San Francisco Cityspan Information Center

sfgov.org

"Bridging government and citizens through technology," Cityspan offers tips for business start-up and links to agency websites. Click on City Services, then select E for Employment to access links to current openings in municipal and county government. Some jobs are never posted, so be sure to call the hotlines.

Job Hotline (updated on Thursday evenings): 415-557-4888. Muni Job Hotline: 415-554-6818. San Francisco International Airport Job Hotline (not airlines): 650-821-2562.

WorkBasePA (Palo Alto)

workbase.com/palo_alto

Looking for work? Fill out one simple online form so that potential employers in the Palo Alto area can find you.

COLORADO

Colorado's Job Bank

ajb.org/co

This is the job bank for Colorado's state employment service.

Colorado Newspapers

newslink.org/conews.html

This gateway from Newslink.org will link you to many of the newspapers for this state.

Boulder Community Network

http://bcn.boulder.co.us

The Boulder Community Network connects you to information about the region and its educational and business opportunities, community organizations, social services, and more. Select Employment on the front page to go to the One Stop Career Network, a collection of links to employment opportunities and career resources in the Boulder area and throughout the state.

Boulder County

co.boulder.co.us/jobs

Search here for employment opportunities with the Boulder County government. You can also call the twenty-four-hour Job Line at 303-441-4555 or send an e-mail to jobs@co.boulder.co.us.

Colorado Virtual Library

aclin.org

Created and maintained by the Access Colorado Library and Information Network, a statewide network of libraries and organizations, the Colorado Virtual Library offers a wealth of community, business, and consumer information. Click on the Best Websites for Coloradoans to access the Employment and Career links.

GUAM

Guam's Job Bank

ajb.org/gu

This is the job bank for Guam's state employment service.

Government of Guam Official Departments

gov.gu/government.html

This page leads to all of Guam's government agencies and the University of Guam. The university and some of the agencies offer employment opportunities online.

Guam's One-Stop Career Service Center

http://onestopcareer.gov.gu

Explore career options, find training or financial aid information, and link to job leads. Unfortunately, at the time of review many of the links were out of date.

JobsonGuam.com

jobsonguam.com

Search by job title or by company, or leave the search box empty to bring up a list of all jobs. You must register (free) to apply online.

HAWAII

Hawaii's Job Bank

ajb.org/hi

This is the job bank for Hawaii's state employment service.

Hawaii Newspapers

newslink.org/hinews.html

This gateway from Newslink.org will link you to many of the newspapers for this state.

eHawaiiGov

ehawaiigov.org

The state of Hawaii offers a great deal of helpful information through this portal. You'll find information of interest to citizens and visitors alike, including the Hawaii Information Link Index that offers easy access to a range of services and agencies. Click on Working in Hawaii to reach the business and employment resources. Under Search for a Job you'll find links to several sources of employment listings for this state.

IDAHO

Idaho's Job Bank

ajb.org/id

This is the job bank for Idaho's state employment service.

Idaho Newspapers

newslink.org/idnews.html

This gateway from Newslink.org will link you to many of the newspapers for this state.

IdahoWorks

idahoworks.org

IdahoWorks is a collaboration of the Idaho Department of Labor and state and local workforce-development organizations whose mission is the continuing development of an educated workforce in the state. Click on Job Seekers to get to the job leads and career resources.

MONTANA

Montana's Job Bank

ajb.org/mt

This is the job bank for Montana's state employment service.

Montana Newspapers

newslink.org/mtnews.html

This gateway from Newslink.org will link you to many of the newspapers for this state.

Discovering Montana

discoveringmontana.com

The official website for the state of Montana features agency and education information, tourist resources, and helpful guides to working, living, and doing business in Montana. Click on the Working link to access the state's Job Service, the Native American Jobs Program, and opportunities in teaching. New to this edition is the Virtual Human Services Pavilion featuring help with child care, links to the Tribal Colleges, online voters' registration, and more.

Montana Job Service

http://jsd.dli.state.mt.us

Check the Montana Job Service for opportunities throughout the state, including the Natural Resource Education Youth Summer Camps that are designed to educate Montana's future natural resource managers. You'll also find additional material devoted to youth services and labor market information.

NEVADA

Nevada's Job Bank

ajb.org/nv

This is the job bank for Nevada's state employment service.

Nevada Newspapers

newslink.org/nvnews.html

This gateway from Newslink.org will link you to many of the newspapers for this state.

Nevada Department of Employment, Training & Rehabilitation (DETR)

http://detr.state.nv.us

http://nvos.state.nv.us

nvjoblink.org

Locate workshops or access the Career Information System open to Nevada residents only. You'll also find a listing of service locations and loads of other DETR resources. The second URL goes to the One Stop Operating System (OSOS) where you can post your resume or register for many of the other services offered by DETR. The third URL leads to the job opportunities and resources for seniors, students, and others looking for work.

NevadaWorks

nevadaworks.com

This northern Nevada initiative works with the business and educational community to enhance the local economy and create jobs. At the time of review, NevadaWorks was seeking to address the nursing shortage in that region by offering programs for former nurses as well as recruiting individuals new to the profession.

NEW MEXICO

New Mexico's Job Bank

ajb.org/nm

This is the job bank for New Mexico's state employment service.

New Mexico Newspapers

newslink.org/nmnews.html

This gateway from Newslink.org will link you to many of the newspapers for this state.

New Mexico Department of Labor (DOL)

http://dol.state.nm.us

The DOL's mission is to promote economic development by matching the needs of employers with the skills of job seekers. Click on Job Seekers to access the Job-Hunting page where you'll find available training programs. The Up to 21 page features publications for different age levels, and links to career information and other useful resources. The Casual Labor Office specializes in matching workers with day labor requests within the community.

NORTH DAKOTA

North Dakota's Job Bank

ajb.org/nd

This is the job bank for North Dakota's state employment service.

North Dakota Newspapers

newslink.org/ndnews.html

This gateway from Newslink.org will link you to many of the newspapers for this state.

Customer Resource Information System for North Dakota (CRISND)

crisnd.com

Don't overlook this warehouse of services in your job search! CRISND is part of the One Stop Delivery System that empowers its users and provides easy access to programs and services in North Dakota. You'll find job links here as well as information about child care, financial assistance, and training programs. Search by type of service, location, or customer type (veteran, adult, etc.).

DiscoverND

discovernd.com

Your gateway to North Dakota offers business information and educational institutions, links to state agencies and to cities and counties within the state, and links to other job and career resources.

Job Service North Dakota: Virtual OneStop

http://onestop.jobsnd.com

The handy menu on the left offers education and training links, resources for youth entering the world of work, resume assistance, support services, and more. Most of the site is accessible to all. You must register to access the whole site, including the self-assessment tools and resources for creating and posting a resume, and to sign up for the e-mail job alert. Click on the Job Search link to start your search for employment.

OREGON

Oregon Employment Department

emp.state.or.us

Among its many services, Oregon's Employment Department oversees a system of safe, affordable, and high-quality child care, including the Child Care Resource & Referral programs. Click on Jobs to go directly to the Oregon Employment Department Job Listings. From the menu on the left, choose from among apprenticeships, job fairs, etc. Government Jobs leads to a convenient listing of links to current job offerings in Oregon county and municipal government. Click on Oregon Jobs to access the Job Bank.

Oregon Newspapers

newslink.org/ornews.html

This gateway from Newslink.org will link you to many of the newspapers for this state.

Business in Portland

businessinportland.org

While Business in Portland does not include job leads, it does offer links to area chambers of commerce, business start-up information, and up-to-date business news.

Multnomah County Library Help for Job Seekers

multcolib.org/jobs

Don't forget the library! It's generally a good first stop when you're conducting a job search, and the Portland area is no different. You'll find some good local job links plus a bit of help in fine-tuning your job search and developing your interview skills.

Portland Business Alliance

portlandalliance.org

Here you'll find information about the community of Portland, Oregon, along with a searchable database of local businesses and a relocation guide. You'll also find links to the schools and services. The Employment link goes to the OED.

SOUTH DAKOTA

South Dakota's Job Bank

ajb.org/sd

This is the job bank for South Dakota's state employment service.

South Dakota Newspapers

newslink.org/sdnews.html

This gateway from Newslink.org will link you to many of the newspapers for this state.

Sioux Falls Chamber of Commerce

siouxfalls.com

The local chamber maintains information about the area's most important industries, links to educational resources, the city government page, and more. One of the most helpful features is the Chamber of Commerce Directory, which is searchable by category or business name. Click on Employment to reach the listing of employment agencies.

Sioux Falls Recruiting Cooperative

sfrc.com

The cooperative, established by a group of local businesses, has as its goal the recruitment of professionals and IT candidates for Sioux Falls industries. Select from among technical, engineering, professional, and sales and marketing positions. Visit the community links or register to post your resume.

South Dakota Department of Labor

state.sd.us/dol

The Department of Labor manages all aspects of employment and job training for the people of South Dakota. At this site, you'll find information about those services, including the South Dakota Occupational Outlook Online, apprenticeship opportunities, and the One-Stop initiative. Click on South Dakota Job Search to access SDWORKS! It features a Quick Search that allows you to browse the job postings by location. Register to post your resume or to do a more advanced job search.

UTAH

Utah's Job Bank

ajb.org/ut

This is the job bank for Utah's state employment service.

Utah Newspapers

newslink.org/utnews.html

This gateway from Newslink.org will link you to many of the newspapers for this state.

Department of Workforce Services

http://jobs.utah.gov

As "Utah's Job Connection," the Department of Workforce Services (DWS) is the lead agency for job- and career-related services in the state. You'll find job-search guides, career-outlook data, and child care resources. DWS also links to employers who are currently hiring, the Job Bank, and the Electronic Job Board, which provides a customized searchable database of jobs and online application capability. You should also contact the office nearest you or call 888-920-WORK to make sure you are receiving the best service possible. This site is growing as it adds services requested by job seekers and employers alike.

Working in Utah

utah.gov/working

The state of Utah has pulled together some great resources here. You'll find all the information you need for living, learning, doing business, and working in the state. From this page, you can link to the Job Bank and the other resources provided by Workforce Services, and link to the state's newspapers, largest employers, and universities. Lots of Utah job leads are accessible from this website. Use the search box if you don't find what you need at first glance.

WASHINGTON

Washington's Job Bank

ajb.org/wa

This is the job bank for Washington's state employment service.

Washington Newspapers

newslink.org/wanews.html

This gateway from Newslink.org will link you to many of the newspapers for this state.

Access Washington

access.wa.gov

Use the easy-to-use menu system or the Ask George search engine to explore Washington's gateway to the Internet. You'll find considerable content, including a selection of online services, education directories and resources, an index to agencies by service category, and more. In addition, there are links to state, local, and federal agencies and services, as well as to business and consumer resources. Employment information can be found under the Jobs/Work link on the right side of the page as well as under the Employment link on the left. You'll find information for teens entering the world of work, apprenticeship program information, the Career Guide, and the Job Bank.

CityofSeattle.net

cityofseattle.net

The official website for the city serves as a public network for Seattle. Search by keyword, by service, or by agency, or browse using the simple menu structure. You'll find all the information you need to live in Seattle, start a business, get around the city, or access online services. Click on the Jobs icon to reach the career resources and job leads, including jobs with city government, King County, and the University of Washington.

Seattle Community Network

scn.org

This free public-access computer network is run by Seattle area volunteers. You'll find loads of information about the neighborhoods, local businesses, and organizations here. Click on Jobs to access job hotlines, career events and resources, and job leads for the community and region.

WorkSource Washington

http://work.wa.gov

workforceexplorer.com

Washington's Employment Security Department sponsors WorkSource, an electronic resource for the state's job seekers and career changers. Get help creating and posting your resume, or find training and educational opportunities. The job leads include access to a handy collection of Washington area newspaper classified ads neatly arranged on one Web page. Unfortunately, at the time of review several of the classified links were out of date. From the WorkSource page you can easily access the WorkForce Explorer, the official source for labor market information and a great place for career exploration. You can also use the second URL to access the WorkForce Explorer.

Your Keys to the City of Spokane

spokanecity.org

You'll find easy-to-access information about Spokane city government and its services, and lots of good links to other area resources. Click on Employment to browse the current job offerings. For more information about any of the jobs listed, call 509-625-6160.

WYOMING

Wyoming's Job Bank

ajb.org/wy

This is the job bank for Wyoming's state employment service.

Wyoming Newspapers

newslink.org/wynews.html

This gateway from Newslink.org will link you to many of the newspapers for this state.

Wyoming Department of Workforce Services

http://dwsweb.state.wy.us

The Wyoming Department of Workforce Services is responsible for all of the services and programs offered by the state to job seekers and employers. You'll find labor statistics, occupational health and safety information, and workforce-development tools. Resources here include the state's employment offices, job-hunting tips, links to other career resources, and the Job Bank.

Wyoming Job Network

http://onestop.state.wy.us

The One-Stop at this site offers a Quick Search that allows you to use keywords or browse by broad category and area of the state you're interested in working in. By registering, you will be notified when a job matching your skills set becomes available, and you will also be included in the state talent bank. Don't overlook the additional links to Teacher Tips, employment resources for teachers; Yellowstone seasonal jobs; employment at the University of Wyoming; and other job leads.

12

International Opportunities

This chapter features Internet resources for locating employment opportunities outside of the United States in North America, Latin and South America, Europe, Africa, the Middle East, and the Pacific Rim. It is arranged by region and then alphabetically by country. Many international recruiters based in one country often work to place employees in other countries, so you may want to check neighboring countries for references.

Using websites with a geographical or industry focus makes it easier for you to focus your job search as well. Yahoo! and other regional portals offer links to government agencies, embassies, and other information about specific countries, as well as access to foreign newspapers and career resources. Northwestern University Library maintains a list of links to foreign government websites that could prove helpful in your job search (library.northwestern.edu /govpub/resource/internat/foreign.html). In addition, many of the larger Internet job sites in Chapter 3 carry international postings, including America's Job Bank. Some international sites listing jobs in a given specialty such as mining or academe have been placed in the chapter that focuses on that specialty. Explore the entire book for possibilities!

Please Note: Unless indicated otherwise by the inclusion of *http://* you must add *www.* to the beginning of each URL listed here.

Services with Listings for Multiple Countries and Regions

Goingglobal

goinglobal.com

Goingglobal offers snapshots of cultural differences, the state of the economy, and other attributes of countries around the world. To access more detailed information, you must purchase the books or hire one of Goingglobal's career counselors.

International Career Employment Center

internationaljobs.org

For a decade, International Careers has published a weekly international employment newspaper for subscribers only. A few job listings are accessible to nonsubscribers via the website, including some jobs that employers are urgently seeking to fill; these can also be sent to you via e-mail.

International Rescue Committee (IRC)

theirc.org/jobs/index.cfm

The IRC is the leading nonsectarian voluntary organization providing emergency relief and resettlement assistance for refugees worldwide. Individuals who register for the Emergency Response Roster are considered for employment as it becomes available.

JobPilot AG

jobpilot.com

After selecting a region, you can browse this site by company or use the search form to locate job leads. Register to post your resume or have job listings sent to you via e-mail. A nice addition is the link to Expat Corner, a practical resource for job hunters who are thinking of relocating to another country. At the time of review, the database listed just fewer than two thousand jobs, primarily in Austria, Belgium, the Czech Republic, France, Germany, Hungary, Italy, the Netherlands, Poland, Switzerland, and the United Kingdom.

JobShark

jobshark.com

At the time of review, we found thousands of jobs listed on this site, most of them in Canada. Unfortunately, the added value career links appear to be fee-based only.

Monster Work Abroad

http://workabroad.monster.com

Career articles, tips and tools, a guide to salaries, and forums for communicating with other job seekers are easily accessible from the opening page. Select the country you want to work in to see the job leads on six of the seven continents.

OverseasJobs.com

overseasjobs.com

Part of the AboutJobs.com network, this website is easy to use—browse by location or click on the Search Jobs link to start your keyword search. Get help with your resume or link to other career resources.

PlanetRecruit.com

planetrecruit.com

From the opening page, select from among the dozens of countries represented to start your job search. This site is simple to navigate and easy to search. Register to apply online, post your resume, or receive job alerts via e-mail.

TopJobs

topjobs.net

Select a category and location for a quick search on the opening page. Or click on New Jobs for access to the newest jobs only. You can also view company profiles, search by sector, or register to have job leads e-mailed to you.

Africa and the Middle East

AFRICA

Career Classified

careerclassifieds.co.za

Simple to use, Career Classified offers a keyword search on the opening page and links to other job and career resources. You can apply online without registering. Click on the JobSeekers' clock to browse the job leads. Register to post your CV.

Jobguide

jobguide.co.za

This site offers an opportunity for recruiters and potential employers to see your CV. You must register (free) to access the job leads.

The Personnel Concept

personnel-concept.co.za

Personnel Concept recruits in the areas of IT, electronics, and finance. Browse the job postings by broad category or search by keyword. Apply online using the resume submission form or contact the site via e-mail.

ISRAEL AND THE MIDDLE EAST

Association of Americans and Canadians in Israel (AACI) Jobnet

jobnet.co.il

AACI brings you this online service—updated daily—with the financial help of the Ministry of Science and the Samis Foundation. Click on the General Index to access a directory of trade associations. Browse the Index by job category or employer, or search for jobs using keywords.

GulfJobSites

gulfjobsites.com

GulfJobSites.com is an independent directory and search engine covering job and employment-related websites from the Arabian Gulf/Persian Gulf region, including Saudi Arabia, United Arab Emirates, Oman, Kuwait, Bahrain, Qatar, Iraq, and Iran. In addition to all of these links, it hosts its own job board. Job seekers are strongly urged to read the article on How to Use This Site before jumping in with both feet.

Asia and the Pacific Rim

REGIONAL RESOURCES

Asia-Net

asia-net.jp

Asia-Net serves the Asia/Pacific Rim business communities by matching job candidates with potential employers. Click on Careers to browse the available jobs. To apply for a job, you must register. Note: At the time of review, none of the postings indicated a posting date, which made it difficult to know how old they were.

JobAsia

jobasia.com

To get the full benefit of this free job site you must register. Use the simple Search or PowerSearch for jobs, or look up companies by industry or name. The Job Hunting Tips include self-assessment tests and other helpful career resources. Register to develop your job-search profile and have JobAsia save jobs for your personalized list.

AUSTRALIA

Australian JobSearch

jobsearch.gov.au

Search for jobs by location and occupation, or click on the section of the Australian map you are interested in to browse the jobs in that geographic area. Access self-exploration and career information, aid for business start-up, or articles of interest. In the menu at the right, Job Juice is intended for young job seekers who have left school.

Department of Education, Science, and Training (DEST, formerly DETYA)

dest.gov.au

DEST supports the lifelong learning needs of all Australians, and it provides a wealth of information. Under Careers is The Job Guide featuring hundreds of occupations. You can also link from here to My Future, the Australian JobSearch, and the Good Guides evaluation of Australian colleges and universities.

EducateIT

educateit.com.au

EducateIT, from IDG Communications, is designed to help IT professionals locate training and educational opportunities. They also link you to job resources from CareerOne.com.au.

Job Review

http://jobreview.camrev.com.au

Maintained by the publisher of *Campus Review*, Job Review offers job listings for international education and health professionals. The site is easy to navigate and simple to search, and users can register to receive job alerts.

JobNet Australia

jobnet.com.au

JobNet offers a comprehensive range of IT career services. Browse the thousands of IT job leads by geographical area, check to see what skills are hot, and search for training opportunities.

My Future

myfuture.edu.au

Australia's Career Information Service offers information for the professional assisting others and for the folks in need of that assistance. Click on the Facts to access financial aid, career and business start-up information, articles, and work opportunities. You'll also find career events and an easy-to-use job-search page. This site is very nicely done.

Sydney Morning Herald

smh.com.au

mycareer.com.au

To start your job search, select Jobs on the menu or use the second URL to go directly to the Job Search page. Choose a sector or type in a keyword. Refine the search by region or job type (full-time, part-time, etc.). Register to create your job folder, have job postings sent to you via e-mail, or post your resume.

INDIA

Naukri

naukri.com

Maintained by Info Edge of New Delhi, Naukri has fast become one of the best resources for job hunters in India. Search for a job by keyword or location.

Register to post your resume or to receive e-mail notification of current opportunities.

JAPAN, HONG KONG, KOREA, AND MALAYSIA

CareerCross Japan

careercross.com

CareerCross is a bilingual recruitment resource serving the English-Japanese business community. Learn about living and working in Japan, and find jobs in Japan and overseas. First select either English or Japanese. Visit the Career Club for tips on interviewing, resume writing, and more. Search by job category, location, or other qualifiers. Register to receive e-mail updates or to post your resume.

Kyushu Japan Association for Language Teaching (JALT)

kyushu.com/jalt

Kyushu JALT offers resources for teachers of English as a foreign language, such as a notice board and an events calendar. Click on Jobs in Japan to access information about working in Japan, links to school websites, and of course, job opportunities.

O-Hayo Sensei, The Newsletter of (Teaching) Jobs in Japan

ohayosensei.com

O-Hayo Sensei is a free-subscription electronic newsletter that lists teaching positions at dozens of schools and companies in Japan. Have the newsletter e-mailed to you, or download it from the website. You'll also find information about living and working in Japan.

SINGAPORE AND THAILAND

Department of Employment (DOE), Thailand

doe.go.th

This is a good source of job leads for Thailand. The DOE supervises Thai nationals working overseas as well as foreign nationals working in Thailand.

Singapore Economic Development Board

sedb.com

Look here for detailed information about specific industries in Singapore. Click on Living or Working in Singapore to access helpful tips about the culture, job market, standard of living.

Eastern Europe

REGIONAL RESOURCES

American Association of Teachers of Slavic and Eastern European Languages (AATSEEL)

aatseel.org

AATSEEL maintains this website for its members. Offering a handy calendar of events, AATSEEL also links to websites of interest to teachers of Slavic languages, and to professional development opportunities, internships, and jobs.

CZECH REPUBLIC

czechjobs.cz

The Czechjobs.cz job-search form is readily accessible from the opening page. Register to post your resume or to have job listings that match your profile waiting for you when you log in.

RUSSIA

American Chamber of Commerce in Russia

amcham.ru

The AmCham online directory of its membership is no longer available to nonmembers. The calendar of events, news update for Russia and for the organization, and advice for living and doing business in Russia can still be viewed by anyone accessing the website.

Bucknell University List of U.S. Firms in Russia

departments.bucknell.edu/russian

The Russian Program at Bucknell maintains this website for students in the program. One of the offerings is a database of U.S. firms operating in the former Soviet Union. It is accessible from the menu on the left. Click on the Jobs link, and the database is the first of many job and career resources listed. You'll also find links to job leads in the Moscow and St. Petersburg newspapers.

Russian and East European Institute Employment Opportunities

indiana.edu/~reeiweb

Indiana University offers this resource for individuals seeking jobs in Russia or Eastern Europe or for those with expertise in the languages, history, or cultures of these areas. You'll find loads of up-to-date links here. Click on the Employment links for internships and jobs. The Find a Job page includes helpful advice for job searchers as well as links to other employment resources.

Looking for jobs by geographic area is one way to focus your job search. We'd also encourage you to search by job category in the sites listed for your industry in this book. Network and target companies that would likely need your skills.

Europe

REGIONAL RESOURCES

EuroPages: The European Business Directory

europages.com

EuroPages is searchable by activity or sector. Once you select a sector, you can then search by country or subcategory. You can also search by company name or service.

EURopean Employment Services (EURES)

http://europa.eu.int/eures/index.jsp

EURES offers a database of living and working conditions in all the member countries. Visitors also have access to all the European national employment services, an overview of labor conditions in each of the regions, and a helpful FAQ area. At the time of review, there were more than eight thousand jobs listed.

European Governments Online

http://europa.eu.int/abc/governments/index_en.html

The European Union maintains this list of links to its member nations and other European countries. It offers a profile of each of the countries, plus a Dialogue with Citizens that provides practical details such as the state of the job market. Other links include news and the countries' official websites.

Exec-appointments.com

exec-appointments.com

To start your executive job search, select the pay scale you're looking for, then enter at least one of your criteria. Click on Search to view your results.

StepStone

http://stepstone.com

StepStone is a major source of European jobs, primarily in Central and Eastern Europe. Select the European country where you wish to work from the menu or click the country on the map of Europe. From there, choose a category and add keywords. Click Search to view the results. Register to post your CV or to receive e-mail updates.

FRANCE, BELGIUM, ITALY, AND SPAIN

Association Bernard Gregory

www.abg.asso.fr

This association supports the training and employment of young French doctorates in engineering, the sciences, and the social sciences. Along with its corporate and other partners, the association offers thesis proposals and support, information on how to move from the academic world to the corporate world, and employment listings through ABG-Jobs.

CESOP, the Service Centre for Career Counseling

cesop.it

CESOP is available in English or Italian. Click on Career Service to get to information about living and working in Italy, the Italian Job Centre, and links to other European job sites.

Le Monde

lemonde.fr

http://emploi.lemonde.fr

The French newspaper of record offers all the news that's fit to print. Use the second URL to go directly to the career page. Search by job function or location.

Prospective Management Overseas (PMO) Vacant Positions Overseas

pmo.be

PMO specializes in the selection, recruitment, and management of experts such as technicians, engineers, or administrators for international projects. Click on Positions to browse the listing of job possibilities. Use the form to apply for positions and submit your CV.

Réseau Européen pour l'Emploi

reseau.org/emploi

You'll find many job listings at this site. Select Offres d'emploi to access the job leads. Register to submit your resume or CV, or to receive job postings via e-mail.

Trabajo.org

trabajo.org

This site is available only in Spanish. Here you'll find listings for jobs in Spain. Easiest search is from the opening page. Simply click Buscar to view all of the jobs. You can also search by region and/or job category.

GERMANY AND AUSTRIA

Breitbach Unternehmensberatung

breitbach.com

Breitbach is a German IT recruiter and consulting company. Select English or German language, and click on Jobs to access a brief description of opportunities available in Germany. Job descriptions as written are deliberately general in scope. You are encouraged to call them if you have any interest in a position.

IRELAND AND NORTHERN IRELAND

irishjobs.ie

The good news about IrishJobs.ie is that its job search is easy to use and you do not have to register to find and apply for jobs. The bad news is that other than a few career articles, IrishJobs.ie does not offer additional content. Instead, it links to books for sale, career coaches for hire, and financial advice that must be purchased. Register to post your resume or receive job leads via e-mail.

NIjobs.com

nijobs.com

This Northern Ireland job site has the job-search form readily accessible on the opening page. Register to post your resume or receive job leads via e-mail.

NETHERLANDS

Nederlandse Laboratorium

laboratorium.nl

The Laboratorium website offers information of interest to employees of Dutch biomedical and chemical laboratories. You'll find news and information about training opportunities, associations, and job leads. Unfortunately, at the time of review, resumes submitted to the site could be read by anyone.

SWITZERLAND

Academic Job Exchange Board (formerly Telejob)

telejob.ch

TeleJob is the electronic job exchange board for the Association of Assistants and Doctoral Students of the institutes of Zurich (AVETH) and Lausanne (ACIDE). Use the Quick Search or click on Job Offers to browse the available positions. You can register to have job announcements sent to you electronically. At the time of review, resumes were easily viewed by anyone visiting the site, raising concerns for the privacy of the candidates. The site is still offered in five languages.

ETH Career Services/pr@cs Online

career.ethz.ch

pracs.ethz.ch

The Swiss Federal Institute of Technology Zurich (ETH) maintains the first job site for its alumni and students; pr@cs Online is maintained by Telejob and the ETH alumni to provide traineeships in the private sector as well as in the university community for ETH students.

JobEngine.ch (formerly StepStone)

jobengine.ch

Search by industry or browse by employer. At the time of review, we found just under two hundred job leads. This site is mostly in German.

UNITED KINGDOM

Agency Central

agencycentral.co.uk

You'll find easy access to recruiters and job sites of all description for England, Scotland, Wales, and Ireland. Click on a specific industry to find lists of associations, businesses, and job leads within that industry. Visit the Career Advice Centre or find information about working abroad.

British Jobs/Scotland Jobs

britishjobs.net

scotlandjobs.net

From either of these sites you can search for jobs in Scotland, Britain, or Wales. Browse by location or by category, or use the Search function that combines location, category, and contract type (permanent or temporary), plus any keywords you want to add.

CASCAiD

cascaid.co.uk

CASCAiD, suppliers of career-guidance software to most U.K. schools, offers this site with career advice for professionals, youth entering the world of work, and lifelong learners. Simply click on the appropriate link to access the information you need.

CityJobs

cityjobs.com

CityJobs specializes in finance, IT, accounting, and legal-sector positions in the United Kingdom. The keyword search on the opening page allows you to get results quickly. For best results use as few terms as possible. Register to post your CV or receive job leads via e-mail.

HERO: Higher Education & Research Opportunities in the United Kingdom

hero.ac.uk

The HERO website serves as a portal for the academic community in the United Kingdom. Offering news of interest and links to colleges and universities, HERO also links to research, science, academic, and management jobs and studentships in the public and private sector through jobs.ac.uk, the "official recruitment site for Higher Education." Under Inside Higher Education you will also find information on careers in higher education along with direct links to university recruiting pages.

JobServe

jobserve.com

JobServe offers one of the largest sources of information technology jobs in the United Kingdom. Simple to navigate, you can browse jobs by agency, or do a more detailed search by location and keywords. Select an industry to start your job search. Register to receive the free newsletter or to have job postings that fit your specifications sent to you by e-mail.

MediaWeek

mediaweek.co.uk

MediaWeek Online offers industry news and articles, industry directories, and job leads. Browse the company links or consult the Career Advice archives. Click on Jobs to search the Media Moves job and career resource. Register to use the CV template, post your resume, or receive job postings via e-mail.

PeopleBank: the Employment Network

peoplebank.com

Browse or search the job ads or find career advice for specific industries. Register to submit your resume to PeopleBank or to have job ads sent to your e-mail account.

Reed Personnel Services

reed.co.uk

Browse the helpful career advice and industry information, or use the salary calculator. Register to apply for the jobs listed. Once registered, you can also post your CV and have the latest job postings sent to you via e-mail.

THES: The *Times* Higher Education Supplement

thesis.co.uk

thesjobs.co.uk

The *Times* Higher Education Supplement (THES) chronicles the latest developments in higher education and provides a forum for issues that affect the world of academe. For subscribers only, THES makes available a searchable archive of articles, research funding sources, and free access to the British Library's journal search service. New academic job opportunities appear every Tuesday. Browse them by broad category, search by keyword, or sign up for e-mail job alerts. Use the second URL to go directly to the Jobs page.

TimesOnline, the *Times* (London)

timesonline.co.uk

Depend on the *Times* for world headlines and business news. Click on the Classified link to reach the Appointments (jobs) and Executive Appointments sections. Browse the listings here by company, or search the jobs by industry or keyword. Register to post your CV. You'll find career advice at the Appointments link.

Totaljobs.com

totaljobs.com

Billing themselves as "serious about jobs," totaljobs.com certainly does deliver. At the time of review, we found thousands of jobs, mainly in the United Kingdom. All visitors have access to the career resources. Register to post your CV or develop a profile for the e-mail job alert. Business news alerts are by subscription only.

Latin America and South America

Bolsa de Trabajo

bolsadetrabajo.com

Here you'll find employment opportunities and resumes for Spanish-speaking professionals. You must register to access the job openings or post your resume.

Latin American Jobs

latinamericanjobs.com

Country profiles, business news from many of the countries, and career advice are available to anyone visiting the site. You must register before you have full access to the job listings.

LatPro.com

latpro.com

LatPro is a comprehensive online career center for Spanish- and Portuguese-speaking and bilingual professionals. Access resources for specific countries, the immigration links featuring an H1B visa FAQ and related job leads, or the other career aids. Use the customized search to find jobs by location and job category, or have job listings sent to you via e-mail. LatPro.com also offers free by subscription several trade magazines and the *Latin Career News* e-newsletter.

North America

Resources for the United States are included in Chapter 11.

CANADA

Sites with resources for the whole country are at the beginning of this section. Those for specific provinces (Alberta, British Columbia, Manitoba, Ontario, and Quebec) follow, in alphabetical order. Most but not all sites in Canada have versions in French and English with easy links to both versions from the front page.

Canada WorkinfoNET

workinfonet.ca

WorkinfoNET is the primary source of career and training information for Canadian job seekers, career changers, and the self-employed. Use URLs that follow to go directly to WorkinfoNET's website for the province of your choice:

Alberta (ALIS)   alis.gov.ab.ca

British Columbia (BCWIN)   workinfonet.bc.ca

Manitoba (MBWIN)	mb.workinfonet.ca
New Brunswick (NBWIN)	nb.workinfonet.ca
Newfoundland and Labrador (NLWIN)	gov.nf.ca/nlwin
Northwest Territory (NorthWIN)	northwin.ca
Nova Scotia (NSWIN)	ns.workinfonet.ca
Ontario (ONWIN)	on.workinfonet.ca
Prince Edward Island (InfoPEI)	gov.pe.ca/infopei/Employment
Quebec	qc.info-emploi.ca
Saskatchewan (SaskNetWork)	sasknetwork.gov.sk.ca
Yukon (YUWIN)	yuwin.ca

Canadian Association of Career Educators and Employers (CACEE)

cacee.com

The Canadian Association of Career Educators and Employers (CACEE) website offers information, advice, and services, primarily for its members. Students and nonmembers have access to a schedule of career fairs and networking events, the Workopolis career resource, and *Career Options* online, a magazine designed for students.

CanadianCareers.com

canadiancareers.com

CanadianCareers covers all facets of the job hunt, from career exploration to presenting yourself in an interview. You'll find job opportunities, information about occupations, career fair schedules, and internship details, all nicely organized and easy to use.

CanJobs.com

canjobs.com

The simple search is easily accessible from the opening page. You can search and apply for jobs without registering; however, to gain access to the career resources, job alerts, and discussion group, you must register.

Career Edge

careeredge.org

Career Edge is a national nonprofit organization whose mission is to improve youth employability. It provides recent graduates with internships and career-related work experience.

CareerClick

careerclick.com

CareerClick offers job leads from many of Canada's daily newspapers. Search for jobs by category and location, or use the advanced search to limit the dates and newspapers searched. You can also register to post your resume or have job listings sent to you via e-mail. At the time of review, some of the events and external links were out of date.

CareerPlace

careerplace.com

An initiative of the Native Women's Association of Canada, CareerPlace assists aboriginal Canadians in finding and keeping jobs and advancing their careers through its network of services, support, and mentoring programs. You must register (free) to use the site.

Charity Village

http://charityvillage.com/applicant/jobs.asp

Charity Village is "Canada's busiest source for nonprofit jobs" and includes hundreds of job listings and continuing education opportunities for the sector. The CharityVillage Learning Institute (CVLI) offers access to continuing education and development opportunities for nonprofit professionals. Browse the jobs by the posting date or search by keyword.

Electronic Labour Exchange (ELE)

ele-spe.org

ELE is part of the Human Resource Development Canada initiative (see HRDC-DRHC). Job seekers supply a work profile that will be compared with the skills needed by employers who are part of the exchange. ELE is simple to use; it uses a uniform vocabulary to match employers and job seekers, which produces highly accurate results.

HRDC-DRHC (Human Resources Development Canada)

hrdc-drhc.gc.ca

jobbank.gc.ca

The Canadian government sponsors this site and other HRDC-DRHC sites in the individual provinces that offer access to a full range of human services. Among the items of special interest to job hunters are the career-planning and self-assessment tools and the training and self-employment resources. The second URL goes directly to the Job Bank and includes a special search for students entering the world of work.

Jobs, Workers, Training & Careers (formerly WorkSearch/ProjetEmploi)

jobsetc.ca

Human Resources Development Canada maintains this straightforward, easy-to-use interface to assist Canadians in finding work and developing a career. You'll find strategies for evaluating your next steps in the career process, financial assistance, and job leads. Recent immigrants can get help in the Newcomers to Canada pages. The Canada Site link offers one-stop shopping for Canadians in search of human services and helpful consumer, business, and education information, all searchable by audience or topic.

Positionw@tch

positionwatch.com

Positionw@tch is an online IT recruiter. Search the entire database by keyword, browse by company, or use the advanced search to specify location, job category, and skills.

Public Service Commission (PSC)

http://jobs.gc.ca

The PSC is responsible for the appointment of qualified individuals to Canadian federal government positions. Search here for jobs, training opportunities, student work experience, and internships with the Canadian government.

Strategis

strategis.gc.ca

Industry Canada supports this wide-ranging business resource. You'll find company directories, business information organized by industry, and labor statistics. You can also get the information you need to start a new business. Consumer information and the latest business news are also accessible here.

Workopolis

workopolis.com

Claiming to be Canada's biggest job site, Workopolis offers thousands of job postings, including all listings from major Canadian daily newspapers. It also provides a bit of humor, good career advice, and a discussion forum. There is plenty of helpful content here.

WorkopolisCampus.com (formerly campusworklink.com)

campus.workopolis.com

Students must register to access the job database and the full range of resources. Endorsed by the Canadian Association of Career Educators and Employers

(CACEE), workopolisCampus.com offers its services free to career centers of Canadian colleges and universities.

YouthPath

youth.gc.ca

Created by Youth Resource Network of Canada (YRNC), this site offers information about the world of work for Canadian young adults. Job opportunities, career assessment and planning tools, training and education resources, and other tools for preparing youth to enter the workforce are at your fingertips.

ALBERTA

Career and Placement Services (CaPS) Resource Center

ualberta.ca/CAPS/CaPS_a2-1.html

The University of Alberta offers this quality resource for its students. You'll find a wonderful collection of career-related tip sheets and schedules for career fairs and workshops. Access to the job bank is now password-protected for students only.

GoEdmonton.Net

ecn.ab.ca/main

Go Edmonton constitutes the heart of Edmonton's Community Information Network. Explore the Careers & Employment link for job opportunities. Check out the business listings for information about local companies, browse the newspapers for job leads, or check the government and education sections to learn more about the nonprofit sector.

Government of Alberta Home Page

gov.ab.ca

Here you'll find everything you need to know about the government of Alberta—phone numbers, news briefings, and more. Click on Service Alberta to access community profiles, information of interest to new residents, and of course, the job leads!

NextSteps.org

nextSteps.org

The City of Calgary funds this career website for the youth of the community. Appealing colors, simple layout, and quality information all contribute to the success of this site, making it a good example of what the Web can do for younger job seekers.

BRITISH COLUMBIA

BC Public Service Agency Job Opportunities

bcpublicservice.ca/postings

Public service offers a wide range of employment opportunities. Click on Current Job Openings to access the newest offerings or use the search for other jobs.

British Columbia Chamber of Commerce

bcchamber.org

Access the business directory or the handy collection of business links.

Greater Victoria Chamber of Commerce

victoriachamber.ca

This site's links include business information, business start-up assistance, and profiles of nearby communities.

Vancouver CommunityNetwork

vcn.bc.ca

Browse the community resources by topic. When we reviewed the site, the Job Posting Boards links were separate from the Employment and Labour links, so do look at both for company information and job leads. The Education and other community links could also be helpful in your search for employment.

MANITOBA

Work and Life in Manitoba

gov.mb.ca/workandlife.html

The provincial government offers this website, featuring everything you wanted to know about Manitoba at your fingertips. Career information, labor statistics, and employment information are listed in separate sections, so be sure to take your time as you go through the site. Click on the Business link on the left to access resources for business start-up and a database searchable by sector or company name.

ONTARIO

Employment News

employmentnews.com

You'll find some good information on this award-winning resource. Employment News is the online equivalent of the free publication of the same name that is available throughout Ontario. You'll find job-search tips, school profiles, up-to-date news, and career articles, in addition to the job leads.

Sheridan College Career Centre

sheridanc.on.ca/career

The Sheridan Career Services page offers helpful advice and career-planning assistance in a straightforward conversational style. Access listings of employers, get help in choosing or reevaluating your career, research an employer, or search for a job.

Student Development Centre

sdc.uwo.ca/career

The University of Western Ontario maintains this Student Development Centre for both students and alumni, and restricts some areas of the website to those groups. The Career Planning and Resource Library pages are two areas that are accessible and helpful to any job seeker or career changer.

Toronto Public Library: Career Bookmarks at the Virtual Reference Library

http://careerbookmarks.tpl.toronto.on.ca

TPL's Career Bookmarks are a wonderful resource for anyone who is job hunting, exploring the world of work, reentering the workplace, or restarting a career. These bookmarks cover strategies to use in the job search, help for specific audiences, and assistance in researching employers.

University of Waterloo Career Services

careerservices.uwaterloo.ca

Starting with Self-Assessment, you'll learn about your strengths and weaknesses. You'll also get valuable tips for the job hunt and helpful advice for successfully building your career. Search the events database by date or category. There are lots of good resources here.

QUEBEC

The Montreal Page

toutmontreal.com (French)

toutmontreal.com/english/index.html (English)

The main page is in French. Select the second URL to access the English version. This site has nicely organized categories of information about living and working in the city, apartments for rent, ride sharing, and more. Click on the Businesses and Services link to access job and career resources.

Scandinavia

Job-Index

jobindex.dk

Since 1996, Job-Index has maintained this Web collection of job opportunities in Denmark. Browse the jobs by category. Register to post your CV or to have job announcements sent to your e-mail account.

Ministry of Labour, Finland

mol.fi

Maintained by the Finnish government, this website is a good starting place for a job search in Finland. Included here are listings for job opportunities all over Finland with additional links to job openings in Scandinavia and the rest of Europe.

13

Resources for Diverse Audiences

This chapter lists websites that offer information and job leads targeted to specific audiences based on gender, cultural background, or other affinity. They are certainly not the only places online where these groups can look for job listings, but users can be assured that the employers and recruiters advertising at these sites are concerned about equality and diversity in their organizations.

Please Note: Unless indicated otherwise by the inclusion of *http://* you must add *www.* to the beginning of each URL listed here.

General Diversity Sites

BestDiversityEmployers.com

bestdiversityemployers.com

This site brings career resources, resume postings, company profiles, job listings, and much more to a diverse population. Select the NAACP Diversity Career Fair button at the bottom of the page for a list of events and employers recruiting at each.

Diversity/Careers in Engineering and Information Technology

diversitycareers.com

The print publication focuses on minority/diversity technical professionals and features career articles and job announcements. The website includes the online magazine and carries a full list of employers placing advertisements in the latest print issue.

Equal Opportunity Publications, Inc. (EOP)

eop.com

The EOP website includes information on the company's family of publications, including *Equal Opportunity*, *Woman Engineer*, *Hispanic Career World*, and *African-American Career World*. Under each magazine title you will find sample articles, subscription information, a list of companies actively recruiting, and help-wanted announcements.

Hire Diversity

hirediversity.com

This national diversity recruitment service links qualified candidates from entry level to senior level with Fortune 500 companies and the government. The Diversity Channels have separate lists of resources and articles for each population (African-American, Hispanic, disabled, and more), but everyone will appreciate the great job bank.

IMDiversity.com

imdiversity.com

IMdiversity.com is an excellent resource for all minority and diversity candidates. It is set up in "villages" for African Americans, Asian Americans, Hispanic Americans, Native Americans, and women. The resources and information in each village are specific for that group, and those without a specific village will find information for their needs in the Global Village. Job listings here are updated frequently and are easy to access. This site was conceived by *The Black Collegian* magazine.

African Americans

The Black Collegian

black-collegian.com

The print publication for college students and professionals of color has set up this extensive online information resource. The website includes job resources, resume information, career guidance, and all kinds of other great articles and resources for everyone. *The Black Collegian* also sponsors IMDiversity.com (see listing earlier in this chapter).

Blackworld

blackworld.com

Blackworld is an enormous Internet directory designed primarily, but not exclusively, for black communities around the world. The Classifieds section includes an area for Jobs, but you should also scroll down and check the Employment category under Business for more resources.

Asian Americans

Asian American Economic Development Enterprises, Inc. (AAEDE)

aaede.org

This full-service nonprofit organization is dedicated to economic self-help for Asian Americans and others. The organization's website lists job opportunities by company name and provides links to additional resources.

Disabled Workers

America's Jobline

nfb.org/jobline/enter.htm

1-800-414-5748

America's Jobline is an audio version of America's Job Bank, which provides job searching and electronic resumes. Any resident of a participating state, including those who do not have ready access to computers or do not know how to use a computer, may use the telephone to locate and apply for jobs in America's Job Bank. (Check the website for a current list of participating states.) You can also use Jobline's resume function to produce resumes by telephone and forward a print copy by fax or e-mail to employers who permit this option. America's Jobline is a project of the National Federation of the Blind, the largest organization of blind people in the United States, with assistance from the United States Department of Labor and state workforce-development agencies. It is available to sighted and blind job seekers free of charge.

Disability Resources Monthly

disabilityresources.org

This is operated by a nonprofit organization that "monitors, reviews, and reports on resources" every day to empower the disabled. It disseminates information to libraries, disability organizations, health and social service professionals, consumers, and family members. Scroll down the menu on the right side to reach the Employment area, a collection of links to sites and services ready to assist you in your job search.

National Business and Disabilities Council

business-disability.com

The National Business and Disability Council is the leading resource for employers seeking to integrate people with disabilities into the workplace and companies seeking to reach them in the consumer marketplace. Disabled persons who are college graduates or soon-to-be college graduates and those who have the equivalent in technical training qualify for the free job-search service, including a resume database and a good job database.

Gay and Lesbian

GAYWORK.com

gaywork.com

GAYWORK.com is an online community for gay and lesbian job seekers, as well as for the global business community seeking diverse job applicants. The job database is easy to search and is filled with good positions, but you must register to see the complete listings. The site has other good resources and information available to unregistered users, including many employer profiles (corporate, college, government and community, and small business). This is a wonderful resource.

Hispanic Americans

Hispanic Online

hispaniconline.com

Hispanic Online is a leading Web and America Online forum for Latinos living in the United States. The site offers job listings (in partnership with Monster.com), chat rooms, message boards, and news, events, and issues of interest to the Latino community based on *Hispanic* magazine, a monthly for and about Latinos, with a national circulation of 250,000 and a readership of more than one million.

LatPro

latpro.com

Dedicated to Hispanic and bilingual (Spanish/English and Portuguese/English) professionals since 1997, LatPro.com offers a searchable resume database and job postings including e-mail alerts. The site also features original articles and resume services along with other career resources. This site is popular with Fortune 100 companies as well as thousands of other employers.

Saludos

saludos.com

This site, dedicated exclusively to promoting Hispanic careers and education, is supported by *Saludos Hispanos* magazine. In addition to the career opportunities, this site offers a free resume database, mentor profiles, and other job-search guidance.

Native North Americans

American Indian Science and Engineering Society

aises.org

This nonprofit organization is dedicated to the "building of community by bridging science and technology with traditional Native values." It helps American Indian and native Alaskan students prepare for careers in science, technology, engineering, and business. The website includes a Career Center with a resume database for members and a job board that is open to the public.

CareerPlace

careerplace.com

CareerPlace is a national career and recruitment site developed to assist aboriginal people in finding meaningful employment and for Canadian businesses to reach qualified and skilled aboriginal job seekers. The organization matches job seekers with employers; it contact the companies, identifies career opportunities, and negotiates the position for the job seeker. It also provides mentoring services.

NativeWeb

nativeweb.org

NativeWeb is an international nonprofit organization dedicated to educating the public about indigenous cultures and issues, to promoting communications among indigenous peoples and organizations supporting their goals and efforts, and to supporting the use of technology by indigenous people. The Community Center area of the website includes job listings, while under Resources users will find Native Economy and Employment, which includes links to additional Jobs and Opportunities.

The Tribal Employment Newsletter

nativejobs.com

This is a recruitment tool for employers who want to increase their efforts to hire diverse populations. For the job seeker, it is easy to access job announcements. The jobs are not dated, but the information on posting says listings are active for only thirty days. There are other resources here that will be of interest to Native Americans.

Older or Disadvantaged Workers

Experience Works!

experienceworks.org

Experience Works! is a nationwide staffing service dedicated to providing temporary and permanent employment opportunities to older individuals, dislocated workers, welfare participants, and other adults seeking employment and needed income. Job seekers must register with their local office to be considered for openings in their area. A list of those offices plus contact information can be found on this site.

Senior Service America

seniorserviceamerica.org

Senior Service America Inc. is a nonprofit organization that helps provide training and employment opportunities to older adults who work to fill real community needs. Potential employees over the age of fifty-five and employers and community organizations interested in hiring can contact the organization for more information.

Religious Affiliations

Christian Career Center

christiancareercenter.com

Professional career counselors run this service, which is dedicated to helping job seekers "integrate their faith with career/life planning and find work that fits their God-given design." They offer a lot of job-hunting help, including career-consultation services, a resume bank, and career resources and guides.

Christian Jobs Online

christianjobs.com

This site is intended as "a place where Christian job seekers and employers can meet." The service posts job openings, positions wanted, and resumes. Many of the organizations that post here are Christian-based nonprofits with a variety of needs (e.g., social workers, architects with experience designing churches). You can search the job database without registering, but you will need to register to apply for any positions you find here.

The Everett JewishJobFinder

jewishjobfinder.com

This site serves Jewish job seekers interested in career opportunities in Jewish education or Jewish communal leadership as well as employers looking to fill openings in Jewish education or Jewish communal work settings. Users will find jobs and internships, career-development information, and a section on the Jewish job market. Registration is not required to search jobs or view some other parts of the site, but it is required for you to apply for positions found here. We found older listings in the database, so you may want to limit your search to jobs posted in the past ninety, thirty, or seven days.

Transitioning or Former Military Personnel

Career Command Post

careercommandpost.com

This site helps bring active-duty military personnel and their spouses as well as veterans of the armed forces together with civilian employers. There are a wide variety of positions listed with salaries ranging from $20,000 to $90,000 per year.

Career Development

cdc-va.com

This firm is one of the leading placement companies for junior military officers in the United States. Based in Alexandria, Virginia, it has been working since 1972 and has placed more than six thousand former military officers in positions in more than six hundred companies across the United States.

Corporate Gray Online

greentogray.com

This site targets job seekers transitioning from military to civilian careers, connecting you with military-friendly companies nationwide. The premise comes from the popular Corporate Gray books for finding jobs in the private sector after a military career—*From Army Green to Corporate Gray, From Navy Blue to Corporate Gray*, and *From Air Force Blue to Corporate Gray*—all distributed by Competitive Edge. All users are required to fill out the free registration form in order to search the job database.

Military.com

military.com

This site offers a variety of information and job opportunities for the military, those in transition, and their families. The site partners with The Destiny Group for the career and job information. Users must fill out the free registration to access the listings.

Transition Assistance Online (TAO)

taonline.com

TAOnline.com provides free services to specific job seekers (separating military service members, retirees, veterans, spouses and dependents, Department of Defense employees, etc.) to assist them in finding a job or career with employers seeking to hire individuals with the unique training, education, skills, and leadership that only the military provides. A division of LucasGroup, the jobs here can be viewed by anyone, but contact information is hidden and the online application process is available only to eligible persons.

Use Your Military Experience and Training (UMET)

http://umet-vets.dol.gov

This is a great site with information on licensing and certification for all kinds of civilian jobs in each state. In addition, it helps translate military experience to civilian experience and includes tuition-assistance services.

VetJobs.com

vetjobs.com

This site is for all transitioning military personnel as well as longtime veterans. Users will find general career information, a resume database, and entry-level as well as middle management positions posted here.

Women

Feminist Career Center

feminist.org/911/jobs/911jobs.asp

This service of the Feminist Majority Foundation Online is intended to increase awareness of a wide variety of feminist issues and to help feminist employers and job seekers find each other. Search for jobs and internships by keywords and region, browse the full list, or view the twenty most recently added listings. You can also submit your resume to the public Positions Wanted database for free.

Womans-Work

womans-work.com

This site lists alternative and flexible opportunities for women, including part-time, work-from-home, flextime, telecommuting, and freelance opportunities. It gives salary information by geographic location or job title. Although no posting dates are listed, the webmaster says that no job is more than sixty days old, and new jobs are added almost daily.

Work, from iVillage

ivillage.com/work

At iVillage, you can find interactive services and support in many areas of interest to women, including working from home and entrepreneurship. The Work channel includes articles and information on salaries, careers, work-from-home ideas, supportive discussion areas, and jobs from CareerBuilder.com.

14

Lifelong Career Planning

Whether or not you want to admit it, your work is critical to your happiness and your life. It affects your standard of living, your lifestyle, and how you spend most of your waking hours. Decisions that affect your career affect your life. They include ideas such as changing jobs, changing careers, moving to a new place because the opportunities there are better, or returning to college because you need a degree to progress in your field. Career planning is not just what happens when you are finishing high school or college. It is a lifelong process of exploration and decision making that affects your life and the lives of those around you.

As you go through life and encounter decision points (either by choice or by force), you need tools to help you explore options, make decisions, plan actions, and execute those plans. This chapter provides resources designed to help you with your job search, interview preparation, career exploration, and much more. It reveals just a small fraction of the beneficial things available online. Even more listings can be found through The Riley Guide (rileyguide.com).

Please Note: Unless indicated otherwise by the inclusion of *http://* you must add *www.* to the beginning of each URL listed here.

General Resources for Lifelong Career Planning

All the sites listed here include numerous resources and information sources to help you with planning and managing your career, from selecting a field to finding a job to moving up, sideways, or out of the market. Many even offer guidance for your life after work.

CareerJournal from the *Wall Street Journal*

http://careerjournal.com

If you use only one site for all your career and life planning, make it this one. CareerJournal covers all the issues. Look over the Job-Hunting Advice with its information on resumes, interviewing, changing careers, using the Internet, and much more. Check out the Salary and Hiring Info section for articles and resources on hiring activity, salaries, and other trends nationwide. Plan to spend some time here.

JobHuntersBible.com

jobhuntersbible.com

Richard Bolles, one of the great leaders in career exploration, has produced a very attractive and informative guide to help job hunters and career changers find the best career sites and advice on the Internet. JobHuntersBible.com supplements Bolles's book *What Color Is Your Parachute?*, but the site is also an excellent resource on its own.

USNews.com

usnews.com

The publisher of *U.S. News and World Report* has produced an outstanding resource for career and life planning. It features one of the best guides to education on the Web, including dedicated sections focused on college, graduate school, and financial aid. Under Work and Careers you'll find great information on careers, employment trends, and job-search skills. Other areas of the website can help with budgeting, investing, and even retirement planning.

Career Exploration

If you are considering a career change, these sources can help with finding information and options, including how to transfer your current skills to new occupational areas and industries.

America's Career InfoNet

acinet.org

This service provides information on hundreds of occupations and describes what you need in order to do each job. The Career Information link shows you wage and trend reports, occupational requirements, and much more. The Career Tools link helps you check your employability, explore careers, look for employers, and review occupational licensing information for various states. You will also find a financial aid adviser to help you find ways to pay for the training or education you may need to move to the next best gig. America's Career InfoNet is a component of CareerOneStop (careeronestop.org), which is sponsored by the U.S. Department of Labor.

Career Exploration Links

uhs.berkeley.edu/students/careerlibrary/links/careerme.htm

The Career and Educational Guidance Library, part of the Counseling and Psychological Services housed within University Health Services at the University of California at Berkeley, provides this well-organized set of links to career resources in a large number of occupational fields. The sponsors are proud to say that this site includes no jobs, just information.

Career Guide to Industries

bls.gov/oco/cg

The Career Guide to Industries provides information on available careers by industry, including the nature of the industry, working conditions, employment, occupations in the industry, training and advancement, earnings and benefits, employment outlook, and lists of organizations that can provide additional information. It's a good way to check out who's needed by various industries and find out whether or not you fit the bill. This is another great guide from the Bureau of Labor Statistics at the U.S. Department of Labor.

Guide to Career Prospects in Virginia

ccps.virginia.edu/career_prospects

This is a database of information about careers that are important to Virginia (and almost every other state). For each career, you'll find a written analysis that includes required educational levels, skills, earnings, and job outlook. It features a set of statistical tables for each career covering wages and job outlook at the Virginia regional level as well as the national level. While most of the salary data is specific to Virginia, descriptions of each career area are general enough to be relevant to all and are very well done. Search by keyword or browse the careers by job family.

Major Resource Kit

udel.edu/csc/mrk.html

The MBNA Career Services Center at the University of Delaware developed these kits as a tool to help its undergraduates. The Major Resource Kits link academic majors to career alternatives by providing information on career paths, sample job titles, and a short bibliography of printed materials available in many libraries. Each kit includes information such as entry-level job titles that previous University of Delaware graduates in that program have attained, brief job descriptions, major employers for the field, and other materials.

O*NET Online

http://online.onetcenter.org

O*NET—the Occupational Information Network—takes the place of the *Dictionary of Occupational Titles*. This online version was created to provide broad access to the O*NET database of occupational information, which includes information on skills, abilities, work activities, and interests associated with more than 950 occupations. You can search by keyword or code, and you'll enjoy seeing what occupations are similar to yours and which use the skills you already have.

The *Occupational Outlook Handbook (OOH)*

bls.gov/oco

This is the current edition of the printed guide produced by the U.S. Bureau of Labor Statistics. You can use keyword searching in this valuable handbook to find out how your interests fit into the top 250 occupations in the country. You can use the index to explore various occupations or select an occupational cluster to see what is included within each group. In addition to this information, you'll find well-written articles on how to find a job and evaluate an offer, where to find career information, and what tomorrow's jobs will look like. This is a great source for employment and career information.

Occupational Outlook Quarterly (OOQ)

bls.gov/opub/ooq/ooqhome.htm

Published quarterly by the Bureau of Labor Statistics, this magazine features articles with practical information on jobs and careers. The topics cover a wide variety of career- and work-related areas such as new and emerging occupations, training opportunities, salary trends, and results of new studies from the Bureau of Labor Statistics. The Grab Bag is a collection of brief items of interest to counselors and students, while the whimsically titled You're a What? section looks at unusual occupational fields and is fun for younger persons to read.

Career-Planning Processes

Career Development eManual

cdm.uwaterloo.ca

Try this six-step process for career- and life-planning success. Starting with self-assessment, this guide will take you through the full job-search process right up to choosing which job offer to accept. This guide is a service of the University of Waterloo Career Services in Ontario, Canada.

Career Planning Process, Bowling Green State University

bgsu.edu/offices/sa/career/students/planning_process.html

Developed by Pam Allen and Ellen Nagy, this site guides you through various steps to evaluating yourself and your career options.

Minnesota Careers

mncareers.org

"What do I want to do with my life? What do the numbers say? Where do I go from here?" This guide from the Minnesota Department of Employment Security will help you answer these questions and plan your career path. While they start by talking to young people just out of high school, older and more experienced people will also find this guide to be extremely helpful. It's not just for Minnesotans!

nextSteps.org

nextsteps.org

This is a great guide to career planning, exploration, and decision making for people fifteen to twenty-four years of age. It features interactive tools you can use as you work through the various steps and exercises tied to great resources. NextSteps.org is a service of the Calgary Youth Employment Center, Canada.

Counseling Assistance

APA Help Center

http://helping.apa.org

Through this site, the American Psychological Association offers useful facts, information, and advice on how psychological services can help people cope with problems such as stress, depression, family strife, or chronic illness. The site provides sections devoted to psychology in the workplace, the health implications of the mind-body connection, family and personal relationships, and psychology in daily life. In addition, you may order a free print brochure, "How to Find Help for Life's Problems," learn how and when to choose a psychologist, and obtain a referral to a psychologist in your area. A detailed site map and an easy-to-use keyword search facility aid navigation of these helpful pages.

International Association of Jewish Vocational Services

iajvs.org

This is a not-for-profit association linking together twenty-eight health and human service agencies in the United States, Canada, and Israel. Through its member agencies it provides a wide range of educational, vocational, career, and rehabilitation services to individuals seeking to improve their lives. Check the list of member agencies to find the one nearest you.

National Board of Certified Counselors (NBCC)

nbcc.org

The NBCC is a national certification agency for counselors. Certification from this group or from a local licensing board assures that a counselor has met certain professional standards. You can use NBCC's CounselorFind to obtain a list of board-certified counselors in your area at no charge. In addition, under Examinations you will find the State Credentialing Boards List. Many states require counselors to go through their own certification process before they are allowed to practice as counselors. You can also contact these agencies for lists of locally certified counselors in your area who may not hold national certification.

National Career Development Association (NCDA)

ncda.org

This association is the career-counseling arm of the American Counseling Association (counseling.org), a group that has been instrumental in setting professional and ethical standards for the counseling profession. NCDA offers its Consumer Guidelines for Selecting a Career Counselor along with a list of frequently asked questions about career counselors and career counseling. NCDA offers special certifications for Master Career Counselors and Master Career Development Professionals, and a list of those who have been awarded these titles along with an outline of the standards that must be met are publicly posted on the site under Consumers and Job Seekers.

Distance Education

Distance Education and Training Council

detc.org

The Distance Education and Training Council (DETC) is a nonprofit educational association located in Washington, D.C. Formerly called the National Home Study Council, it serves as a clearinghouse of information about the distance-study/correspondence field and sponsors a nationally recognized accrediting agency called the Accrediting Commission of the Distance Education and Training Council. Through the website, you can find accredited high school and college degree programs, a single directory of all institutions accredited by this group, and a list of study subjects available from the many programs.

Globewide Network Academy (GNA)

gnacademy.org

The Globewide Network Academy is "dedicated to promote the access to educational opportunities for anybody, anywhere. To do this, GNA pioneers and develops distance learning relationships and facilities for the worldwide public to use." Search the catalog for distance-learning opportunities ranging from precollege to postgraduate and anything in between. Once you've found a program that interests you, you will need to contact the listed institution directly for admissions and registration procedures. With more than twenty-three thousand courses in more than two thousand programs worldwide, you can almost certainly find just what you need.

Education and Training Resources

Don't forget to check USNews.com listed earlier in this chapter. This site includes financial aid information as well as the annual College Rankings and Graduate School Rankings published by *U.S. News and World Report* (usnews.com/usnews/edu/eduhome.htm).

Carnegie Library of Pittsburgh: Education Resources

carnegielibrary.org/locations/jcec/education

The librarians in the Job and Career Education Center in this library have created a terrific tool for finding information on educational institutions plus financial aid! Check out their listing of print resources, databases, and Internet resources that offer information for anyone seeking assistance with the costs of higher education. There is a special area with information for foreign nationals.

College and University Rankings

library.uiuc.edu/edx/rankings.htm

This collection of links and references to print and online rankings of colleges and universities around the world is provided by the Education and Social Science Library at the University of Illinois at Urbana-Champaign. Be sure to read the information on the controversy of ranking services before you start perusing the rankings.

CollegeNET

collegenet.com

CollegeNET lets you browse information on colleges by various criteria, including geography, tuition, and enrollment. More than five hundred college applications are available here for you to fill out and submit online. Financial aid and scholarship information can also be found here.

Collegiate.Net, the Center for All Collegiate Information

collegiate.net

Collegiate.net not only lets you search for colleges and degrees, but it also lets you tap the manufacturers of collegiate products, alumni associations, and other sites related to the college scene.

COOL: College Opportunities On-Line

http://nces.ed.gov/ipeds/cool

According to the site sponsors, "College Opportunities On-Line (COOL) is your direct link to nearly 7,000 colleges and universities in the United States. If you are thinking about a large university, a small liberal arts college, a specialized college, a community college, a career or technical college or a trade school, you can find them all here." COOL can be searched by location, program, or degree offerings either alone or in combination. COOL is a product of the National Center for Education Statistics (NCES) Integrated Postsecondary Education Data System (IPEDS).

GoCollege

gocollege.com

This is another searchable guide to colleges, but GoCollege has teamed up with Cliffs to help you prepare for the SAT and ACT exams. You can even access the full version of the practice tests for free on specific dates. You'll want to check the site's front page regularly for these dates. Users are advised, "Our practice tests are written by testing experts. Your tests are saved under your user ID for future reference." Free registration is required for the test area and to access the scholarship search area.

RWM Vocational School Database

rwm.org/rwm

This is a database of private postsecondary vocational schools in all fifty states offering bachelor's and master's degrees, online degrees, and technical and management degrees. Except for the Distance Education programs, the site is organized by state and occupational training, and all schools listed are state licensed or accredited. The Distance Education list is a short list of institutions meeting the stated requirements of the site. The information provided for each school is either an address and telephone number or a link to its website; either allows you to easily contact the school to request a catalog and further information. Each state's page also includes a link to resources for that state from the U.S. Department of Education.

Employment Projections and Hiring Trends

Reviewing this information can help you discover if your career field is growing or declining and if that trend is just in your area or if it affects the entire country.

Employment Projections from the Bureau of Labor Statistics (BLS)

bls.gov/emp

This section of the BLS website provides many reports from the Office of Employment Projections, which develops information about employment trends, the national labor market, and the implications of these data on employment opportunities for specific groups in the labor force. Assessments are also made of the effect on employment of specified changes in economic conditions and/or changes in federal programs and policies. You will find a link from this page to several useful resources, including the *Occupational Employment, Training, and Earnings* report, the *Occupational Outlook Quarterly*, the *Career Guide to Industries*, and the *Occupational Outlook Handbook*, all of which also carry information on projected employment trends and earning potential.

Labor Market Information State by State

rileyguide.com/trends.html#gov

Labor Market Information includes statistics on employment, wages, industries, and other factors affecting the world of work. These links from The Riley Guide take you to labor market information for the individual states so you can see how the industry or occupation you are exploring is doing wherever you want to be. While the Bureau of Labor Statistics and the other federal agencies give us data based on national averages, you might find the state you are targeting to be in a different, uh, state.

Occupational Employment Statistics (OES), U.S. Bureau of Labor Statistics

bls.gov/oes

The OES produces an annual survey of occupational employment and wages for more than 750 occupations. You'll find all kinds of very useful information, from wage and compensation data to occupational descriptions and employment projections.

State Occupational Projections

http://almis.dws.state.ut.us/occ/projections.asp

This site contains projections of occupational employment growth developed for all states and the nation as a whole. Allowing you to review state-level data lets you make a more informed decision about what is going on in your neighborhood rather than trying to guess based on the average for the whole United States. One of the most important uses of the projections is to help individuals make informed career decisions. You can review information on projected employment growth for an occupation and compare this among several states or select several occupations and compare their growth projections in just one state. The projections found here are usually updated on a two-year cycle, so you will see new data regularly added.

Financial Aid

College Is Possible

collegeispossible.com

This is a resource guide for parents, students, and education professionals from the Coalition of America's Colleges and Universities. This site walks you through preparing, choosing, and paying for college with simple information as well as links to additional resources and information. Some material is in Spanish, much of the cited resource material can be downloaded at no cost, and the advice and information is of very high quality. There is also a section dedicated to adults who have decided to return to college or to attend for the first time. With two out of every five college students now over the age of twenty-five, these people will not be alone.

FinAid, The SmartStudent Guide to Financial Aid

finaid.org

Established in 1994, FinAid is a gold mine of information and resources for financial aid for education, including scholarships, loans, military aid, and other funding sources. The site also has calculators for figuring out your debt load and payback, facts and alerts about scams, and much more. Make this site your starting point for financial aid information.

FSA for Students: Federal Student Aid from the U.S. Department of Education

http://studentaid.ed.gov

The Federal Student Aid (FSA) programs are the largest source of student aid in the United States, providing nearly 70 percent of all student financial aid. This site provides users with access to and information about the products and services needed throughout the financial aid process. There is information targeted to parents, counselors, returning (adult) students, and international students as well as students in college and graduate school. Under Funding you'll find links to information on state aid, tax credits, the Department's Free Application for Federal Student Aid (FAFSA), and the Student Guide. Updated each award year, the Student Guide is a comprehensive resource on student financial aid from the U.S. Department of Education. It includes information about the various aid programs and how to apply for them. The entire FSA site is available in English and Spanish.

SallieMae

salliemae.com

Founded in 1972, SallieMae provides funds for educational loans, primarily federally guaranteed student loans originated under the Federal Family Education Loan Program (FFELP). Through its website, SallieMae allows you to access information to help you plan for college, apply for a loan, manage your loan payments, and even search for a job. There is information for parents as well as students. SallieMae's family of services also includes WiredScholar, a site to help you plan for college, and TrueCareers, a major online job bank.

Other Education and Training Options

Apprenticeship Information from the U.S. Department of Labor

doleta.gov/jobseekers/apprent.cfm

Apprenticeship is a combination of on-the-job training and related classroom instruction in which workers learn the practical and theoretical aspects of a highly skilled occupation. Apprenticeship programs are sponsored by joint employer and labor groups, individual employers, and/or employer associations. This page will give you information on how to find and apply for apprenticeship programs in the United States.

The Job Corps

jobcorps.org

The Job Corps is the nation's largest residential education and training program for at-risk and disadvantaged youth between the ages of sixteen and twenty-four. It operates more than one hundred centers around the country and in Puerto Rico, offering participants the integrated academic, vocational, and social-skills training they need to gain independence and get quality, long-term jobs or further their education.

Professional and Trade Associations and Unions

These resources will take you to hundreds of associations and organizations representing many occupations and professions. See what they have to offer in internships and apprenticeships, networking and support, mentoring, certification programs, professional development and training, and publications.

American Society of Association Executives

asaenet.org

The American Society of Association Executives (ASAE) is a terrific resource for anyone trying to locate a professional association for a particular field or interest. Click on Find Associations, People, Businesses, and then pull down the extensive menu of searchable directories on the site. We suggest starting with the Gateway to Associations and then trying other sources.

Labor Unions, from Yahoo!

http://dir.yahoo.com/business_and_economy/business_to_business/labor/unions

Yahoo! maintains this list of labor unions covering many occupations and industries.

Organizations, from Yahoo!

http://dir.yahoo.com/business_and_economy/organizations

This is Yahoo!'s entry to its list of organizations, including professional and trade associations.

The Scholarly Societies Project

scholarly-societies.org

You can search or browse this list of national and international associations, societies, and unions focused on "scholarly, academic, or research goals." This site has been online for several years; it is maintained by the Library at the University of Waterloo, Ontario (Canada).

Salary and Compensation Information

In addition to using the following resources, surveying listings in the many job banks will provide some salary information. You'll find more sources in the resources already cited in this chapter, such as CareerJournal and the career guides. Check The Riley Guide (rileyguide.com/salary.html) for more resources and salary-research ideas.

JobStar Salary Surveys

jobstar.org/tools/salary

JobStar has put together what many consider to be the finest collection of salary surveys online anywhere. Combined with lists of books to request from your local library and articles from experts such as Jack Chapman, this site will point you in the right direction for your salary search.

Salary.com

salary.com

This site is much more than just salary resources and an easy-to-remember URL. It is dedicated to total compensation—not only what is in your paycheck but the additional benefits and perquisites you receive as a part of your earnings. The Salary Wizard is fast and easy to use, allowing you to search for base, median, and top-level earnings in hundreds of jobs for many occupational areas, and much of the data applies to your local jurisdiction. Salary.com has a team of compensation specialists working to add value to salary surveys done by such organizations as the Bureau of Labor Statistics. The team knows what it is doing (and you should take advantage of it). If you are serious about your salary and compensation research, the Personal Salary Report is well worth the moderate fee. This site also includes helpful articles and exercises to help you figure out things like benefits, stock options, bonuses (and how to get them), and even negotiations.

SalaryExpert.com

salaryexpert.com

A free service of Baker, Thomsen Associates, SalaryExpert.com offers free access to extensive international compensation information prepared by these extremely knowledgeable experts. Click on Free Salary Tools to access the Basic Salary Reports for the United States and Canada or the International Salary Report covering many other countries. Each allows you to select a job title and region and returns a nice report showing salary averages, salary levels, benefits, and cost of living. Other premium reports are available for a moderate fee, including the Premium Salary Report, The Executive Compensation with Comparables Report, and the U.S./Canada Employee Benefits Report. College students will want to visit the related SalariesReview.com to order personal earnings reports. Sample reports are available for review before you buy.

Self-Assessment

Sometimes a self-assessment test can help you to understand yourself better, but sometimes it can lead to more questions, best answered with the assistance of a counselor.

Campbell Interest and Skill Survey

http://assessments.ncspearson.com/assessments/tests/ciss.htm

If you are interested in a career that requires some postsecondary education, the CISS (Campbell Interest and Skill Survey) assessment can help point you in the right direction. Developed by David Campbell, Ph.D., the CISS uses targeted questions and analysis to help you understand how you fit into the world of work. This survey has been a popular tool with career counselors, and Pearson is now making it available to the public through the Internet for a fee. The report you receive upon completion of the survey compares your results to the results of people who are successfully employed in the fields you're interested in. Nearly sixty occupations are covered in your personalized report, which also includes a comprehensive career planner to help you interpret your results and plan for your new career.

Career Interests Game

http://career.missouri.edu/holland

Based on Dr. John Holland's work (see the listing later entitled "Self-Directed Search"), this free game is designed to help match your interests and skills with similar careers and to suggest occupations to consider. This is a service of the Career Center at the University of Missouri at Columbia.

Keirsey Temperament Website

keirsey.com

This is the official website for the test developed by David Keirsey. Based on the Myers-Briggs Type Indicator (MBTI), the Keirsey Temperament Sorter helps people discover their basic personality type as indicated by their preferences and personality. You can take the Keirsey Temperament Sorter and the Keirsey Character Sorter online at no cost and learn basic information about your type and how it might affect your career choices and work style. Some of the tests are available in languages other than English.

Self-Directed Search (SDS)

self-directed-search.com

The SDS was developed by Dr. John Holland, whose theory of careers is the basis for most of the career inventories used today. His theory states that most people can be loosely categorized with respect to six types—Realistic, Investigative, Artistic, Social, Enterprising, and Conventional—and occupations and work environments can be classified by the same categories. People who select careers matching their own type are more likely to be happier and more successful. You can take the SDS online for a small fee. You'll receive a report indicating your three-letter Holland code along with occupations that match your skills and interests and recommendations on how to proceed with developing and planning your career.

15

Executive Job Searching Online

This chapter contains selected resources for mid- to senior-level executives engaged in a job search. These resources were selected because users have reported them to be very helpful. Many other resources listed throughout this guide also include job listings at this level. The good news is that, yes, executives can search for new job opportunities online. The bad news is that most of the better sources are fee-based, but they are usually worth the expense based on the quality of the listings and the confidentiality of your information.

Please Note: Unless indicated otherwise by the inclusion of *http://* you must add *www.* to the beginning of each URL listed here.

General Services and Resources

CareerJournal from the *Wall Street Journal*

careerjournal.com

As noted throughout this book, this site is an excellent source of career news and great job leads. The content changes daily and is made up of new articles written for this site as well as relevant articles from the *Wall Street Journal*. While we feel that the articles are the best part of the site, we know many of you will be more interested in the job listings. Many of the postings are from various search firms; others are direct postings from employers; still others have been taken from the print version of the *Wall Street Journal*. CareerJournal also offers several resources to assist you in your search—from searching directories of recruiters to salary surveys and interview and negotiation advice. Take the time to explore all the offerings.

ChiefMonster.com

chiefmonster.com

ChiefMonster.com is a service of Monster.com. Although it is free, it is a club that requires application for membership. Members get exclusive access to "senior-level opportunities from today's top employers, executive search firms, and venture capital companies. As a member, you'll also have the opportunity to benchmark your skills and compensation against peers, expand your networking circle, and arm yourself with personalized real-time tools and information. Membership is free and completely confidential." For those who do not meet the qualifications for ChiefMonster, Monster Management (http://management.monster.com) is a valuable alternative.

Exec-U-Net

execunet.com

Exec-U-Net is a career-management and job-search membership organization for executives earning $100,000 and up. It offers job listings along with a resume-review program and face-to-face networking meetings organized around the country. Several membership options are offered, depending on how long you want to be active with the organization. This service has been available for several years and has always received very good comments from members.

ExecutivesOnly

executivesonly.com

This service offers executives who earn upward of $70,000 a year the opportunity to review job leads and get assistance from a career-management consultant in preparing a resume, presenting themselves, and planning their next career move. The people behind this service have extensive backgrounds in recruiting and outplacement and offer quality service based on what they know. They offer several membership options based on how long you wish to be a member and what services you will take advantage of during your tenure. Discounted memberships may be available to those who are currently enrolled in an outplacement program or who recently ended a program without making a successful transition to a new opportunity. Contact them for information.

Netshare

netshare.com

Netshare is a fee-based service offering listings of exclusive confidential job leads, a resume database, and career-management tools for senior executives earning $100,000 and up. If you haven't heard of Netshare, don't be concerned. Think of the company as "the quiet guys" who don't do as much general advertising as the competition but have a terrific reputation through word of mouth. The database is updated daily, and Netshare offers varying membership options designed to meet your current search needs.

Additional Sources for Leads and Connections

These are services and resources you can use to locate job leads or present your information to executive search firms. You will find other resources and services listed throughout the book, so don't limit yourself to just these few.

BlueSteps

bluesteps.com

BlueSteps is a service of the Association of Executive Search Consultants (AESC), a professional association that represents retained executive search consulting firms worldwide. BlueSteps offers two services for executives seeking new career options, Executive Profile and SearchConnect. Executive Profile allows you to submit your resume for consideration by the members of AESC. SearchConnect is a searchable directory of all AESC members that you can use to make direct contact with firms that handle searches in your industry and functional field. These services can be purchased separately or as a package. If you are actively seeking new opportunities, we recommend that you purchase the package for better exposure and better connections at a lower cost.

CEO Job Opportunities Update

ceoupdate.com

CEO Job Opportunities Update is a biweekly publication that lists senior-level nonprofit opportunities in trade associations, professional societies, cause-oriented organizations, and foundations. In addition to accepting announcements from HR professionals and executive search firms, it actively seeks out listings in newspapers, magazines, websites, specialty publications, and newsletters; checks the status and accuracy of each posting; and verifies the compensation offered. According to the website, CEO Update "tracks over three hundred searches in a typical two-week publishing cycle." The twenty-eight-page print version of the newsletter is published every other Thursday and contains details about the newest 100 to 150 searches. This is really a print publication; the website allows subscribers to access information about an additional 100 to 150 job openings previously announced in the newsletter for which employers and recruiters are still actively seeking candidates. Current subscription information and costs can be found on the website.

6FigureJobs.com

6figurejobs.com

6FigureJobs offers experienced professionals the opportunity to confidentially seek and be considered for some of the most prestigious jobs in the country. The service is free but is intended only for those qualified for executive-level placement; however, it also offers those who are ready to move into the c-suite a great opportunity. You must submit your complete resume, which is then reviewed to be sure you qualify for membership based on your years of experience, educational background, job titles, job progression, job responsibilities, and current compensation. Once you are accepted you have access to the job database and your resume is included in the database. You then have the option of controlling how public your resume will be.

Directories of Recruiting Firms

You can use the following resources to locate recruiting firms in your local area as well as those specializing in your target industry or occupation discipline. Many career consultants suggest that you contact the firms to let them know of your interest in being considered for searches that they might be handling and submit a resume for review. If you know the name of an individual search consultant, particularly one a colleague can recommend, then address your approach to this person. If you have never worked with an executive search firm or recruiter before, we suggest checking out some of the articles in the Executive Recruiters section of CareerJournal (careerjournal.com) for advice and information to help you understand and work effectively with these firms.

BlueSteps from the Association of Executive Search Consultants

bluesteps.com

Please see its entry earlier in this chapter.

Custom Databanks, Inc.

customdatabanks.com

If you are familiar with the CareerSearch product found in many college career centers and outplacement firms, then you have already met Custom Databanks. This company provides the database of executive search firms used by CareerSearch, and it also makes this and other databases available to the public for a fee. To start your search, click on Download Data, and then select your search criteria. The results will tell you how many records have been found and the cost before you buy, but they will also tell you how many firms have listed e-mail addresses, fax numbers, or merely postal addresses. You can buy whichever list you want based on your needs and contact plans, but we suggest you avoid limiting yourself to those firms with e-mail addresses only. The data file you are buying can easily be imported into any word processor or spreadsheet program for mail-merge and campaign management. This is a competitive product to Kennedy's (see next listing), but we found in many cases it provided more contact names for each firm listed.

The Directory of Executive Recruiters from Kennedy Publications

kennedyinfo.com/db/db_der_bas.html

Kennedy's is probably the best-known name in this field and is worth the cost of the search. When you initially search the directory it tells you how many records (search firms) match your criteria and how much the resulting list will cost you. You can then alter your search based on how many records you've found (too many or too few) or how much it costs. If you wish to save money you can find print copies of the directory in most major bookstores as well as in public and business libraries. Many colleges and universities have Kennedy's in their reference collections. Kennedy's also offers a separate International Database of Executive Recruiters as well as a searchable database of Hiring Companies, other options you may want to consider in your campaign.

FindARecruiter.com

findarecruiter.com

Part of the Recruiters Online Network (recruitersonline.com), FindARecruiter is a free searchable database of third-party recruiters, headhunters, executive search firms, and staffing agencies. You can search the directory by job field or industry, location (not limited to the United States), or company name. See Chapter 3 for more information on Recruiters Online Network.

Headhunter E-mail Address Lists from Avotek

avotek.nl/emailgds.htm

Based in the Netherlands, Avotek is a marvelous resource for an international job search. It now offers lists of recruiters from several countries, allowing you to contact them directly via e-mail and submit your resume for consideration in searches they are conducting. Each list tells you what country is covered, how many addresses are listed, when the list was last updated, and the cost.

The Recruiting and Search Report

rsronline.com

These are print directories listing contingency and retained executive search firms that specialize in various industry and functional areas. You can also order the directories on diskette for the cost of the directory plus an additional fee. The file is in ASCII for easy import into any spreadsheet or word-processing program. The list of available directories, including the number of entries in each, is on the website along with order information.

RiteSite.com

ritesite.com

"RiteSite's purpose is to provide the strongest and most comprehensive possible help to job-hunting and career-building executives." John Lucht, author of *Rites of Passage*, offers members a specially designed Custom Career Service to "help you with everything you can do to advance your job search and long-term career development." This includes resume preparation and posting, ability to confidentially forward your resume to others, and connectivity to his select group of retained executive search firms. The site's central core is devoted to helping you find, contact, and build relationships with these firms. He has job listings here that are open and free for anyone to view. He charges a moderate annual membership for those who want the Custom Career Service.

SearchFirm.com

searchfirm.com

SearchFirm.com is a free searchable directory of retained and contingency recruiters and interim staffing firms from around the world. Intended for employers, job seekers will find this very useful.

Executive Compensation Information

At some point in a successful search, you will be asked what you expect to receive in compensation. What salary are you asking, and what additional perquisites and benefits might attract you to a particular position? The following resources along with many already listed can help you in preparing your answers and in the negotiation process that will inevitably follow. Many of the resources noted earlier in this chapter will also have information and guides for you. You can find even more information in The Riley Guide (rileyguide.com).

Articles and Reports on CEO Pay from Forbes.com

forbes.com

Forbes publishes several articles plus special surveys on executive compensation throughout the year, including the annual report on Best Paid CEOs. When you connect to the website, look for the Careers section or search the site using the keyword *compensation*.

BusinessWeek

businessweek.com

BusinessWeek presents frequent articles on pay and perquisites for management and executive professionals throughout the year, and it also publishes an annual survey of CEO salaries every April. To start finding this information online, connect to the site and head to the Careers area. Select Pay and Perks from the left menu to gather all of the articles on pay and perquisites published over the past year. Then use the Search feature to find the keywords *executive pay*. Search the entire site, and you will find some reports and articles from more than a year ago. Some content on *BusinessWeek*'s website is for subscribers only, but much of it is open to the public.

CareerJournal from the *Wall Street Journal*

careerjournal.com

CareerJournal's section on Salary and Hiring Info contains articles and charts on pay, perquisites, options, and anything else you need to know before talking money with a company.

DEF 14A Reports from the EDGAR Database of Corporate Information, U.S. Securities and Exchange Commission (SEC)

sec.gov/edgar.shtml

Compensation for the top executives and members of the boards of directors of every publicly traded company in the United States must be reported to the SEC. While some fee-based EDGAR (Electronic Data Gathering, Analysis, and Retrieval system) services will pull this information out for you, it's easy enough to find using this free database. Select two or three competitive companies similar in size and industry to your preferred employer, go to EDGAR's Search for Company Filings, and use the Quick Forms Lookup to search EDGAR for the DEF 14A form for each, and then use the Find command in your Web browser (usually control-F) to scan for the word *compensation*. This will not only reveal salary and stock information, but it also may give you some ideas for additional compensation considerations, such as cars, travel expenses for your spouse or partner, cell phones, and much more.

Ecomp, the Executive Compensation Database

ecomponline.com

Yes, it's just spitting out the same information you can find yourself by searching the DEF 14 reports filed by each company, but this site does it so much faster. And you can search by company or ticker name if you are looking for a particular organization. It will not give you a summary of the noncash perquisites, severance packages, and stock options awarded to the chief executives of each company. For that type of information you will need to go to EDGAR and search the full DEF 14 reports.

Index of Cited Resources

Subject Index

Academic jobs. *See* Education and academic jobs

Accounting and finance jobs, 54–56

Acting and entertainment jobs, 80–81

Actuaries, 56–67

Advertising jobs, 57

Aeronautics and aerospace, jobs in, 111–12

Africa, job opportunities in, 208

African Americans, job opportunities for, 229

Agre, Phil, 12

Agriculture, jobs in, 95–97

Alabama, state-sponsored job service sites for, 178–79

Alaska, state-sponsored job service sites for, 189–91

Alberta, job opportunities in, 223

Animal sciences, jobs in, 97–98

Anthropology jobs, 66

Apparel and footwear, jobs in, 122–23

Archaeology jobs, 66

Architecture, jobs in, 112–13

Archives, jobs in, 86–87

Arizona, state-sponsored job service sites for, 191

Arkansas, state-sponsored job service sites for, 179–80

Arts, jobs in the, 81

Asia, job opportunities in, 209

Asian Americans, job opportunities for, 229

Ask the Headhunter: Reinventing the Interview to Win Jobs (Corcodilos), 25

Associations, jobs in, 75–76

Astronomy jobs, 98

Australia, job opportunities in, 209–10

Austria, job opportunities in, 215

Automotive jobs, 114

Aviation jobs, 114

Baker, Wayne E., 26

Baking arts jobs, 83

Beauty and fashion jobs, 84

Belgium, job opportunities in, 214

Biology jobs, 99

Biotechnology and biomedical engineering jobs, 115

Bolles, Richard, 5, 24, 25, 51, 238

Bookbinding jobs, 89

Britain, job opportunities in, 216–18

British Columbia, job opportunities in, 224

Broadcast media jobs, 90–92

Browsing, 7

Business directories, 151

Business jobs, starting points for, 54. *See also* specific field of business

California, state-sponsored job service sites for, 191–94

Call centers, jobs at, 58

Canada, job opportunities in, 219–25

Career exploration, 239–41

Career planning. *See* Lifelong career planning

CareerXRoads (Crispin and Mehler), 25

Cartooning jobs, 82

Chemical engineering jobs, 115

Chemistry jobs, 99

Child care jobs, 82

Chimney sweep jobs, 115

Chiropractic jobs, 99–100

Church business administration jobs, 57

Civil engineering jobs, 116

Coates, Tom, 132

Colorado, state-sponsored job service sites for, 194

Communications jobs, 57

Community information networks, 150

Compensation information. *See* Salary and compensation information

Complete Idiot's Guide to the Internet (Kent), 15

Computing jobs, 116–18

Construction, jobs in, 118–19

Contacts, identifying good, 12–13

Cool Careers for Dummies (Nemko and Edwards), 5

Co-ops, 142–45

Corcodilos, Nick A., 25

Counseling assistance, for career planning, 242–43

Counseling jobs, 76–77

Court (verbatim) reporters, 78

Cover letters, 30
  resources for writing, 39–41

Crispin, Gerry, 10, 25

Culinary jobs, 83

Customer relations jobs, 58

Czech Republic, job opportunities in, 212

Dance, jobs in, 83–84

Defense industry, jobs in, 132

Delaware, state-sponsored job service sites for, 166–67

Denmark, job opportunities in, 226

Dentistry jobs, 100

Department of Defense, U.S., 139

Directories
  business, 16–18
  Internet, 8
  of recruiting firms, 256–59

Disabled workers, job opportunities for, 230

Disadvantaged workers, job opportunities for, 232–33

Distance education, for career planning, 243

District of Columbia, state-sponsored job service sites for, 167

Diverse audiences, general sites for, 228–29

Drilling, mining, and offshore jobs, 126

Earth and environmental sciences, jobs in, 101

Eastern Europe, job opportunities in, 212

Economics jobs, 67

Education and academic jobs
  college- and university-level, 67–69
  kindergarten through twelfth-grade, 69–70
  for new teachers, 70

Education resources, for career planning, 244–45, 248

Edwards, Sarah, 5

Elder care jobs, 82

Electrical, mechanical, and plumbing industry, jobs in, 125

Electrical engineering jobs, 120

Electronic resumes. *See* Online resumes

E-mail
  obtaining free, 15
  for resumes, 30–31

Employers
  researching and targeting, 16–18
  websites of, 19

Employment projections, for career planning, 245–46

Engineering jobs, general resources for, 110–11

English as second language/English as foreign (ESL/EFL) jobs, 71

Entertainment and acting jobs, 80–81

Entomology, jobs in, 100

Environmental and earth sciences, jobs in, 101

Equal opportunities, general sites for, 228–29

Equipment leasing jobs, 59

Europe, job opportunities in, 213–18. *See also* specific country

Event and meeting management jobs, 60